JOSÉ
MOURINHO
Up Close and Personal

ROBERT BEASLEY

Windsor and Maidenhead

This paperback edition first published in 2017
First published in hardback in Great Britain in 2016 by
Michael O'Mara Books Limited
9 Lion Yard
Tremadoc Road
London SW4 7NQ

A CIP catalogue record for this book is available from the
British Library.

Papers used by Michael O'Mara Books Limited are natural,
recyclable products made from wood grown in sustainable forests.
The manufacturing processes conform to the environmental
regulations of the country of origin.

ISBN: 978-1-782438-34-2 in paperback print format
ISBN: 978-1-78243-887-8 in ebook format

3 5 7 9 10 8 6 4 2 1

Front cover image: Alexander Hassenstein / FIFA via Getty Images
Back cover image: Dominique Faget / AFP / Getty Images
Flap image: Jamie McPhilimey / The Sun Online

Designed and typeset by Mark Bracey

Printed and bound by CPI Group (UK) Ltd, Croydon, CR0 4YY

www.mombooks.com

Contents

	Introduction	1
1	Bolton Away	6
2	Glory Hunters	11
3	Phantom Goal	15
4	Ashley Cole	21
5	Mour of the Same	29
6	Jennifer	33
7	Ready for War	39
8	Quadroubles	44
9	Match of the Day	49
10	I'll Be Back!	54
11	England	60
12	Tottenham	66
13	The Greatest Prize	72
14	Goodbuy, Zlatan	78
15	Re-United	83
16	Broken Dream	90
17	Park the Bus	95
18	Spying Mission	100
19	Special Son	107
20	Cris and Cross	114
21	Breaking News	120
22	Show Me the Money!	127
23	Pep Talk	133

24	Happy Days!.	138
25	Dead Man Walking	143
26	Strike Threat	148
27	Over to Roo	154
28	On the Deck	162
29	One Out of Five	167
30	The Little Horse	172
31	Stumbling at the Final Hurdle	176
32	Costa Bravo	182
33	Frank's a Lot!	188
34	Food for Thought	195
35	Criminal Damage	200
36	Hazard Warning	205
37	Pot, Kettle	211
38	Insulting Behaviour	217
39	Medals, Mementos and Memories	221
40	Game Time	225
41	Beating Wenger	231
42	You're Not Wanted Here	239
43	Poor Relations	248
44	Fame and Fortune	254
45	The Home Front	258
46	Close and Personal	264
47	The Sack Race	268
48	From Blue to Red	277
	Epilogue	282
	Acknowledgements	293
	Picture Credits	294

To Saskia and Joshua, who've made my life complete
and who never cease to amaze me.

INTRODUCTION:
OLD TRAFFORD, 2004

José Mourinho first burst into my consciousness on the evening of Tuesday 9 March 2004. I'm sure it was the same for millions of other football fans that night. Certainly every supporter in England was suddenly talking about him: the crazy guy in the dark overcoat who'd just gone running and jumping along the touchline at Old Trafford.

Mourinho had every right to be excited. Portuguese star Costinha's last-gasp equalizer against Manchester United was a huge moment for the manager and his Porto side. It was the first knockout stage of the Champions League, and the defensive midfielder's goal sent United crashing out and put Porto on their way to winning the cup with the big ears. It was a seismic moment for Mourinho on many levels, not least because, ultimately, the convincing 3–0 Champions League final triumph over Monaco in Gelsenkirchen, Germany, on 26 May meant that within a month the man in the overcoat would be announcing himself as a 'special one' as he took charge of Chelsea. Now that really put him at the forefront of my mind.

At this point you should know that I am a Chelsea fan and have been since their 1967 FA Cup final against Tottenham. I was seven years old at that time and football mad. England had won the World Cup the previous summer and, believe it or not, the 1967 Cup final at Wembley was the next big match to be shown 'live' on television way back then. It beggars belief now in the multi-channel world of digital television in Ultra High

1

Definition and 3D, where we can enjoy wall-to-wall football on our screens virtually every day. Not in the swinging Sixties you couldn't, which is why FA Cup final day was so special back then and why it was such a huge occasion for the nation, not just the followers of the finalists.

In May 1967 I didn't support a specific football team, although my dad frequently used to take me down the road to Nuneaton Borough FC, my home-town club, which I loved. It wasn't quite as glamorous as watching the Cup final, though, so on 20 May I was hugely excited. In the morning my friends and I went over to the rec (the recreational playground at the Miners' Welfare and Social Club in Heath End Road, Nuneaton) and played out the final. I was on the Chelsea team and the rules were simple: the first team to ten were the winners. We won, and we won easily: something like 10–5, maybe 10–6. Anyway, that was it.

On the basis of that great victory I went home and confidently told my mum and dad and elder sister Alison that Chelsea were going to win that afternoon. They didn't. Goals from Jimmy Robertson and Frank Saul saw to that as Spurs won 2–1 with Chelsea only managing an eighty-fifth-minute consolation score from the great Bobby Tambling. I suppose I could have been a glory hunter and swapped allegiance to winners Tottenham and forgotten all about the losers in blue, but something deep inside me had stirred that day, had been awakened by that defeat, and my lifelong love for Chelsea was born.

Little did I know that twenty years later I'd be living the dream as a sports journalist regularly covering my beloved Chelsea and getting to know the stars and key figures at the club, from the boardroom to the dressing room and on to the pressroom. Which is why I made sure that I was there that day when Mourinho was unveiled at Stamford Bridge and took control of 'my' Chelsea.

I wanted to see what this guy was all about, introduce myself to him as soon as possible and try to forge the sort of close relationship with him that I'd previously enjoyed with the likes of Ken Bates, Matthew Harding, Glenn Hoddle, Ruud Gullit and Luca Vialli. So on Sunday 2 June 2004 I strode to the Bridge to hear Mourinho come out with that famous 'special one' line, which would, from that moment on, become his moniker worldwide. He was brilliant. He was spellbinding. He was box office.

Unfortunately the organization on the day was a complete shambles. For some reason Chelsea had decided to try to stage the press conference in their pressroom, a pretty small space close to the tunnel and dressing rooms for ease of access after matches for managers. However, the arrival of Mourinho was international news. TV film crews, radio reporters and journalists from all over Europe were in attendance, some from even further afield. The room and its facilities were nowhere near big enough. So it was decided to do the press conferences, in stages.

First, there was the official unveiling in front of everyone, with far too many people crammed into the pressroom for comfort or safety. Afterwards there was a series of other conferences with selected, smaller groups such as the international press, the British TV and radio boys, the UK's daily newspaper reporters and finally the UK's Sunday newspapers. Each group was looking for something specifically for themselves, something exclusive to their outlets over and above Mourinho at the general press conference. It's not an unusual situation but it is unusual for a club to try to do all of this in one of the smallest rooms at the stadium.

Now, I was a Sunday newspaper man at the time and, as usual, we were the last in line. That's because, unlike that of the others', our deadline for reports was not until the weekend, rather than on that day. Therefore our need for access was not as immediate. The problem, though, is that managers and players quickly get tired of question after question and by the time they have done all the other interviews and finally get to the Sunday newspaper guys they are fed up and just want to get away. Often, an expected twenty-minute slot can end up as just a few short minutes.

The other problem for the Sunday press is the need to monitor what questions and answers the TV, radio and daily newspapers have already asked in the earlier conferences. It's not about spying or eavesdropping; it's to avoid repetition and to ensure the questions asked gained a new, fresh angle on the story. Let's face it: no one wants to pick up their newspaper or go online on Sunday to read information and comments that they saw on TV, heard on the radio or read in the daily newspapers days before, but how can you monitor all of that when you are outside standing on the tarmac? So, suffice to say, I was not best pleased at facing the very real possibility that anything we got from Mourinho could turn out to be old news by the weekend.

So, just before Sunday's press conference was finally about to begin, I made my protest in a feisty clash with Chelsea's press chief Simon Greenberg. He was sitting alongside Mourinho at the top table when I ripped into him. It was a short, sharp, controlled blast about the chaotic nature of the press conference. I'm pretty sure I would have done it anyway, because the proceedings thus far had been a complete shambles, but I admit I also viewed the occasion as an ideal opportunity for me to force my way into Mourinho's mind right from the start. It worked. He couldn't help but be aware of my brief but forceful interruption. I knew I had succeeded in making an early impact. It might just have been, 'Huh, who's this stroppy, mouthy guy?', but at least I'd made myself stand out. It was a start.

The challenge now was to exploit that impact by working to forge a close and, hopefully, ongoing relationship. I did that, and more. And so it all began.

1

BOLTON AWAY

There were still five minutes left, but two goals from Frank Lampard had surely settled it, so I pressed the 'send' button on my laptop and emailed my match report early. My rationale was that if anything dramatic did happen in those final few minutes I could always ring the office and add the extra information over the telephone. However, in my mind it was already 'job done' – not just for me but for Chelsea and for José. It was Saturday 30 April 2005.

I got up from my desk, slipped out of the press box and hurried down the stairs at the Reebok Stadium into the reception area. I was moving quickly and purposefully because I didn't want to miss the moment. The Bolton receptionist looked up and asked, 'Are you with Chelsea?' I just smiled at her and said 'Yes' and marched unchallenged through the doors to the changing rooms, down the tunnel and then stood pitchside as the seconds ticked away.

Chelsea's Head of Communications Simon Greenberg was right beside me with Mourinho sitting expectantly on the Chelsea bench just a few feet away, waiting for that fateful, final whistle. Within moments referee Steve Dunn duly signalled the end of the game to confirm a 2–0 win for Chelsea and, most importantly and significantly, the prized Premier League crown to go with it. I watched closely, trying to take it all in, both from a sports writer's perspective and as a lifelong fan who never thought his team would win the league.

I kept a particular eye on Mourinho who, in my opinion, was the main man behind this incredible triumph. Naturally, he was on the pitch celebrating with his players and his staff and that's when I made my move, walking out towards the centre circle to meet him. I said, 'Congratulations, boss, well done, thank you,' and we shook hands. Then I asked him a series of quick questions. 'How long ago did you realize you were going to be champions? How does it feel, what does it mean to you? Was there a key moment when you knew you could do this, would do this?'

The answers weren't great, but Mourinho was caught up in the moment and quite emotional and it didn't really matter anyway; I was content enough to be sharing a key moment with him. Finally I said, 'What are you going to do now?' He smiled and replied, 'I'm going to ring my wife.' Sure enough, he walked back to the dugout, sat down and called Matilde Mourinho to tell her he was a champion yet again.

That one act told me a lot about the man rather than the manager, a man who wanted to share this magical moment with his wife and family as soon as he could. He said Matilde was a nervous spectator and, because of that, didn't enjoy going to matches. She preferred to sit at home and wait for the phone call from her man. It became a recurring theme over the years, with José proudly and repeatedly telling me how much his wife and children meant to him.

José didn't linger long with his Chelsea 'family' after the call, though, preferring to head down the tunnel and leave his players and staff to savour the moment. He explained, 'This [moment] is for them, for the players. Fantastic. It's time for me to disappear, it's time for them; they are the men.' I looked around the pitch to survey and savour the scene. In front of the celebrating Chelsea fans I saw match-winner Frank Lampard with his arms around skipper John Terry and owner Roman

Abramovich, all of them bouncing up and down singing. There were players celebrating everywhere. I made a move to grab Eidur Gudjohnsen, who'd once played for Bolton. It was a good call as he revealed that José had asked him to do the pre-match team talk for this vital title clincher. That was a nice line for the newspaper. I saw my old buddy Steve Clarke, Mourinho's trusted assistant, and dropped to my knees in a jokey salute to the ex-Chelsea star, who I'd known since his playing days.

Inevitably, I ended up in the Chelsea dressing room, watching Abramovich, chairman Bruce Buck, Greenberg and all the players and staff celebrating wildly, some of them singing the Chelsea anthem 'Ten men went to mow' while others sprayed champagne all around. Joyous scenes, but no José.

It seemed that from his point of view his work was done and now it was about the next match, the next challenge and the next trophy. Indeed, the next match just three days later was a decisive Champions League semi-final, second-leg clash with Liverpool at Anfield. No time to celebrate, little time to recuperate, but already plenty to look back on and commemorate.

Whatever subsequently happened at Anfield, the Special One had already proved just how special he was by winning the Premier League title at the first attempt, and in record-breaking fashion. It was a truly remarkable league campaign as the Londoners rewrote the history books of club and country, and was the first time Chelsea had won the title for fifty years, their one previous success coming way back in 1955. What's more, Mourinho achieved the remarkable feat in Chelsea's centenary year to add a fitting gloss to the celebrations.

The Portuguese hadn't wasted any time in his bid to achieve that. He announced his arrival into the English game in style as Chelsea kicked off the 2004–05 season with a 1–0 win over Sir Alex Ferguson's Manchester United, courtesy of an Eidur

Gudjohnsen goal. Arsenal were still clear title favourites, though, and a 5–3 win on the second weekend of the season saw the Gunners surpass Nottingham Forest's English record of forty-two top-flight matches unbeaten. Yes, they were the team to beat, and Arsène Wenger's side continued in majestic form, winning eight of their opening nine league matches to set the early pace. It was a pace they could not sustain, however, and it was their arch-rivals United who finally halted Arsenal's imperious forty-nine-match run. A 2–0 defeat at Old Trafford opened the door for Chelsea and a 1–0 win at Everton saw the Blues go top on 6 November. They would not be moved, staying there for the rest of the season. By Christmas they had forged a five-point lead and then eight straight wins saw them go 11 points clear at the start of February. The contest was essentially all over. All that remained was to wait for the final confirmation and a majestic coronation.

It wasn't just a timely title triumph to savour; it was also an astonishing statement of intent that reverberated throughout the league. Mourinho's men finished eight points ahead of the 'Invincibles' of Arsenal, who were the defending champions, 18 points clear of third-placed Manchester United and an incredible 34 points in front of fourth-placed Everton. They had amassed a Premier League record of 95 points after notching an impressive 29 wins – another Premier League record – and eight draws throughout the campaign, with just one defeat, a surprise 1–0 reverse at Manchester City. Chelsea won 15 games away from home, another Premier League record, kept 25 clean sheets, another Premier League record, and conceded just 15 goals all told, another Premier League record. Mourinho was voted Manager of the Season. Frank Lampard, who scored 13 league goals with 18 assists, was voted Player of the Season. Perennial also-rans Chelsea were now the dominant force in English football.

But that first season wasn't all about the Premier League for him: for a long while, his team was remarkably fighting on four fronts.

2

GLORY HUNTERS

Chelsea began a make-or-break week on Sunday 20 February 2005 with three of the four trophies they were chasing now at stake in the next eight days. It began badly. The first silverware to topple was the FA Cup, with the Blues knocked out at Newcastle in the fifth round.

Mourinho had made bold changes for the match, leaving a number of key names out with an eye on the upcoming Champions League last-sixteen trip to Barcelona in midweek, which would be followed by the Carling Cup final with Liverpool the following weekend. But with Chelsea struggling and behind at half-time, he displayed the daring and speed of thought for which he became renowned, by making all three of his substitutions there and then. It was a brave move – a sign he wanted to win and he meant to win. On this occasion it backfired spectacularly.

Chelsea finished the match with only eight fit men after Wayne Bridge was stretchered off injured, Damien Duff was hurt but limped on and stand-in goalkeeper Carlo Cudicini was sent off, all of which consigned them to a rare defeat. But Mourinho was pumped up by the display, and praised his players effusively: 'Sometimes you lose and you are still very proud of the team, even more than when they win. I thought they were magnificent. The way they reacted against a very good team, when they were a goal down ... the way they fought was fantastic.'

This was a signal indicating the way the still relatively new Chelsea boss would operate: to seize back the initiative if proceedings were going against you, and if you failed in trying, at least you could show you failed giving it your all, showing your desire and playing with passion, something the Portuguese himself was not short of. It was a refreshing approach to management in England, where often coaches wouldn't want to take unnecessary risks or try ideas out. Mourinho was showing he was a different kind of boss.

Chelsea lost again on the Wednesday night in Barcelona, the only time they suffered back-to-back defeats all season, but again the match was immersed in incident and controversy. The Londoners were winning 1–0 and looking comfortable until referee Anders Frisk sent off Didier Drogba in the fifty-fifth minute after a challenge with goalkeeper Victor Valdés.

Drogba, who had already been booked, received a second yellow card, then a red. It was a contentious, disputed decision. But the home side took full advantage of Frisk's ruling and their extra man. Substitute Maxi López and striker Samuel Eto'o both scored to secure a 2–1 lead to take to Stamford Bridge. It didn't end there.

After the match Chelsea lodged an official complaint with UEFA, claiming that Barcelona boss Frank Rijkaard had been seen meeting with Frisk in the referee's dressing room at half-time, something the two accused both denied. The clear inference was that Frisk had been influenced by the meeting, which could have explained his decision to dismiss Drogba. It was a most unsavoury drama, with claim then counter-claim, and the matter would escalate further the following month, with significant consequences for Frisk, Mourinho and Chelsea.

At that point, though, a season that promised so much was suddenly teetering on the brink. Dreams of a quadruple had already gone, and the treble was in dire danger when Liverpool's

John Arne Riise volleyed the Reds ahead on 27 February in the opening minute in Cardiff in the Carling Cup final. Here, then, was a real test of the Londoners' nerve, resolve and character.

Chelsea responded positively and pushed hard for an equaliser but saw a flurry of chances go begging. It needed a helping hand (well, head, actually) from Liverpool's Steven Gerrard, whose own goal levelled it up with just eleven minutes to go. Mourinho showed his passion once again, although not in a way appreciated by many: his decision to put a finger to his lips to shush the Liverpool fans triggered an immediate reaction from the match officials and the Blues' boss was banished from the dugout for the rest of a pulsating, nail-biting encounter.

Fortunately for Mourinho it didn't affect the outcome, although the match did require extra time to settle it, with José just a frustrated spectator in the stands. He needn't have worried. Didier Drogba and Mateja Kežman both scored in the second half of extra time to put Chelsea in control, and a late Liverpool score through Núñez was purely cosmetic. After just six months at Stamford Bridge, Mourinho had already handed the club's new owner, Russian billionaire Roman Abramovich, his first trophy.

These were heady times at a club unused to being serious contenders on so many fronts. Mourinho was a proven winner and had delivered yet again, but there was absolutely no question that life at Chelsea under the new manager was anything but high octane, high drama and high stakes. So it would prove yet again when Barcelona came to the Bridge for a highly charged return leg on 8 March. There was no Drogba of course, after his red card, but there was more incident-packed action.

Mourinho's side romped into a 3–0 lead inside nineteen minutes and looked unstoppable. They were 4–2 ahead on aggregate and in full flow after goals from Gudjohnsen, Lampard and Duff. But Barca had other ideas, especially the world's greatest player, Ronaldinho. His thirty-first-minute penalty was followed by an unbelievable goal seven minutes before the break, which threatened to transform the outcome. From the edge of the box, with barely any backlift, the Brazilian superstar had somehow bent the ball around defender Ricardo Carvalho and beaten goalkeeper Cech. That moment of genius meant it was the Spaniards who were suddenly back in control and on course to go through on the away goals rule.

Chelsea needed inspiration of their own and it came from a familiar source, captain John Terry leaping highest to head home a Duff corner in the seventy-seventh minute to put Barca out and Chelsea into the quarter-finals.

On the final whistle Mourinho, in his trademark overcoat, ran on to the pitch, windmilling his right arm in delight, and leapt on to the backs of his celebrating team. The treble was still on.

3

PHANTOM GOAL

The Champions League quarter-finals of 2005 brought German champions Bayern Munich to Chelsea, but this time there was to be no Mourinho, not even sitting up in the stands. The toxic fallout from Barcelona had engulfed the Blues boss. First, a frightened and fearful Anders Frisk had announced he was quitting as a referee, explaining his decision by saying he'd received death threats from enraged Chelsea fans. Then, in a furious response to Frisk's demise, came an outburst from Volker Roth, chairman of UEFA's referees committee. He didn't blame Chelsea fans and he didn't blame Chelsea for Frisk's decision; he blamed Mourinho.

The wrathful Roth raged, 'It's the coaches who whip up the masses and actually make them threaten people with death. We can't accept that one of our absolutely best referees is forced to quit because of this. People like Mourinho are the enemy of football.'

Roth was claiming that the Portuguese had effectively instigated the supposed death threats by persuading Chelsea to protest about the half-time antics of Frisk and Rijkaard. It was nonsense of course, but it was a phrase that would be repeated about Mourinho in all sorts of contexts in the years ahead.

Mourinho was banned for two matches for 'bringing the game into disrepute' and 'making false declarations'. UEFA also fined him £8,900 and Chelsea £33,300. The upshot was that Mourinho would have to serve his stadium ban for the home and away games against Bayern. It didn't seem to affect Chelsea at all in the first leg. They again hit four at the Bridge in thrilling style, although Bayern captain Michael Ballack took the gloss off the result a little with a ninetieth-minute penalty to make it 4–2 on the night and give his side hope in the return leg. It appeared Chelsea could win very well without their inspirational manager.

However, there were rumours that Mourinho's absence didn't affect Chelsea too much because he was there all along. Yes, the inside story was that José's desire to be with his team was so strong that he actually defied UEFA and showed up anyway, sneaking into the home dressing room long before kick-off and being smuggled out in a laundry basket just before the end of the game. He supposedly sat watching the game on TV in the dressing room, and it was even claimed that he sent right-hand man Rui Faria clandestine messages throughout the game via an earpiece hidden under his assistant's beanie hat. UEFA officials were alerted to the possibility of the messaging between manager and assistant at half-time and quizzed Faria.

The conspiracy theories were in overdrive. In the second half, it was José's other assistant, Silvino Louro, who was now under suspicion after repeated trips up the tunnel saw him allegedly returning with scraps of paper bearing instructions from the boss. The official line is that Mourinho had watched the game in the Chelsea leisure centre, just behind the Matthew Harding stand. The official outcome was that Chelsea had one foot in the semi-finals.

Now the circus moved on to Munich. Mourinho would find it far more difficult to evade detection at the Olympic Stadium home of his opponents. It didn't stop the rumours of more cloak-and-dagger behaviour, though. There was talk he would disguise himself and be sitting in the crowd, watching the game and again relaying messages. Sure enough, before kick-off José was spotted high in the stands by a TV crew. He didn't stay long, but it set UEFA staff and Bayern officials on edge, which, knowing Mourinho and his mind games, may well have been the point all along.

Then there was talk of a sound system complete with transmitter in the Chelsea dressing room to enable Mourinho to broadcast his pre-match and half-time talks to his players from afar. (The club's line was that he stayed and watched the game at the team hotel.) It was far-fetched stuff, but all of this chatter was given credence by the suggestion that the ex-special forces bodyguards of Chelsea owner Roman Abramovich had the necessary covert skills to make it happen. It was a distracting sideshow to the main event, the match, but being there as it all unfolded certainly made me think.

My relationship with Mourinho was already good, albeit very much in the early stages back then. It was a much closer connection than I enjoyed with many other managers I'd known and worked with over the years. He was a breath of fresh air, a dynamic new figure who made an immediate impact with his spiky personality and bold statements. He was a journalist's dream. Day to day he was certainly nothing like the confrontational, controversial figure I sometimes saw in full flow from the press box or in press conferences. He was very engaging, easily approachable, friendly, funny and had the knack of making you feel special. He had time for you and seemed genuinely interested in you, your family and your life. He'd stop for a chat, was always ready with some banter and loved to play the joker, sometimes with such a good poker face that he had people second-guessing whether he was serious or jesting. You'll have seen it for yourself in many of his press conferences: José sitting there with an impish look on his face, suppressing a grin but with his sparkling eyes betraying him and giving the game away.

Those early press conferences were a hoot and, as a reporter, if you couldn't get a big hit from a José presser (journalist slang) you weren't doing your job properly. It was all pretty exciting. Okay, I was nowhere near his inner circle at that point but the guy I knew and got on with so well bore no resemblance to this 'enemy of football' who was seemingly capable of such Machiavellian acts and had such a win-at-all-costs attitude. It did not match with my experience of him, although clearly there was far more for me to learn about this man. Above all else, though, his most important attribute for me, especially as a fan, was that Mourinho was a winner, and a winner through and through.

So it proved in Munich. An early Frank Lampard goal put Chelsea 5–2 ahead on aggregate and the Blues' boss could relax, wherever he was. Claudio Pizarro pulled a goal back for Bayern in the sixty-fifth minute but Didier Drogba made it 6–3 overall just ten minutes from the end. It was all over and not even two late Bayern goals could stop Chelsea's march into the semi-finals.

The distinctive and familiar figure of Rafa Benítez now stood between Mourinho and a second, successive Champions League final. The Chelsea boss had got the better of his Liverpool counterpart in the Carling Cup final, but this was an even bigger date with destiny and what happened in the second leg of the semi-final would forge an intense rivalry and dislike between the opposing managers that still goes on today.

The first leg at the Bridge was a lively enough affair but had ended goalless, so all eyes were on the match at Anfield on Tuesday 3 May. Within four minutes Liverpool were awarded a debatable goal that proved decisive. This was before goal-line technology so it was Slovakian linesman Roman Slysko who decided that a close-range effort from Luis García had crossed the line, despite protests to the contrary from Chelsea. TV replays were inconclusive. They didn't prove at all that the ball was all over the line, but they didn't prove it wasn't.

No one will ever convince Mourinho that the ball had crossed the line. I sat there listening after the match when he said, 'You should bring the linesman in here and ask why he gave the goal. To do that you have to be 100 per cent that the ball went in and my players said it was not. It was a goal that came from the moon, from the Anfield Road stands, I don't know from where. You can't tell from TV. Only one person has decided the future of a team. I make mistakes, my players make mistakes, he made a mistake. The best team lost, that's for sure, but football is cruel sometimes. You have to accept the reality of it. They scored, if you can say that, or what you should say is that the linesman scored. Of course we are disappointed, but I am very proud of my players.'

Years later García's ghost goal still rankled with Mourinho. 'Losing a Champions League semi-final to a goal that didn't cross the line will stay in my mind for ever. I cannot forget it. It still hurts, of course it does.' And when I chatted with him about it in 2013, he went even further. I actually asked him about the accuracy of his 'win-at-all-costs reputation' and he scoffed at the idea, saying, 'But if I win a big match with a goal that is not a goal, if I could I would change [it] ... So for example that semi-final Liverpool versus Chelsea, if Chelsea wins and goes to the final with a goal that is not a goal, I say, "No, zero-zero, let's go for extra time." So I don't know why people connect me with these feelings because I'm exactly the opposite, so I don't understand.'

Misunderstood, misinterpreted, much maligned, maybe. Special, certainly. His first season had brought a league and cup double and a Champions League semi-final to Chelsea – extra special for a club like them back then. If Mourinho had achieved nothing else in his career at Stamford Bridge he was already assured of a place in the Chelsea Hall of Fame. What we didn't realize at the time, though, was that this was just the start.

4

ASHLEY COLE

Everything was going so well for Mourinho and Chelsea, and then Ashley Cole came along and threatened to spoil it. The England and Arsenal defender certainly presented me with a dramatic dilemma in my burgeoning relationship, professional and personal, with José Mourinho. It was Tuesday 25 January 2005; a day I'll never forget. The information I received that morning threatened consequences, serious consequences. Potentially very good for me, as a journalist, but also potentially damaging for my dealings with my favourite football team Chelsea, their manager Mourinho, Cole himself and the player's big-time agent Jonathan Barnett.

It all started like this. I was working from home in Rickmansworth, Hertfordshire, when I received a phone call from a regular contact who'd proved a very good and successful source for stories in the past. I still can't name them, even so long after the event, but they were very well connected, especially at Chelsea. The source was excited and convinced their information could lead to a huge scoop; they were right. A smile spread across my face as I listened to the information being imparted.

Chelsea had organized a secret meeting with Ashley Cole to mastermind a move from Highbury to Stamford Bridge. The meeting was to take place on Friday afternoon in central London. Chelsea chief executive Peter Kenyon was going to be there to try to seal a deal with Cole and his adviser Barnett.

The source added that Cole and Barnett were very keen for the move to happen.

Great information. We knew the date, the time and the main protagonists. So I asked, 'Where's the meeting taking place?' hoping to nail the final piece of the jigsaw. 'No idea,' came the reply. 'What?' I spluttered. 'You've got all the other details ... can you find out where?'

Disappointingly the response was negative as the source explained the unique circumstances by which they'd come by details of the meeting in the first place. Straight away I knew they were right. There was just no way of going back to find out any more without raising suspicions and maybe blowing the story. It was a setback, but I was still convinced we could solve the scenario with a bit of detective work. After all, it was only Tuesday, which meant we had plenty of time on our side. All I needed was a plan.

I called the office and spoke to my boss Mike Dunn, Head of Sport at the *News of the World*. I told him about the conversation and he was suitably excited at the prospect of a big scoop for that Sunday's newspaper. Obviously the great unknown, the venue, was the stumbling block. I couldn't simply ring Peter Kenyon, Ashley Cole or Jonathan Barnett to ask them the whereabouts of their clandestine meeting. The fact was they were all up to no good, because such a meeting was completely against football rules: Cole was contracted to Arsenal Football Club and Chelsea had no right to speak with or meet with the player without Arsenal's permission. Proceeding without such permission is what's known in the game as 'tapping up', and getting caught would leave Chelsea, Cole and Barnett wide open to disciplinary action by the Premier League and/or the Football Association. Similarly, we couldn't ring every hotel in the capital and ask, 'Excuse me, it's the *News of the World* here, are you hosting a secret meeting between Chelsea and Ashley Cole on Friday afternoon?'

However, after a bit of thought, I realized there was one way we could find out the venue. After all, we knew who was going to the meeting and on what day, so I suggested we just follow one or all of them on Friday and they'd lead us directly to the meeting place. Simple. Or so I thought.

I was amazed when this course of action was immediately frowned upon and quickly rejected as a way forward. I argued, 'We're only following them, it's not illegal, what's the problem?' But, for some unknown, unfathomable reason, and I'm still not sure what it was, it was deemed to be an unacceptable, unsavoury course of action. I was stunned. This was the *News of the World*, for goodness sake, not the *Church Times*!

The obvious consequence was that we were in dire danger of missing out on a top scoop with this squeaky-clean approach. I began to fear the story would be lost because I could not conceive of another way we could find out where the meeting was to be held. That meant we had little, if any, chance of being able to prove that a meeting had taken place. And no proof, no scoop. I was downcast but not despondent. What else could I do?

I suggested setting up an interview with Ashley Cole, to be published at the weekend. That way we'd at least have a big hit on the man at the middle of the story, which would be a very timely piece if he did quit Arsenal and join Chelsea in the next few days. It wouldn't seem too suspicious either. The Gunners' left back was already embroiled in protracted and difficult contract talks with Arsenal at the time. (He later revealed in his autobiography how he nearly swerved off the road when the Gunners offered him only £55,000 a week instead of the £60,000 he was seeking, a revelation that earned him the moniker 'Cashley'.) I argued that we could use all of his unhappiness and unrest at Arsenal as the basis for the interview request. Who knew what Cole might say in the circumstances?

This idea was seized upon and an interview was duly arranged. I went along to conduct it and sure enough it was dynamite stuff. Cole was very forthcoming. He didn't even need encouraging, let alone enticing, to let rip over his perceived predicament at Arsenal. It was the sort of interview a player gives to a newspaper in a bid to force his way out of his club and of course we already knew Cole wanted out, so it all worked perfectly. Brilliant. Job done. Admittedly we couldn't break the big story but at least we'd got a superb 'second-best' alternative. It meant we'd have a controversial, agenda-setting feature for Sunday that would once again have us well ahead of the game and our rivals on Fleet Street.

The afternoon of Friday 28 January duly arrived and sure enough we had drawn a blank on discovering where the covert Cole talks were going to be conducted.

On the Saturday morning I had an early start, travelling to the south coast for the Southampton versus Portsmouth FA Cup tie, which kicked off at lunchtime. So it was only after I had filed my match report that I got to have a proper chat with the sports desk. They were in overdrive, and not with the afternoon's football results. No, some guy had rung into the office claiming he'd seen Peter Kenyon, José Mourinho and Ashley Cole meeting in a London hotel on Friday afternoon. He was a businessman who'd gone to the Royal Park Hotel near Hyde Park for a meeting of his own. He was also a keen football fan so immediately understood the significance of seeing Messrs Kenyon, Mourinho, Cole, Barnett and a football fixer called Pini Zihavi all together at the same hotel.

As I said, the informant was a businessman and quickly realized that this was a moneymaking opportunity. He rang one newspaper that Friday afternoon to try to sell his story but they did nothing. So in the evening he called the *News of the World*. Deputy sports editor Tim Allan took the call, which was perfect.

As a senior executive on the sports desk he already knew we'd been seeking confirmation of this very story, so his reaction was instant and decisive. Whereas the other newspaper had been sceptical and suspicious of the information, Tim knew that this was the breakthrough we'd been waiting for and sprang into action. First he interviewed the man over the phone to get all the details of the meeting. Then he arranged for a reporter to go straight down to the hotel to try to get independent confirmation of what he'd just been told.

Encouragingly, on the Saturday morning the reporter despatched to the hotel announced that he had managed to get an off-the-record confirmation from a member of the hotel staff saying that, yes, Mourinho and Cole had been there. It wasn't enough for the lawyers. They told Allan we needed to bring the businessman into the office to give us an affidavit, a statement under oath confirming what he had seen. This presented us with a surprising obstacle: no one could find a Bible for him to swear on! There was a frantic scouring of offices, of drawers and bookcases before a copy of the Good Book was finally found somewhere in *The Times* building, which was alongside the *News of the World* offices in Wapping. The businessman swore his oath on the Bible in front of the lawyer and then gave his full version of the events he'd witnessed at the Royal Park Hotel the previous day. The rest is history.

We dropped the Cole interview from the newspaper and instead ran the huge 'tapping up' story on the Sunday. It caused an uproar, not just on the day but throughout the next week. Barnett shamelessly denied there'd been a meeting, and Chelsea were briefing that the story was wrong. All their desperate denials were in vain, though.

The following Sunday, 6 February, the Premier League started a formal investigation into the matter. It was to be a long, drawn-out affair, although by March the protests of 'innocence' had gone quiet as the evidence mounted. Arsène Wenger, for one, was now convinced of Chelsea's skulduggery. This was no surprise really, as I'd arranged for Arsenal vice-chairman David Dein to come into the *News of the World* offices to meet our executives and lawyers and see the evidence first-hand. Soon afterwards Wenger complained, 'This case is very sad and very unfortunate because you expect your neighbours in the same city, with that power, not to behave like that. I am convinced that a meeting did take place – although that has not been confirmed.' He went on to blast the Blues as 'arrogant' and 'naive' and asked sarcastically, 'Why not do it in the middle of the M25 and then at least everybody knows?'

Finally, on Wednesday 23 March, Chelsea, Mourinho and Cole were charged by the Premier League. The evidence the League had gathered on Barnett and Zahavi, who were not subject to Premier League rules, was forwarded to the Football Association for the game's governing body to consider their own disciplinary actions against the two agents. Then on 19 April the Premier League at last announced that an independent commission would be convened to consider the charges on 17 and 18 May, almost four months after the story appeared. It was not soon enough for Wenger, who later moaned, 'We are now in May and the situation happened in February [actually January]. It has still not gone to a hearing. It looks like an international war is quicker sorted out.'

He had a point. Incredibly, it wasn't until Thursday 2 June that the outcome was eventually announced. It was worth the wait. Chelsea, their manager Mourinho and transfer target Cole were all found guilty as charged. All three were hit with record fines. Chelsea were ordered to pay £300,000 and given a suspended three-point deduction. Mourinho was hammered with a £200,000 fine while Cole was ordered to cough up £100,000. Subsequently, though, Mourinho and Cole did both successfully appeal against their fines, with both reduced to £75,000. Still, the truth and accuracy of my story had been totally vindicated despite all the denials and half-truths from some of the accused along the way.

There was another incidental penalty that was arguably even more expensive for the guilty men. Chelsea's hopes of signing Cole from Arsenal were scuppered for another nineteen months. It was a costly affair all around, and I was the man responsible for it. The dilemma now was how would this affect my relations with Chelsea, Mourinho, Cole and Barnett, who had himself been fined £100,000 by the FA and banned from practising as an agent for eighteen months, nine of those suspended, for his role in the shady dealings.

Not surprisingly there were repercussions: Cole and Barnett never cooperated with me again but, while Chelsea were not happy with me, they did at least maintain a line of communication, albeit a somewhat frosty one in the immediate aftermath.

So, what of Mourinho? He was brilliant. He didn't blame me at all. He blamed himself for going along, explaining to me later that he'd wanted to look into Cole's eyes to see if he really had a burning desire to play for Chelsea or was just after a big payday or, even worse, would use Chelsea to get a pay rise to stay with Arsenal. He was actually impressed that I'd broken the story, and realized what a good operator I was and what an ally I could be to him and to Chelsea. So instead of fracturing our fledgling friendship, it actually strengthened it and brought about an even closer bond and working relationship between us. What a result! Cole and Barnett I could cope without, but to lose Mourinho as well would have been nigh on disastrous. Yes, of course I knew the risk I was taking when I first wrote the article but I believed it was too important a story to ignore and that I would have to suffer the consequences if those involved reacted badly. I stand by that decision and I'm certain I would still have felt the same, even if Mourinho had snubbed me too.

Having said that, I was grateful for his mature and reasoned response, which I thought spoke volumes about the integrity of the man, his honesty and his fairness. I was even more grateful to him when the Sports Journalists' Association later awarded me the prestigious Sports Story of the Year award for 2005. That was followed up by the Chris Blythe Award for 'Scoop of the Year', which was presented to the journalist who'd delivered the best story published in the *News of the World* that year. The final recognition came later when my exposure of the Ashley Cole scandal was voted the newspaper's twenty-seventh best story of the Noughties. Thanks, José.

5

MOUR OF THE SAME

You could argue it was my fault that it was Asier del Horno, not Ashley Cole, who arrived as Chelsea's new left back in June of 2005. The twenty-four-year-old Spanish international was signed in June from Athletic Bilbao, a deal that was ultimately overshadowed by the £24-million arrival of Michael Essien from Lyon and the £21 million paid out for Shaun Wright-Phillips from Manchester City.

In comparison, del Horno's £8 million fee was a modest one. The problem was that his impact at the club would be much less than modest. As a result he managed just a year with the Blues and his most memorable moment was an inglorious one: a red card for a wild lunge on a certain Lionel Messi. It was Wednesday 22 February 2006 at Stamford Bridge, with the Blues yet again matched against the mighty Catalans in the Champions League last sixteen.

A cagey opening erupted in the thirty-sixth minute with del Horno's rash challenge and dismissal, although Chelsea did still manage to go in front when Frank Lampard's fifty-ninth-minute free kick deflected in off Thiago Motta. The ten men couldn't hold on, though. A John Terry own goal and a Samuel Eto'o strike gave Barca a win that would eventually prove enough to see them through to the quarter-finals; the return leg in the Camp Nou ended 1–1. Not surprisingly, del Horno disappeared at the end of the 2006 season, Chelsea selling him on to Valencia for a cut-price fee of £4.8 million.

The following month the Blues spent £5 million on another left back. Yes, it was Ashley Cole. The unsettled William Gallas, fed up with being played out of position as a full back by Mourinho, happily went the other way and joined Arsenal. José had finally got his man, although we'll never know what might have been if he and Chelsea had tried the legitimate approach for the England star in the first place. He certainly couldn't have done any worse than del Horno. That said, the Spaniard did leave as a champion, something Cole wouldn't achieve at Chelsea until four years later with Carlo Ancelotti at the helm.

While del Horno and Chelsea had been found wanting in Europe, it was a totally different story in the Premier League that year. It was simply Mour of the same at home as Mourinho's men again dominated to become back-to-back champions. The league was all but won by the turn of the year when the Blues were an incredible 11 points clear, but the destination of the title only finally became official on 29 April 2006. An emphatic 3–0 win over second-placed Manchester United at Stamford Bridge sealed a second successive title and more special memories for the Special One.

Chelsea were imperious on the day and had been so throughout the season and now it was time to pour the champagne, break out the cigars and get the party started. It was quite a party, too. The coveted trophy was presented afterwards: there were pyrotechnics, ticker tape and a glorious lap of honour to make it an unforgettable day all around. Mourinho even threw his winner's medal into the Matthew Harding stand to add to the spectacle and ensure some lucky fan in the crowd would pocket a unique and tangible memento of the day. What an occasion and what a first match for my son Joshua, who I'd brought along with my daughter Saskia, although I did have to explain to him afterwards that it wasn't like that at every game.

Mourinho was Manager of the Year again. Frank Lampard

was Player of the Year again, boasting 16 league goals in 35 games. Chelsea notched 91 points and equalled their own record of 29 wins, nine of them coming in a row at the start of the season. Hernan Crespo's last-gasp winner at newly promoted Wigan Athletic had kicked it all off on the opening day and Chelsea went on to sweep aside Arsenal, West Bromwich Albion, Tottenham Hotspur, Sunderland, Charlton Athletic, Aston Villa, Liverpool and Bolton Wanderers, scoring 23 goals in the process while conceding just three. It was a remarkable opening run which set the tone for the season.

The Blues went on to amass an amazing 20 wins in their first 22 games of the campaign, meaning the destination of the title was never seriously in doubt.

There had been setbacks, though. Just a week before the visit of United they'd lost 2–1 at Old Trafford in the FA Cup semifinal against Liverpool to wave goodbye to securing a second successive league and League Cup double. Lowly Charlton had become the first English team to win against Mourinho at the Bridge with a penalty shoot-out victory against the holders in the Carling Cup.

Nevertheless, Chelsea were still without doubt England's top club: they finished eight points clear of United, and Mourinho was undeniably the top manager. Even the great Sir Alex Ferguson was forced to pay due deference to Mourinho and his men. The United manager confessed, 'Chelsea deserve all the plaudits they will get, especially on their home form. They are worthy champions.'

Mourinho, moods and all, was definitely the journalists' favourite manager too, with his box-office press conferences full of wisecracks, banter or controversy. He made news, he guaranteed headlines and all backed up by the fact that he couldn't just talk the talk, he could walk the walk to success and silverware, too. It was a win-win scenario for sports reporters like me and, as a regular on the Chelsea beat, I was now developing a great working relationship with him.

A pre-season tour to the East Coast of the US in the summer of 2005 had certainly helped ensure there was no lingering hangover from my involvement in exposing the Ashley Cole scandal in the January. So by the time Chelsea went off to the USA as English champions again in 2006, we were forging a very good rapport and were both dreaming of more good times to come.

6

JENNIFER

It's not often you witness José Mourinho totally lost for words. Normally he'll talk football with you all day long and even when he's not addressing his favourite subject, he's often the joker, full of banter, telling funny stories and playing pranks – there's never a dull moment. However, on this particular day, even he was momentarily stumped for something to say. Fittingly, we were in sunny Los Angeles when the man of five different languages got stage-struck. We weren't actually in Hollywood, we were in Beverly Hills at the time, but that's close enough given it's the playground of the rich and famous of Tinsel Town. The lobby of the world-renowned Beverly Hills Hotel, to be precise. And it was noisy.

Chelsea were on a pre-season tour of the USA. They were staying in the hotel and had set up their summer camp at UCLA's sports complex just around the corner. Everyone was assembled together in the hotel lobby waiting for the team bus to arrive to take them to the practice session. There were twenty-six or so footballers, the team's associated coaches, medics, physios, kit men and hangers-on. Spirits were high and so was the volume.

I was sitting with Mourinho, who was telling me about his disastrous summer holiday to Brazil. 'It rained like it was the end of the world,' he complained. 'Every day!' But suddenly José's holiday tales were stopped in their tracks. Not only that, but the whole Chelsea contingent fell into an immediate silence.

The transformation was dramatic. One moment a cacophony of voices all clashing with each other, the next a proverbial 'pin-drop' scenario. What could have possibly brought such a vocal, excitable group to total silence in the batting of an eye? A sight that made those present blink not once, but twice, just to persuade themselves that they were not imagining the star that had just appeared in their midst. Startled eyes stared, jaws dropped and every man there was rendered immobile. That's the effect Jennifer Aniston had.

José was no different. He did what everyone did as the *Friends* star breezed through the front doors and into the hotel reception area: froze on the spot with only his eyes moving to track the actress as she strode through the lobby towards the Polo Lounge.

It was one of those moments in life one will never forget – great for repeating as an anecdote at every opportunity. For Jennifer Aniston was absolutely gorgeous that day. She wasn't dressed up to the nines in some designer gear, with perfect make-up and hair – it didn't even look as if she was wearing make-up and her hair had simply been pulled back into a ponytail. She was wearing a vest top, a pair of faded jeans that ended mid-calf and a pair of flip-flops. Simple but stunning, and she knew it. Jennifer clearly realized the impact she had made on this body of men. She even glanced over at the motley collection of mesmerized individuals and flashed us a beaming smile before continuing confidently and contentedly on her merry way.

All too soon she had disappeared from sight into the corridor and inevitably José was the first to react. 'F***ing hell, Brad Pitt – what a wanker!' Everyone burst into laughter. Pitt had of course dumped Jennifer the year before and turned his attentions to Angelina Jolie instead. A fact Mourinho was equally quick to seize upon. In a flash he added, 'Jennifer

Aniston one, Angelina Jolie nil,' and as he mentioned Jolie's name he pouted to mimic Angelina's famous full mouth, her trademark feature. More guffaws all around. José was japing around of course but he was probably thinking what everyone else was: who would possibly give up Jennifer Aniston?

It was certainly a surreal incident. Anywhere else on the planet Mourinho and his players would have been the absolute centre of attention. Not in America and certainly not in LA. No, in the film capital of the world the Chelsea 'stars' were way, way down the pecking order. Even the likes of captain John Terry and star midfielder Frank Lampard could regularly walk down the street unnoticed and unmolested. Remember too that soccer, as the Americans call it, is not one of the major sports in the USA, and this was also at a time when Chelsea were only just emerging as a major force in English and European football. It was Mourinho's first spell in charge and, while Chelsea were Premier League champions, that didn't mean much at all to the disinterested locals.

Some of the players loved the anonymity; others craved the usual recognition. And they were all a little bit star-struck when the Hollywood 'A-listers' were around. Frequently Chelsea would throw an official party when they stayed in LA on tour. The likes of Snoop Dogg, Matthew McConaughey and Jason Statham would show up and it certainly made for an intriguing contrast when the football stars rubbed shoulders with the Hollywood elite.

José and I reminisced and laughed about the Jennifer Aniston episode years later when Mourinho was boss of Real Madrid, and it was then that he told me of another meeting with a top Hollywood star that was not quite so memorable.

José is a big fan of the movies and his favourite actors are Al Pacino and Anthony Hopkins. Pushed on the two, he will admit Pacino is his number-one choice. So José's meeting with Pacino should have been an awesome experience for him: the coming together of two great men, two revered figures, two heart-throbs even. José was, of course, pleased, producing his mobile phone to show me a picture of him and Pacino together. There was a touch of jealousy, though, as Mourinho revealed that the whole room, and especially the women in it, had flocked to Pacino, not Mourinho. Now that was something that didn't normally happen to José and I suspect his famous ego had been a bit bruised by it because he joked that Pacino was old, was small and his face was heavily lined and wrinkled. He couldn't understand how everyone swarmed around him, swooned over him and preferred the company of the actor compared to the super-cool football manager.

It was all said in jest but my feeling was that there was a definite edge to the joke. José's career has been built on him believing he is a 'special one', a match for anyone and better than most. To find himself overlooked, ignored and unappreciated would not have been to his liking. Perhaps denigrating one of the people he admired most, even with tongue in cheek, was his way of coping with a perceived snub. It gave me a clearer insight into the mentality of the man; someone who believed he had few equals, if any, and liked it that way, thank you very much. It's that attitude, self-belief and self-confidence that make him the magnificent manager that he is, one of the most successful in the history of the game. Just now and again, though, it also manifests itself in a way that is not as positive or attractive: sometimes in private, as on this occasion in his office in Madrid, but sometimes very much in the public eye. Think Arsène Wenger and Rafa Benítez.

Those sort of feelings didn't show themselves often. The vast majority of the time the man was a joy to be around. Easy-going, down to earth and so approachable and engaging. There were plenty of times when he craved to be able to do normal things without all the fuss and attention. Like on that trip to LA.

It was the day of the official Chelsea party, a star-studded, glitzy affair planned to match the LA setting. José didn't want to go. Part of the reason was that he wanted the players to be given free rein to enjoy themselves without the manager being present and potentially watching every move, every drink, every dalliance. He also fancied a break from the group, a change of scenery and a change of company. So I told José that fellow journalist Paul Smith and I were heading to a famous Malibu restaurant that night, a place called Moonshadows. It's a fabulous place, with great seafood and wines in a terrific setting right on the beach. It's where the beautiful people hang out to see and be seen. Best of all, if you book a table in the window, you are treated to the Pacific Ocean rolling in right beneath you as you dine. It's equally famous for being the establishment where Oscar-winner Mel Gibson got intoxicated in 2006. He was stopped just down the highway on suspicion of drink-driving and his anti-Semitic outburst to traffic cops made headline news around the world and really put Moonshadows on the global map – a bit of a tourist attraction.

José said he loved the idea of a night out with us and told us he wanted to come along too, so I rang Moonshadows and amended the reservation from two to three. José didn't make it. He later explained that the club had pointed out that as Chelsea manager he had to attend the party and carry out his official 'meet and greet' duties to promote the club and schmooze among the VIP guests. It was a shame really because he missed a great night. Mel Gibson wasn't there, neither was Al Pacino or Jennifer Aniston, but Demi Moore and Sarah Jessica Parker were. Well, two astonishing lookalikes anyway. It was unbelievably hard to accept that the girls were not the actual actresses they resembled so incredibly.

We shared a pot of green tea with them and lots of laughs

and Demi even gave us a lift back from Malibu to Santa Monica in her silver Mercedes. Nothing untoward, all good, clean, honest and platonic fun and the sort of evening Mourinho would have thoroughly enjoyed. Great food, great views, great company, and boy did we tease José about missing out when he asked us all about it the next day.

7
READY FOR WAR

It wasn't all Hollywood glitz and glamour on these pre-season trips to Los Angeles and the USA. There was plenty of hard work and planning going on too, but most fascinating of all was observing the dynamic of the squad. It was intriguing and revealing to monitor which players hung out together, how the new signings were finding their feet and who was happy and who looked out of sorts.

In the build-up to José's third season in charge, the 2006–07 campaign, there was certainly plenty to observe. There were two massive arrivals into the Chelsea 'family' and a controversial no-show. The biggest news of the summer was the £30 million club record signing of Ukraine and AC Milan's superstar striker Andriy Shevchenko. Germany captain Michael Ballack had also joined on a free transfer from Bayern Munich and English football sat up and took full notice. This was a powerful statement of intent from the Londoners, who had cruised to two league titles in a row. Suddenly the best had just got even better.

Or had they? Rumours quickly abounded that the pair were actually signed by the board on the wishes of owner Roman Abramovich rather than in response to a request from manager José Mourinho. Abramovich was a huge fan of the Ukrainian and Chelsea had tried to sign him in 2004 and 2005 before finally getting him at the third attempt in the summer of 2006. As for Ballack, who was he going to replace? One of the established stars like Frank Lampard, Claude Makelele, Arjen Robben or Joe Cole? Or one of last year's big-money boys, £24-million Michael Essien or £21-million Shaun Wright-Phillips?

There was another consideration. On the face of it, Shevchenko and Ballack certainly didn't appear to fit the Mourinho profile. He tended to favour recruiting players he already knew and trusted like Paulo Ferreira, Ricardo Carvalho and Tiago, or young, hungry players who were eager to succeed like Michael Essien, Shaun Wright-Phillips, Florent Malouda and John Obi Mikel. Shevchenko and Ballack were older, established stars who already knew the taste of success and were coming towards the twilight of their careers. The popular theory was that players of that stature and age would be far less likely to respond to Mourinho's intensive and demanding approach in training and in matches.

Mourinho did his best to dispel the gossip surrounding his new big-name additions. 'Today is a day when the dream became reality,' Mourinho said after Shevchenko signed his Stamford Bridge contract. 'Andriy has always been my first choice for Chelsea since I arrived. Before it was not possible, now it is for real. He has ambition, discipline, tactical awareness and of course he is a great goalscorer.'

His welcome for Ballack was equally generous. José declared, 'He [Ballack] believes in us, he believes in Chelsea, he believes he can have success. He believes in the Champions League, he believes in three, four years' success for him in a crucial time of his career. He had a lot of other chances as you can imagine. He decided on Chelsea and I think we are very happy and I think also English football should be happy to have such a player playing in the Premiership.'

Later, as the Shevchenko tittle-tattle intensified, Mourinho was even more strident, insisting, 'Never, never during my time did the owner interfere in the basic things of the manager:

training sessions, team selection, the profile of player I want to bring.'

The trouble was he also contradicted himself. His 'first-choice' forward wasn't actually his first choice. For Mourinho added, 'Do you want to know the truth about Shevchenko? I hope the board is not upset with me. We wanted to buy Samuel Eto'o; he was our target. We wanted Eto'o and the owner was more than ready to do everything to bring Eto'o here. He was the player I wanted. Why? Because Eto'o was the only player I could play with Didier Drogba, changing the system for two strikers. But he was also ready to play with Drogba with the system we had at the time, with three attacking players with Eto'o coming from the sides. We wanted Eto'o and the boss did everything to bring Eto'o and Peter Kenyon did everything. In the end, Barcelona said, "We don't sell, forget it, forget it. Not any price." The owner did everything to get him, but it was not possible. After that, we went to other options and got to Shevchenko. I was happy with him.'

There was a 'but', though, with José confessing, 'Even with the top dogs – when you buy for £30 million, £40 million, £50 million or £60 million – sometimes it doesn't work. It doesn't mean you or the club made a big mistake. It just doesn't work.'

The early signs on tour were not encouraging. Shevchenko always seemed on the periphery of the group, always looked deadpan, miserable even. The £30-million man did not exude £30 worth of confidence, happiness or togetherness. In contrast, freebie Ballack had all the swagger and attitude of a superstar who knew himself and his worth; not in an arrogant, aloof way, but in an arrogant, self-confident, contented manner. It made him an imposing, impressive, important figure in the squad. What's more, he was a man who loved to smile and chat, who was relaxed, clever and über cool in the way he acted, dressed and performed. Straightaway I formed the opinion that he would fit in well while the sheepish Sheva might struggle.

That being said, Ballack's arrival was the one that had caused the most immediate impact on the Chelsea 'family' and sparked almost instant controversy. Mourinho was behind it. After initially refusing, José suddenly changed his mind and agreed that Ballack would be allowed to wear the number 13 on his shirt. It was Ballack's favourite number and he had worn 13 for Bayern Munich and Bayer Leverkusen. Now at his official unveiling in LA he told us of his surprise that he had been given the number at Chelsea too. He revealed, 'Initially, I wanted 13 and I was sad because it had already been taken. I had accepted number 19, but two days ago the coach came and said, "Okay, it's fine for you to have the 13 after all."'

It was Mourinho's way of slapping down want-away defender William Gallas, who was facing disciplinary action by the club after failing to fly over to join the tour in Los Angeles as agreed. Gallas wore the number 13 at Chelsea and, even though he was asking to leave, he was still furious to see Ballack given 'his' shirt. It only served to harden the Frenchman's desire to quit the club. That might have been the idea all along as Gallas was subsequently used as bait to finally clinch Ashley Cole's £5-million switch across London, another superstar and proven winner joining the fold, with Gallas going the other way.

A further concern in the camp was the behaviour of flying winger Arjen Robben. He'd suffered an ankle injury in training and spent much of the tour limping around and looking disconsolate. There was more unrest with the Dutchman being linked with Real Madrid and wanting to go, by all accounts. Certainly when I asked him if he was happy to stay at Chelsea he was not forthcoming in affirming that intention. He didn't say he wanted to go, indeed he didn't actually say much at all, which spoke volumes. When you are around people every day you get a vibe from them, and Robben's was that of a man who

(Left) The night José Mourinho burst into the public's consciousness as his Porto side put out Manchester United in the Champions League in 2004. The world, and Roman Abramovich in particular, took notice.

(Right) The Special One: Mourinho announces his arrival in English football by labelling himself a 'special one' to the world's assembled media.

(**This page and opposite, top**) Mourinho has always shared a special bond with his Chelsea players, which quickly translated into trophies in his first two seasons.

I feared my coverage of the Ashley Cole 'tapping up' scandal would damage my relationship with Mourinho, but he proved to be a bigger man than that.

(Right) Completing the set: Mourinho won all domestic trophies on offer in his first three seasons at Chelsea.

(Left, with Chelsea owner Roman Abramovich) But some relationships don't work out, which ultimately cost Mourinho his job in 2007.

England's loss, Inter's gain: a Scudetto in his first season as manager of Inter Milan was followed by an historic treble in his second.

(**Above**) Past, present and future Chelsea: José playing his old club, now managed by Carlo Ancelotti, with Inter Milan in the Champions League in 2010.

(**Below**) Little did Harry Redknapp know that Mourinho could have been standing in his shoes at the end of that 2010–11 season.

(**Left**) Mourinho's record-breaking Real Madrid side celebrate after managing to wrest La Liga back from Pep Guardiola's dominant Barcelona.

(**Right**) Embracing his star player Cristiano Ronaldo.

Mourinho generously arranged an interview with Ronaldo for me, and later on that same trip suggested he may eventually answer Chelsea fans' pleas (**below**).

wanted away but who wasn't quite sure if it would happen. Unlike Gallas, he wasn't prepared to play hardball with the club to try to force an exit and in the end Robben stayed, but only for one more season, and a pretty ineffective season at that. He played just 16 league games and scored two goals before switching to Madrid for £24 million in 2007.

Consequently there were clear and obvious signals for me that all was not well in the Chelsea camp in the summer of 2006. Two consecutive league titles and now three incoming superstars should have seen them as certainties to make it three league crowns in a row. However, there was now a catch-22 scenario at the club resulting from all of their success with Mourinho. They were able to attract a better class of player to add yet more quality to the squad, but with that came increased competition for places, and frustration and loss of confidence among those left most frequently on the sidelines. The success of Chelsea's stars also made them targets for other clubs and heads could be, and were, turned as a result.

As a consequence the mood and the faces were changing. Former key players like Eidur Gudjohnsen and Damien Duff saw the writing on the wall and moved on, Gudjohnsen bagging a dream move to Barcelona while Duff joined Newcastle United. The 'in' and 'out' doors at Stamford Bridge were revolving and a new Chelsea was evolving. Even Mourinho had changed. He'd turned up after the summer holidays sporting a severe crew-cut hairstyle which he announced showed he was 'ready for the war' in the new season. They were prophetic words but not, I suspect, in the way he intended.

8

QUADROUBLES

The final whistle blew at Arsenal to signal that Mourinho was not a champion any more. He'd reigned supreme for four years after celebrating two consecutive titles at Porto followed by his back-to-back successes at Stamford Bridge. Now he had to stomach being a runner-up for a change. A 1–1 draw with the Gunners meant that Manchester United had deposed Chelsea and won the Premier League with two games to spare. It was Sunday 6 May 2007 and there was just a week of the season left. It was a bitter blow, all the more painful as just six days earlier Chelsea had suffered the agony of being knocked out in the semi-finals of the Champions League in the cruellest fashion: losing on penalties to old rivals Liverpool at Anfield.

It was tough for José to take. At the beginning of May the Blues had still been on course for the quadruple. They'd already won the Carling Cup after beating Arsenal 2–1 in Cardiff's Millennium Stadium, and they were through to the FA Cup final on 19 May; they'd also started the week just one step away from a first Champions League final, as well as battling United for the league. Now the 'big two' had gone inside a week and a remarkable campaign was suddenly in danger of appearing a lot less successful in terms of silverware.

Mourinho remained defiant. His first reaction at Arsenal was to stand up and hug his assistant Steve Clarke and shake hands with assistant Silvino Louro. Then he marched on to the pitch towards the Chelsea fans. He gave them a 'chin-up' signal and pointed to his players, urging the supporters to salute them on their efforts to claim a third successive league crown. It was also a rallying call for them to lift the players to go for glory one last time that term: in the Cup final against United in eleven days' time.

Sure enough, Chelsea showed their character and responded to the challenge of winning the first FA Cup final at the new Wembley. Didier Drogba's goal in extra time separated the two teams and saw Mourinho complete the full set of domestic trophies: two Premier Leagues, two League Cups, the Community Shield and the FA Cup, and all in just three years. What's more, it created yet more history for the Stamford Bridge club: they were the last team to win the Cup beneath the twin towers of the old Wembley (beating Aston Villa 1–0 in 2000) and were now the first team to win it under the arch of the new stadium.

It was a joyous season to remember for Drogba, too. He won the Golden Boot as the Premier League's top goalscorer, having notched 20 league goals in 36 appearances. In total, the inspirational Ivory Coast star scored 33 that season, including both of Chelsea's goals in the Carling Cup final against Arsenal followed by his Wembley winner against United. There were also hat-tricks against Levski Sofia and Watford, key goals home and away to secure a win and draw with Barcelona in the Champions League, and winners against Liverpool, Everton and Newcastle. It was the greatest goal-scoring haul of his career and certainly put £30-million new boy Shevchenko well in the shade. 'Sheva' had managed just 14 goals in all, prompting talk that he was looking a very expensive flop. In some ways he was, although he did play 51 matches for Chelsea in that long campaign and it could also be argued that his presence and threat had taken Drogba to an even higher level. So maybe it was £30 million well spent after all.

Mourinho was certainly full of praise for one of his star strikers, declaring, 'He [Drogba] deserves the Golden Boot; to be top scorer in the Premiership without taking penalties is more than deserved. Every goal was a proper goal and I am happy for him.'

His end-of-season review of Shevchenko's contribution was far less flattering and immediately sparked questions about the famous forward's future in the team, even the club. When asked if Sheva would be staying at Stamford Bridge, Mourinho replied in underwhelming style, 'It's up to him. Hopefully he is not happy with what he gave to the team; if he's not happy, that's a start. Sheva's season was not what everyone was [expecting], including myself. In his defence he has a history of many years in a completely different culture; that can be on his side.' Abramovich was on his side too, and he was the most powerful ally of all.

Mourinho had given the big-money buy every chance to succeed; or fail, if you look at it from another perspective. For at times it looked as if Mourinho was playing him on purpose just to prove a point. By Christmas, though, the situation had become toxic. Mourinho was playing Russian roulette when he said, 'If [Abramovich] doesn't trust the manager, he has enough money to sack me, to give me my compensation, send me home and bring another one in. Sheva is not untouchable because [of] the way he is playing.'

The feud festered. On New Year's Day 2007, Chelsea found themselves seven points adrift of United, and the Chelsea boss knew he needed to act. He wanted to bring in a new striker to help Drogba and a centre back to cover for injured skipper John Terry, who'd undergone surgery on his back in mid-December and was not on course to return until February. No signings were made.

According to the Mourinho camp, none of José's proposed

signings were even considered by the board. It seems strange now, but part of the reason for the friction was said to be a petty, jealous dispute over who was truly responsible for the club's rise to prominence. According to senior sources at the club, Mourinho believed his coaching and motivational skills were the primary reason. In contrast, Abramovich felt that it was his generosity and power in the transfer market that was key, and that most managers with that sort of backing could achieve success. It appeared Abramovich was one of the few who thought Mourinho was just 'one out of the bottle' and not a 'special one'. Perhaps not giving into his January demands for new players was a way of proving José couldn't succeed without his cash.

Whatever the real reasons were for the fallout, the unfortunate consequence was that in that vital, final half of the season, with all four trophies still up for grabs, there existed a tense Mexican stand-off between the Russian owner and the Portuguese manager; and yet the Blues still almost did the quadruple. Such discord inevitably bred uncertainty and out of that came constant speculation about Mourinho's future.

For instance, I received a call to say Inter Milan had come in for José and that he might go. It was from a good source, one that I trusted, so I felt it could well be true. Clearly there was only one way to find out for sure and that was to go and ask José face-to-face, man to man. I drove to his home, which was tucked away in a quiet close just off Eaton Square in London's upmarket Belgravia district. I knocked on the front door and it was Mourinho himself who came to open it. He looked surprised to see me standing there but I'd already decided that this was an important enough situation to risk his wrath by turning up at his home unannounced and uninvited. He was okay about it, and so I put the speculation to him. We had a frank chat about it all, Mourinho repeatedly telling me he was going nowhere, he was staying at Chelsea. I looked hard into his eyes and I believed him, so I wrote the story and, sure enough, he stayed.

Eventually a turbulent 2006–07 season was over. It was now time for everyone to take a break, take a breather, take a step back and re-evaluate. It's hard to justify sacking a manager who has brought six trophies in the last three years. It's just as hard to dismiss a season as 'a failure' when you've won both domestic cups, reached the semi-finals of the Champions League and chased for the league right into the last week of the season. That was an astonishing effort, one to be applauded and appreciated, and all the more remarkable because of the constant unrest, rifts and rows throughout it all.

So the football world watched on and wondered which way it would go. Surely the Russian oligarch wouldn't dare axe the most successful and popular manager in the club's history.

9
MATCH OF THE DAY

Abramovich did not sack Mourinho that summer. Instead he appointed Avram Grant above him, as Director of Football and with a place on the board. It was a very public slap in the face for the Chelsea manager, but he took it. He also swallowed an uninspiring summer in the transfer market. Arjen Robben was finally sold to Real Madrid for £24 million and replaced by French international Florent Malouda for £13.5 million. Full back Glen Johnson also left, with Juliano Belletti arriving from Barcelona. Three free transfers also signed on: Steve Sidwell from Reading, Tal Ben-Haim from Bolton and Claudio Pizarro from Bayern Munich. It wasn't really much of a statement of intent from England's most dominant club, especially compared to the previous summer. How would José react?

Well, I jumped on a plane to Los Angeles to find out. Yep, happily the 2007 Cup kings were again doing their pre-season preparations in the famous, celebrity-filled Californian city. This year there was even more of a buzz about the trip as there was one more celebrity about to join the 'in crowd' in LA: a certain David Robert Joseph Beckham.

The England captain and former Manchester United star had stunned everyone in the game by quitting Real Madrid, one of the world's most glamorous and successful clubs, to play Major League Soccer with LA Galaxy. He was to be unveiled in full Hollywood-style on Friday 13 July and would coincidentally be making his debut for the Galaxy in a friendly against Chelsea on Sunday 22. This promised to be some trip, though Mourinho was the main focus for me.

While 5,000 fans and 700 from the worldwide media turned up for the big Beckham extravaganza on Friday the 13th, I instead headed for the Beverly Hills Hotel. It seemed a no-brainer to me to try to get up close and personal to José on a day when you had absolutely no chance of getting up close and personal with Beckham. I swapped a media scrum for an intimate chat and came away with a notebook full of stuff that would last me throughout the tour, including a splash story of him talking about Beckham that would do nicely for the weekend.

José was in good spirits: full of energy and focus and looking forward to another campaign. He insisted all was well with the world, with 'the Chels' and between him and Roman. His mind was not on the Galaxy game, though; he had a more important match in mind before then.

He challenged me to organize a press team to play against his Chelsea staff in a match at their UCLA training ground. Naturally there was no shortage of willing volunteers from my fellow hacks on the trip.

It was a great day. Chelsea provided one of their authentic electric green kits for us, although a couple of churlish pressmen tried to black out the Chelsea badge on the shirt and shorts with gaffer tape because they were not Blues fans. It did not go down well and in the end the tape was removed, albeit reluctantly and with much swearing. Adidas provided a selection of brand-new boots too, which created an unseemly scramble as certain journos dived in to make sure they got their pick of the best available. Most wanted the trendy ones with 'blades' on the bottom but I went retro, picking a beautiful pair of traditional black boots, in lovely soft leather and with good old-fashioned studs. It was the right choice because those studs were needed: it was not what you would call a 'friendly' game.

It started off fine. The pre-match banter was brilliant and the atmosphere was heightened by a decent-sized crowd. The entire Chelsea squad was on the touchline accompanied by all the back-room staff. Even the top brass were there, including Abramovich, who caused a stir by appearing with his new girlfriend, Darya 'Dasha' Zhukova. That had the photographers in a tizz – it was a picture they all wanted but the protocol of the day dictated this was an 'off the record' event not for publication. So the lens caps stayed on and the match kicked off.

José, the son of a goalkeeper, played in goal, while new arrival Avram Grant played in midfield. It was quickly apparent that the 'pros' didn't want to be turned over by a bunch of amateurs from Fleet Street, especially in front of the club's players and directors. The likes of Rui Faria and Steve Clarke were especially pumped. How Faria stayed on the pitch still amazes me now – he wanted to fight everyone and should have had three yellow cards, not one. Clarke was just as competitive, at one point trying to con a penalty when I went in hard on him on the edge of the area. I slid in fast and got the ball but he then kicked my thigh and dived into the box as if I had scythed him down. The American referee wasn't falling for that shameful piece of simulation.

Finally it all went off when Mark Skipp, Head of Security for Abramovich, started sticking the boot in on a prostrate Matt Dickinson. I came running in blind side and shoved Skipp forcibly to the floor. Now this guy is not someone you want to mess with: he's ex-Army, ex-Special Forces and a highly decorated officer too. So I was glad when he jumped up and turned on an innocent Neil Ashton, clearly thinking he had been responsible for flooring him. Abramovich was chuckling away, the players hooting and hollering as I then innocently moved in as a peacemaker between the two.

Chelsea went 1–0 up; I can't remember who scored, but I do remember Mourinho limping off with a pulled hamstring after rushing from his area to make a slide tackle. That meant his assistant, Silvino Louro, became their goalkeeper. That was some switch as he'd been a top-flight keeper for twenty-three years in Portugal, including earning twenty-three caps for his country. So there was plenty of pressure on our striker Ian McGarry when we were awarded a penalty late on. We needn't have worried. He coolly slotted it passed Silvino to earn us a 1–1 draw, a result we were quick to celebrate and rub in the faces of the Chelsea staff. It was a memorable day, all thanks to José, whose idea it was and who was in the thick of it on and off the pitch.

Chelsea's first 'real' match on the trip was against Japanese side Suwon Bluewings on 17 July. They won 1–0 at LA Galaxy's Home Depot Stadium. The Galaxy were up next against UANL Tigres from Mexico. Beckham was not playing but was there in a hospitality box with his manager Terry Byrne and Aaron Lincoln, who looked after John Terry.

I knew Terry and Aaron well. They had once been on the back-room staff at Chelsea but forged fantastic careers for themselves after developing great relationships with Becks and JT respectively. They tipped me off that there was a bit of a soirée going on in the bar of the Beverly Hills Hotel that night, so I rushed back to the hotel to change into something appropriate for an LA party and popped along.

I had a drink and chat with the pair of them as they sat in a corner by the entrance of the bar, so was in pole position when a bare-footed John Terry strode in looking very underdressed in a Chelsea polo shirt and rolled-up tracksuit bottoms, a state he quickly explained by announcing: 'I've broke my f***ing toe, haven't I?' He certainly had, so I bought him a string of 'medicinal' drinks at the bar to help ease the pain and maybe loosen the tongue. It was a lively chat – and my wallet was lighter for it – but that's a story for another day.

The interest for me that night was what would the Chelsea manager be like around the Chelsea owner. First of all came the arrival of Abramovich, looking casual in an open-necked shirt and jeans, trademark stubble and a whimsical smile. He sat down at a table in the middle of the room, with the LA beauties around him totally unaware of who he was and his vast wealth. Shortly afterwards Mourinho strode into the room and headed straight for his boss. I tensed, but Abramovich stood up, smiled and the pair hugged, laughed and then sat, talking and clearly joking together. Abramovich looked relaxed and calm, Mourinho looked mellow (that was his buzzword on the trip) and content. Peace in our time. Or so it seemed.

10

I'LL BE BACK!

Sadly the Hollywood tour rapprochement between owner and manager didn't last. Reality soon kicked in when the pair swapped the palm trees and sunshine of California for the streets of London. Once all the beautiful people were gone the mood quickly turned ugly. There could only be one winner.

So, early in the new season I was back at José's front door. This time the talk was that he was doomed, even so soon in the campaign. For once, José couldn't deny it. His whole demeanour, his body language and especially his face, told the story. Nothing for quoting, but that was the moment I knew the end was near and I could barely believe it.

Sure enough, on 20 September 2007, it was all over. I got a phone call tipping me off that José was finished. I tried to phone him. I rang everybody I could, but hardly anybody was answering because most of the Chelsea squad and staff were at the premiere of Chelsea's *Blue Revolution* film in Fulham Broadway that night with their phones switched off. I did get hold of Joe Cole's dad George and told him what I'd heard. His response was 'Good', but he admitted he didn't know anything. George's reaction was maybe understandable. Back then he wasn't happy with Mourinho's handling of Joe so he wasn't bothered he was on his way out. (In retrospect, he might now acknowledge that his years under José were actually Joe's best, most successful and most productive.)

Next I tried to get through to Chelsea chairman Bruce Buck

on his mobile and was surprised when he answered. There was no time to waste so I immediately put him on the spot, asking about the swirling rumours. He replied, 'I'm sorry I can't talk now, I'm busy.' I said, 'Yes, I know, busy sacking José!' and he hung up. Later a statement on the Chelsea website confirmed it: 'Chelsea Football Club and José Mourinho have agreed to part company today (Thursday) by mutual consent.'

It was stunning news. The new 2007–08 season was just weeks old but already the bitter divisions had resurfaced, the feud reignited, and both men knew it had to stop for the good of the club and the individuals concerned. So the deal was done for Mourinho to go with a full pay-off, with the only proviso being that he couldn't work in England for a year. Abramovich didn't want José coming back to haunt him in the Premier League, and who could blame him? Mourinho's record at the club was remarkable. In 185 matches he'd won 124, drawn 40 and lost just 21. He never lost a home game in the Premier League and he put two Premier League crowns, two League Cups, an FA Cup and a Community Shield in the once bare and dusty Chelsea trophy cabinet. Two Champions League semi-finals had seen him go agonizingly close to European glory, too.

It was a painful experience for all concerned but it simply had to be done, had to be endured. Man in the middle Peter Kenyon, Chelsea's chief executive, summed it all up at the time saying, 'I've done everything over the last twelve months to try and keep this thing together. Not because of being a friend of José's but because at that time it was the right thing to do. There's been a great effort on everybody's part but it's just overtaken what the job is. There's a point where you're spending more time on the problems than dealing with the issues ... You can't point to a single item that made us say "enough". Relationships are complex things. A brilliant club, a brilliant team; there's a lot of complexities. I can't give you a single factor. It was just a combination of things. José's a tremendous person, he's done an unbelievable job and he's a good friend. Often with somebody who's that successful comes other issues. Basically, if this thing was going to work long-term then the relationships between the key people in the organization have to be right. Fact. And it hasn't been right for a long time and it finally got to the point where it wasn't going to be right in the future. For all those reasons that have been written about, and I'm not going to go over it all, we've reached the point where we have to regroup, and that's what's happened.'

So that was it – the end – well, almost the end. Inevitably José had the last word – of course he did. With perfect timing he chose the day that Chelsea's recently appointed Director of Football Avram Grant was unveiled to the media as his successor as Chelsea manager. Grant gave a stilted, downbeat and, quite frankly, boring press conference at Stamford Bridge. As I was heading back to Fulham Broadway Tube station afterwards I was feeling far from impressed and far from inspired. My mood was quickly changed by a tip-off that José was out and about just down the road at Chelsea Harbour. No surprises for guessing what I did next. I headed straight across from the Fulham Road to the King's Road and quickly scampered down Lots Road towards the River Thames to try to find him.

Sure enough Mourinho had dramatically and charismatically re-emerged to steal Grant's thunder. As I arrived he was doing a brief television interview surrounded by a gaggle of fans and intrigued passers-by.

As quickly as I could, I swept in to steal him away for a big sit-down interview of my own. On the TV news that night there were shots of me linking arms with him and walking alongside and into the Chelsea Harbour Hotel as it was then, the Wyndham as it is now. I was trying to steer him away from the gathering crowd and into a room where I would have him all to myself.

I must admit the footage looked a bit odd, a bromance-type image of two blokes arm-in-arm, but I didn't care. My mission had been to get José out of the crowd and on his own, so I wasn't going to let him go! It worked and the happy outcome was that I got what I thought could be my last big hit with him. José was certainly signing off in style, because it was stunning stuff from a proud man battling to control his emotions after a chastening experience.

He fought back tears during the interview as he described how he felt, saying, 'This is the most hurtful, painful experience of my life. You have to believe this is my worst moment at any time, at any club anywhere. It hurts me more than anything that has gone before. Remember this was the longest period I was ever at a club and it is true, I really loved this club because we had so many good moments in this Chelsea family. So I have to control myself. I have to fight not to be too emotional. Did I cry? There was a tear? Yes, but just as it was coming out I caught it, I stopped it. But it's difficult because I feel so sorry to leave so many good people behind, people I have worked with for a long time. It is not easy, it is very sad, but there's no anger. Not a single part of me is angry. There's no anger at all. My decision to come to Chelsea in 2004, when I could choose from virtually every club in every country, was the right decision.'

He did accept that there had been an irretrievable breakdown in relations with Abramovich but refused to accept any responsibility for it. 'Do I blame myself?' he said. 'No. I'm José Mourinho with all my good qualities and all my bad qualities. I'm José Mourinho and I don't change. I don't want to change anything I do – so blame myself? No, no, no!'

And he went on to insist he had not been sacked, he had not quit. It really was an agreement by mutual consent. 'They didn't sack me; I didn't close the door. It is true that we both agreed I should leave. You know me and that I'm not the kind of guy who someone can buy not to say what I want to say. No chance. If I was sacked, I would say I was sacked. If I had closed the door, I would say I'd closed the door. So when I say the relationship broke down, you know I am telling the truth. Chelsea don't say why the relationship broke down and I'm not going to say why it happened. It just happened. The truth is our relationship broke down not because of one detail or because of something that happened at a certain moment, it broke down over a period of time.'

Unsubstantiated rumours abounded at the time that Mourinho's successor had played a significant role in his departure but José shrugged and said, 'I don't care if I was stabbed in the back, I don't care if that's true. I don't want to spend my time and energy fretting about that. It is over. Chelsea is over. I don't care about anything that happens at Chelsea any more. Who they buy, who they sell, who is the manager. I just don't care because I'm not a part of it any more. But I'm very happy with what I did – the way I started and finished. How will I be remembered? Time is the best judge. I believe my best moment was winning the FA Cup last season. Wembley was a fantastic moment. As a kid, I had grown up watching Cup finals at Wembley and I was frustrated at not having won the FA Cup. So that day was very special.'

Yet, four months after that triumph, his winner's medal had been followed by his P45. However, the Special One was adamant his reputation in the game would be undiminished by his shock departure so early in the new season. 'This has not damaged me. It is not a problem for me. I have had two offers already but I don't tell you from where, just that I wasn't interested in either. But I'm taking time out not because I'm tired, not because of stress, not because I need a break, not because I want to go around the world for three months. I'm only taking time off because of the circumstances of football.

Nobody sacks managers in September or October, well, not normally, so I'm ready when a job comes.'

And as he prepared to leave, Mourinho even predicted he'd come back to England to manage again one day, maybe even return to Stamford Bridge. The terms of his pay-off meant it couldn't be for at least a year but he felt then, even at his lowest ebb, that he had unfinished business at Chelsea. How prophetic that was and how happy I am at what I did next.

After we'd hugged and said our final goodbyes I slipped him my business card and asked him to keep in touch. He promised he would, although I admit I was sceptical. I was very wrong. José proved to be a special friend and didn't let me down.

11
ENGLAND

Mourinho was as good as his word. He sent me a text with his new mobile number within days of him returning to his native Portugal where he'd banked his mega Chelsea pay-off and was licking his wounds. I was chuffed, but the best was yet to come.

Just over a month after he'd left Chelsea he sent me a memorable text. The bombshell message announced its arrival on the afternoon of Thursday 22 November 2007 with a couple of loud beeps, which was slightly embarrassing because I was at the Sopwell House Hotel in Hertfordshire listening to Steve McClaren in his farewell press conference as England manager (the Three Lions had failed miserably to qualify for Euro 2008 and the 'Wally with the Brolly' had been axed by the English Football Association the previous day). Nevertheless I reached for my mobile phone, opened up the message and saw it was from my man, Mourinho. It read simply: 'Is the England job interested in me?'

What a question! What timing. I knew what my answer would be – 'YES!' I was pretty sure England fans would have exactly the same response. The FA was another matter, though, but nothing ventured, nothing gained. So I decided to find out.

In any event I had immediately lost all interest in McClaren's words of failure and farewell and couldn't wait for him to shut up and shuffle off. As soon as he did I went down to the front, shook his hand, wished him well and emphasized that my long-standing criticism of him in the job was purely my professional opinion and nothing personal. Then I went off to try to get José his job.

I approached the Football Association's then Head of Communications Adrian Bevington, asked for a quiet word in private and then showed him the text. He was immediately excited by the possibility. I handed over José's phone number and email and promised I would keep the 'story' quiet for now but expected to be kept in the loop if things progressed. He readily agreed and said he would go and discuss the matter with FA chief executive Brian Barwick straight away. I duly reported back to José and we both sat back to await developments.

This being the FA, though, matters did not proceed with any real speed or intent. Unbelievable, really. As the days dragged by, José was clearly frustrated and impatient because he subsequently sent me a second message. 'Still no news from FA.'

Obviously they had still not made any contact at all. So again I took the matter into my own hands. It couldn't have been easier actually, as I'd just boarded a plane for South Africa to attend the draw for the qualifying groups for World Cup 2010 and sitting just a few rows behind me were Barwick and Bevington. I went over, showed them José's second message and asked them what they were messing about at. Were they interested or not? They insisted they were and asked me to apologize to José, explain they had been very busy with the sacking of McClaren and preparing for the World Cup draw and would be in touch very soon. I did just that and this time they did get in touch. Talks went well so that later Mourinho secretly came to London for further meetings and a deal was all but agreed.

So well, in fact, that on the evening of Friday 7 December José confirmed he was ready to become England boss. He texted me to say, 'I have decided I will go to England if they want me. So now let the FA choose what they think is best for them. I certainly don't want to put pressure on them or push them to give me the job. Because this is the kind of job where everyone must be together in their opinion. The FA, the fans, the players and the press. The chosen one must be the manager for everybody. So I will now wait patiently and I will wait calmly and let's see what they decide.'

Privately he felt the job was his and even spoke of taking control straight after Christmas. He'd added, 'I am going away on holiday now but if everything goes well I can be in England on January 1.' He then explained how it was the clamour from England's fans and players that had convinced him he should lead the Three Lions. 'I love English football and I have to say that I have been amazed by the England fans. Their support for me has been out of this world. That's why I am now mentally ready to take charge of England. Honestly, I just couldn't say no to this job now. Yes, it is a massive job, a massive challenge, but when the English people say they want me and the players say they want me; well, I can't say no. It would be an honour to be manager of England and I am excited by the responsibilities of this England job.'

José's agent Jorge Mendes had told Barwick exactly the same in a clandestine meeting in the capital that Friday and laid out Mourinho's vision for England, a way ahead for the mother of the game to restore its reputation and ranking. José was planning to bring in his trusted Portuguese back-room staff, coach Baltemar Brito, assistant coach and fitness expert Rui Faria and goalkeeping expert Silvino Louro. Barwick did not object. Mourinho insisted, though, that he wanted his right-hand man to be an ex-England star, a figure loved and respected by the nation. A man with a great history with the Three Lions and a good personality. Former England skipper Tony Adams, by then a coach at Portsmouth, was one possibility for that key role. Alan Shearer was another contender. Suddenly, there was a flurry of activity at the FA: McClaren's coach, Steve Round, and his mentor, Bill Beswick, were told they no longer had a place in the FA's set-up, as the English game's governing body cleared the decks for the imminent announcement.

Throughout it all I was kept right in the loop by Mourinho and, best of all, José finally told me I could write the story that weekend. What a scoop! Brilliant. Admittedly, by now it was no secret that José was in the running for the job – I'd written stories to that effect; I'd revealed he'd come to London for talks – but this was definitive: he was taking the job and here's the reason why and in Mourinho's own words. That's what you call an exclusive. I sat down at my laptop and wrote a back-page lead and a two-page spread for the inside sports pages of the *News of the World* that Sunday, giving chapter and verse on the whole deal. On the Saturday morning I went through all the stuff from José again to make sure I had got everything I possibly could into the story. Then I triple-checked the copy and sent if off to the *News of the World*. I was elated. This was one of the biggest stories of my career and I couldn't wait for Sunday morning to come.

First, though, I had to go to cover Chelsea's match with Sunderland at Stamford Bridge – not a bad way for me to kill time before publication of my big hit the next morning. Except I never got there. For as I was driving down the M40 in my Chelsea-blue Mercedes there was a beep beep on my mobile phone to alert me to an incoming text message. A quick glance down showed it was from Mourinho, so I pulled in to the Oxford services to find out more. My heart sank as I opened it up. It began: 'Don't go so far with that England story ...' What!? The text went on to reveal how a 'big club' (Inter Milan) had come in with a fantastic offer and he was almost certainly going to take it. He said working day to day with players was the clincher but reiterated how much he loved England, English football, the players and the fans. He asked me to include how close he was to taking the job but how in the end his preference for the regular cut and thrust of club football had prevailed over his desire to reawaken England as a real force at international level. Finally he asked me to make the quotes from a close and trusted friend rather than directly from him.

So in the resulting story I said a confidant of Mourinho's had told me: 'José wants to be Portugal's golden son forever so it is very difficult for him to go and coach another country. He feared he would lose respect from his own people, his own country and that was too much for him. The other complication was that late on Friday a big club put a great contract on the table for him to be coach next season. I expect he will wait for June with a signed contract in his pocket. That should be good, but José is still in pain because he would love to take on the England challenge, love to do it but I believe he will now reject the job.'

I was gutted. It saddened me on a professional level and a personal level. As an England fan I knew the Three Lions had just missed out on somebody truly special who could have transformed the nation's footballing future. As a journalist I knew I had missed out on enjoying a special relationship with the next England manager, not to mention a fantastic story. Not that José Mourinho turning down England wasn't a massive scoop too. Of course it was. It was huge and it certainly set the agenda the following morning when the story broke. A great tale for sure, especially as a lot of the other Sunday papers ran with stories saying José was now nailed on for the England job. Oh no he wasn't!

I wrote the story on the Saturday afternoon instead of watching Chelsea's 2–0 home win against Sunderland. Then in the evening, at around 9.30 p.m. when the first editions of the papers were about to hit the streets in London, I sent a text to the FA's Adrian Bevington telling him José was not interested in the England job any more as he'd landed a top job with a big club on the Continent. Safe to say he was shocked and stunned, understandably so as England's loss turned out to be Italy's gain. If only the FA had been quicker off the mark they would have sealed the deal before Inter came calling.

They'd carelessly let José slip through their fingers and must have been cursing as Mourinho went to Milan and won the lot inside two years: two Serie A titles, the two domestic cups and the biggest of them all, the Champions League trophy. No one could say it was not a deserved triumph, as José had to overcome the champions of England, Spain and Germany to lift his second European crown and an historic treble for Inter. Now that's what you call special.

12
TOTTENHAM

England weren't the only ones to miss out in the autumn of 2007. Tottenham also failed in their own effort to entice the Special One to be their coach. The North London club had made repeated attempts to try to lure Mourinho to White Hart Lane and José was certainly interested. Timing was always the issue, though, but it wouldn't surprise me if it does finally happen one day. The thought of reawakening a once-famous club like Spurs to make them champions again really appealed to him. It's an English club and he loves England and English football. It's a London club and he loves London and owns a house in the capital. It would also give him the chance to embarrass his ex-Chelsea boss Roman Abramovich on his own doorstep. However, for one reason or another, it's not quite happened yet.

José told me he first spoke with Tottenham chairman Daniel Levy about the job in 2007, shortly after his shock departure from Chelsea by mutual agreement on 19 September that year. Spurs were actively looking to replace their manager Martin Jol at the time. The club's intent had been made very public after a not-so-secret trip to Spain in August when Tottenham vice-chairman Paul Kemsley and club secretary John Alexander were caught red-handed trying to lure Seville coach Juande Ramos to North London.

That Friday 17 August meeting at the King Alfonso XIII Hotel was set up by a well-connected London property tycoon called Tony Jimenez, a close friend of mine, as well as of

Kemsley's and Levy's, who has family links to Seville, speaks fluent Spanish and already knew Ramos. Unfortunately the clandestine meeting between Kemsley, Alexander and Ramos embarrassingly became public when the trio were photographed together in the hotel. The clumsy cock-up forced Spurs to back off quickly and make a public statement backing Jol instead.

It didn't fool anyone and Levy's chat with Mourinho shows that the Dutch coach was in real peril. The White Hart Lane club had wanted Mourinho to take charge of Spurs as soon as possible but immediately found out it was a complete non-starter. Mourinho's settlement with Chelsea prevented him from going to another English club so Levy and Tottenham were thwarted on that occasion. They returned their attentions to Ramos, who duly agreed to take charge after Jol was finally sacked in October.

Mourinho remained on Tottenham's radar for years. In spring 2011 he was back in the frame when the future of the then Spurs manager Harry Redknapp was under discussion. In 2010 Redknapp had been charged by police with tax evasion, something he vehemently denied. The matter was set to be decided in the Crown Court, leaving Tottenham facing the prospect of their manager being embroiled in a long and involved court case rather than running the team. Worse, the possibility of the manager being convicted would have been damaging to the reputation of the club. It was a real dilemma for Tottenham at that time. (Redknapp was cleared of all charges in 2012 but Spurs could not have been sure of the outcome of any trial as they considered what to do in the spring of 2011.)

So when Spurs were drawn against Real Madrid, managed by a certain José Mourinho, it seemed an ideal opportunity for the North Londoners to sound out the ex-Chelsea boss about a return to England at the end of the season. Mourinho was known to be unhappy and unsettled in his first season at Madrid and

Tottenham hoped to exploit the situation. Despite his problems in Spain, Mourinho's side duly thrashed Tottenham 4–0 in the first leg at the Bernabéu on 5 April 2011.

The beating served to concentrate minds at White Hart Lane still further and I subsequently got a call to see if I could set up a meeting with José when Madrid came to London for the second leg on 13 April.

The call was from Tony Jimenez. He's a great guy, a very successful and generous man who is incredibly well connected in the football world, especially in England and Spain. I was first introduced to him by Tottenham vice-chairman Kemsley and we immediately hit it off very well, perhaps because we were both lifelong Chelsea fans who knew a lot of the same players and people. As a Blues brother he was well aware of my close links with José. He also knew I was discreet and could be trusted to keep things a secret. We'd worked together when he was a vice-president at Newcastle United, when he was helping the Toon's billionaire owner Mike Ashley recruit a new manager in 2008 after the departure of Sam Allardyce. (Funnily enough, Harry Redknapp was the man Ashley initially settled upon to replace Allardyce and I was told that Harry, then in charge at Portsmouth, had agreed to take the job, only to do a U-turn soon afterwards.)

This latest collaboration with Jimenez would be the biggest deal of all, though. I wasn't convinced Mourinho would go for it but I knew it wouldn't do me any harm to make contact and talk him through it. Quite the contrary: it showed I was well connected and working with his best interests at heart. So I messaged José on the morning of 10 April to see if he would agree to the meeting with Tottenham. I told him 'they are very, very keen to talk to you about a return to English football'. I explained the meeting would just be a discussion at this stage with Tottenham chairman Daniel Levy's representative Tony

Jimenez, who wondered if the Real Madrid boss could spare fifteen minutes during his trip to London this week to have a chat. Mourinho wouldn't agree to the meet, well not then anyway. He explained, 'I can't do it now. I go the day before the match with the team and focus on the match.' But he added, 'I will when I go to London on a free [day].' In the event, though, no meeting was necessary as Harry stayed at Tottenham that summer and José stayed at Madrid.

However, in February 2012, Jimenez was back in touch with me again about meeting up with Mourinho for Tottenham. Redknapp was now favourite for the England manager's job after the departure of Fabio Capello. José was again the man that Spurs wanted. It was widely expected he'd be leaving Madrid at the end of that season so would he meet them this time? Again I said I'd ask the question and do my best to persuade him. I mentioned to Jimenez that Mourinho was thinking of coming over for the Carling Cup final at Wembley later that month so that could be a possible date. Tony was keen. He had access to a private box at Wembley that could provide the perfect meeting place. He said Daniel Levy was even prepared to fly back from Phoenix, Arizona, in the United States to see José face-to-face. Alternatively Tony was in Spain the following week so could meet the Madrid boss and his advisers there.

On the morning of Friday 10 February I contacted José and briefed him on Tottenham's renewed interest. He wasn't surprised, replying, 'I know, I know, I know Levy likes me a lot because when I left Chelsea we spoke but I couldn't go there for contractual reasons. Now I can.' The problem this time was that there were a lot of other clubs manoeuvring around him too. There were whispers about Manchester United, Manchester City, Paris St Germain and maybe even a return to Chelsea. Mourinho was up to speed on it all. He was already scanning the possibilities of jobs back in the Premier League. So he stalled, saying, 'I will wait to see what happens in England. Who is champion, if Harry goes or stays. I will wait and see the direction they go [in].' And then he added, 'AVB in trouble now I guess.' Which made me think his main focus remained on Chelsea and how his former assistant André Villas-Boas was faring at Stamford Bridge. Not good enough was the answer, and the following month he was fired.

Intriguingly, this time José did find a free day for a trip to London later that February. Did he meet Tottenham? Did he meet Chelsea? I can't say. I can say nothing was agreed; well, nothing except that he would be buying a house back in London. That was one of the reasons for his visit and afterwards Mourinho explained away the need for secrecy by telling me, 'I went [to London] and back, didn't want to say because I am buying [a] home and if [the] owners know that it's me I am in trouble. In a few weeks [the] deal is done and I will have a new house in London. Now I need a club.' That was on 29 February 2012. It was a leap year and Mourinho appeared ready to jump ship.

Tottenham and Chelsea were the obvious candidates as both were looking for new managers. The only other club he mentioned was Millwall. It may seem too far-fetched an idea to take seriously but I must admit I was not sure if he was joking or not at the time. Over the years he had repeatedly talked of a desire for a project, to build a club and take it to the very top. Maybe Millwall was that project.

In March 2012 he quipped, 'In a couple of months I hope to have back page of the *Sun*: "The Only One is back! ... to Millwall."' I sent him a non-committal reply saying simply: 'Owner, chairman and manager!!?' and he replied, 'All ... and boss of Hooligans!'

Okay, he was joking after all, so it was the Bridge or the Lane, then. Once again, though, the timing was not quite right for Spurs: it was just too soon for José. There was no way he would contemplate leaving Madrid until the end of the campaign. It was a good job, really, as that season he went on to win La Liga in record-breaking fashion, but he was clearly analysing the situation from afar and preparing himself to return to English football. He even told me the six clubs he'd consider if he were to leave Madrid in the summer. They were Manchester United, Manchester City, Liverpool, Arsenal, Tottenham and Chelsea.

It was another false dawn, though, and ultimately Mourinho stayed at Madrid. A stunning title-winning season in Spain earned him a new four-year contract at the Bernabéu, so the Premier League would have to wait once again.

13

THE GREATEST PRIZE

That spectacular 2011–12 season in Spain is not the one that Mourinho considers his finest hour, even though he gloriously overcame a team that was widely regarded as the best club side of all time: Pep Guardiola's Barcelona. It was yet another dazzling achievement to be added to his glittering curriculum vitae – it just wasn't his all-time favourite. For José Mourinho is a specialist in success and there are a lot of contenders to be considered as his ultimate moment, the one that ranks highest above all the others.

Just consider the stats. When José left Chelsea in December 2015 he'd amassed twenty-two trophies since 2003. He'd won every big prize there was to be won – usually more than once. For example, at that point Mourinho was one of just five managers in football history to have won the Champions League with two different clubs, enjoying glory with Porto in 2004 and repeating the feat with Inter Milan in his second season there in 2010. Only Carlo Ancelotti, Jupp Heynckes, Ottmar Hitzfeld and Ernst Happel have matched that. José had also won eight league titles in four different countries: two in his native Portugal, three in England, two in Italy and one in Spain. Twice in his career he'd even won the treble, something achieved only a handful of times in European football history. In his first full season at Porto he claimed the Portuguese league and cup double and then added the UEFA Cup. At Inter, seven years later, he went even better and won the Serie A title, the Copa Italia and the Champions League.

That was a special moment, so much so that when I asked him in 2014 to name his greatest success so far, Mourinho confirmed, 'It was to win the Champions League with Inter. It was a special group of players, it was that night or never. It was a team of, not frustrated people because they had won a lot of Italian competitions, but it was a group of people, a team that [previously] could not reach [the Champions League prize] despite the owner making amazing investment season after season for a couple of decades. It was players who gave everything to Inter, some of them thirty-eight, thirty-seven and thirty-six who were there forever. They gave everything to arrive there, so, when I saw what it meant for them, I felt completely realized. Why? Because I knew I had pushed them to that moment. So, more than for me, because it was the second time for me, it was the pleasure of seeing these people [do it], it was fantastic.'

Coincidentally, as it turned out, this most joyous occasion had come at Real Madrid's Bernabéu stadium, his next port of call as coach. Inter beat Louis van Gaal's Bayern Munich 2–0 there, clinching the club's first European Cup since 1965 and, even more significantly, claimed the first treble in the history of Italian football. That May night in Madrid proved to be Mourinho's last match with Inter, with José using the celebrations to wave 'goodbye' to the ecstatic Italian fans in the Spanish stadium that was to be his new home.

It was an emotional split encapsulated by the tearful, final farewell with Inter's veteran defender Marco Materazzi that night as both men hugged and sobbed together in the bowels of the stadium afterwards, as TV cameras looked on. It demonstrates the amazing bond that Mourinho can forge with kindred spirits who are driven by the same intensity and desire as him. Ask Didier Drogba, John Terry, Frank Lampard, Petr Cech, Wesley Sneijder, Zlatan Ibrahimović, Javier Zanetti,

Ricardo Carvalho, Michael Essien, Mezut Özil and plenty more besides. Materazzi was a Mourinho man for sure and, at thirty-six, was one of the thirty-somethings Mourinho had in mind when he spoke about why that 2010 triumph had been so special.

It was a mature squad led by thirty-seven-year-old captain Zanetti, the Argentinian international midfielder. In the starting line-up for the final, goalkeeper Júlio César, defenders Lúcio and Walter Samuel, and strikers Samuel Eto'o and Diego Milito were all at least thirty. The bench was even older, with second-choice goalkeeper Francesco Toldo almost forty, and Iván Córdoba and Dejan Stanković alongside Materazzi in the twilight of their careers. So to win European football's most important prize at that stage of their careers, and against all the odds, proved to be the pinnacle for most of the players. Mourinho found deep joy in having been able to make it happen. What's more, his success was then recognized on high when he was named FIFA World Coach of the Year for 2010, the first time world football's governing body had presented such an award.

It was the ultimate moment for Mourinho, who was again close to tears at the presentation ceremony when Inter's Wesley Sneijder paid a glowing tribute to the manager who had led the way. Sneijder told the assembled dignitaries and stars of the game, 'It was a pleasure to work with José Mourinho and I want to tell him this: he is, for me, the best coach in the world.' Afterwards Mourinho modestly tried to share the moment and his award, saying, 'It was given to me but it is also for my players and everyone who works with me and alongside me, like my family and the people who give me the motivation, support and confidence to keep going. The [season] with Inter Milan was perfect and I will always celebrate this moment.'

However, collecting the first-ever Ballon d'Or award for a

manager and an historic treble were still not quite enough for him. Mourinho wanted something more personal and lasting to mark this memorable moment in his career. He wanted a 'James Bond car' as he called it, an Aston Martin, so he went out and treated himself to one. Mourinho explained his buying of the magnificent marque car, saying, 'When I won the FIFA Gold Ball in 2010, which was the first time FIFA gave the gold ball to a manager, we thought in the family it was a special moment in my career. I was always telling them, "That car is a beautiful car, that car is an amazing car." So my family was pushing, "Why don't you buy, why don't you buy, why don't you buy?" So we decided to buy and we decided to put inside the car a plate with the date and José Mourinho, FIFA Gold Ball 2010 blah blah ... and I told the kids that "This car will never be for sale, it is for you one day to own an old Aston and remember what your father did in 2010."'

Mourinho's two-year stint in Italy ended in spectacular fashion, and the end-of-season celebrations, plus all the trophies and awards, makes it easy to overlook the fact that his time at the San Siro had actually been an attritional and sometimes tempestuous affair, complete with plenty of controversy and confrontation. Not internally at Inter, but externally with the Italian FA and the Italian press. Why pick one fight when you can pick three seemed to be the Mourinho mantra back then. Not for the first or last time, it was his deliberate way of creating a bunker mentality within his group, an 'it's us against the world' approach. It worked well, but it wasn't pretty.

In his first season in Italy Mourinho had taunted AC Milan's Carlo Ancelotti and Roma's Luciano Spalletti, saying they'd win 'no titles' that campaign. It was a phrase that Mourinho actually mispronounced in Italian. He said 'zeru tituli' instead of 'zero titoli', but that didn't stop it resonating throughout the climax to the campaign. Mourinho was proved right, with Inter crowned 2009 champions and Lazio winning the Copa Italia, leaving both Milan and Roma empty-handed.

Roma had pushed Inter hard, though, and José admitted afterwards that it was never a foregone conclusion that his side would ultimately be champions. There was even one occasion when he feared his side might have blown their chance, tossing a vital victory away by conceding a goal late into injury time. Mourinho was incensed and decided he needed to demonstrate his anger in spectacular fashion. Unfortunately it backfired in spectacular fashion.

José can laugh about it now and tells the story in self-deprecating fashion, but back then it was definitely no laughing matter – for him or his players. Mourinho recalled, 'We played Fiorentina in Florence and we were fighting with Roma for the title. We were losing 1–0 with five minutes to go and suddenly we do 1–1 and we do 2–1 as [Samuel] Eto'o scores two goals and now it's a big victory. After the second goal the game was over 2–1, but my players were celebrating and they forgot there was one more minute to play. So we'd scored [in] minutes ninety-one and ninety-two and they [Fiorentina] go up and in the ninety-third minute they scored a second goal and it was 2–2 and we lost two points. We go to the dressing room and I need to kick something and I saw a bag. But the floor was wet so when I kicked the bag I slipped and fell to the floor and almost killed myself. No one does nothing, nobody could laugh, nobody could react. Nothing.'

Luckily, the embarrassing slip-up – by the team on the pitch and the manager in the dressing room – had a happy ending, complete with José's first piece of silverware for the Inter trophy cabinet.

Mourinho added, 'Three days later we played the Cup final against Roma in Roma and we win. So when I go into the dressing room all the players were doing what I did, everybody was going down [to the floor]. There are stories like that and that's the good part of football. When you are surrounded by people you really like and the feeling is mutual, you have fantastic times.'

The perfect dressing-room scenario for José: everyone in it together for the common cause and for the common good.

14
GOODBUY, ZLATAN

The intense togetherness that Mourinho had forged in the Inter camp in his very first season didn't stop him from making a spectacular and controversial change to his squad as he prepared for what would be his historic treble-winning campaign. It was on Inter's pre-season tour to California when José Mourinho brokered the mega deal to sell Zlatan Ibrahimović to Barcelona. The Nerazzurri had flown into Los Angeles on 12 July 2009 ready to start pre-season training at the famous UCLA sports complex and take part in the World Football Challenge tournament, a prestigious competition hosted in the USA. On this occasion the four teams competing were Inter, their arch-rivals AC Milan, Mourinho's former club Chelsea and top Mexican side Club America. The big kick-off was just a week away with Inter's first match against Club America in Palo Alto, California, on Sunday 19 July, but by then the spectacular deal to sell Ibrahimović was pretty much done and dusted, although yet to be signed and sealed.

In fact, Mourinho's jet lag had barely worn off when the big switch was being put together. I was waiting to have a prearranged chat with him as he checked into the plush Four Seasons hotel in LA where the Inter squad would be based. We had a happy catch-up conversation during which he invited me along to an official Inter event at the famous Ricardo Montalbán Theatre in LA on 16 July. It proved to be quite an occasion. It was the launch of Inter's new kit for the forthcoming season.

They were the reigning Serie A champions and the shirt was a special centenary strip celebrating 100 years since they won their first Scudetto.

It was a typical, glitzy, Hollywood-style affair with the Inter players arriving in a cavalcade of stretch limousines, greeted by searchlights, booming music and a VIP carpet, not a red one (no, red is for AC Milan) but a special one made in Inter blue. South California radio star Matt 'Money' Smith was the host for the night and Nike vice-president Bert Hoyt and Bedy Moratti, sister of Inter president Massimo Moratti, were introduced on stage to mark the occasion and make the obligatory speeches. Then out came the Inter stars themselves, including Ibrahimović, wearing the new kit and parading it for the TV cameras, photographers, journalists and assembled guests in the 'invite-only' audience.

It was during all this razzmatazz that Mourinho discreetly slipped out of the side of the theatre for a breath of fresh air on the fire escape. I followed along and, as we stood there enjoying a balmy, California evening, he could barely contain his excitement. He told me, 'We're selling "Ibra" to Barcelona for 50 million euros and we get Samuel Eto'o to Inter. Amazing deal, hey?' It was stunning news. My very first reaction was not so much shock but to wonder if Ibrahimović knew anything about it at this stage. After all, only moments before I'd watched the Swede posing away happily on stage in the new Inter shirt without any hint of embarrassment. What's more, Mourinho's pumped-up behaviour made it obvious that this was a brand-new development. So I asked José, 'When will it happen?' and he revealed that Ibrahimović would be flying back to Europe as soon as the two clubs had finalized the details of the deal.

So, after a happy half-hour with an ecstatic José, I slipped off and quickly filed the story. Talk about breaking news! It didn't happen quite as fast as we expected, though. A few days later Zlatan played and scored for Inter in that opening fixture against Club America and then, on the Tuesday, he faced off against Chelsea at the Rose Bowl Stadium in Pasadena, California. Few people realized it at the time, but the match was to be his final appearance for Inter and it didn't end well. Chelsea won easily thanks to goals from Didier Drogba and Frank Lampard, while Ibrahimović broke his hand during the game. Shortly afterwards he broke the hearts of Inter fans by flying back across the Atlantic alone to head to Spain to sign for Barca.

Little did 'Ibra' know then that his big move would be a big and expensive mistake. After three great years with Inter from 2006 to 2009, winning three titles in a row, the Swede managed just one season at Barca before being shown the door. Admittedly, he didn't leave empty-handed, having helped Barca win the UEFA Super Cup, La Liga and the World Club Championships, but in the same year Inter did an even better treble: winning the Scudetto again, the Copa Italia and finally, and most famously, claiming the prized Champions League crown.

In truth Mourinho was sad to see Zlatan leave. He was a huge fan of the big man and in an ideal world would have kept him. However, José is a pragmatist and realized the deal was impossible to resist. Relationships run deep with Mourinho, though, and the pair have stayed in touch – there is a mutual appreciation of their individual qualities. Mourinho told me, 'A player who gave me as much as Ibra will always be in my heart. He did a lot for Inter. Ibra is a player I'll never forget, because he's very good ... I never forget the players who helped my teams to win. He was very important. I like seeing Ibrahimović. I greet him whenever I get the chance to see him and I wish him all the best, except when he plays against me, because he is very special, he is one of the best strikers in the world.'

In February 2012, when I told Mourinho I was heading to Milan to interview Zlatan about his new book, he replied, 'Zlatan is a super player ... tell him that I say I will be the coach winning in Spain, Italy and England ... and he should be the player ... he has to play in England ... in my team!' Mourinho was of course still manager of Real Madrid back then but he'd always told me his next stop would be back in England so it seemed as though he was already sowing seeds.

Two years later, in April 2014, José was back at Chelsea and heading into a Champions League quarter-final with Paris St Germain, a side which now boasted a certain Zlatan Ibrahimović as their striker. Inevitably we spoke about the 6 ft 5 in frontman and the memories came flooding back for Mourinho. He told an hilarious anecdote about how he'd had to play 'dumb' to stop a stroppy Ibra from storming off the pitch during a game in their final season together at Inter Milan.

The Special One revealed, 'It was the last game of the 2009 season and Inter were already champions. We were playing at home against Atalanta, a match we should win easily. Ibra was desperate to finish as top scorer in Serie A. So he's trying to score a few goals to make sure, but all the other strikers, all the other players, are trying to score too. He got very angry. He thought they should be helping him to score the goals, not trying to score themselves, and he was right, the team was being selfish, the team was not playing for him. We were champions, and if you are champions, and if your striker is trying to win the Golden Ball, you help him. But it looked like the team had forgotten that. They were all enjoying themselves but nobody was playing for him.'

Ibrahimović had scored a superb solo goal as early as the thirteenth minute, when he broke from halfway to run clear and then nonchalantly slid the ball past the exposed keeper and into the net. But with just over ten minutes to go he still had not scored again and was losing patience with all around him. Eventually he erupted in anger when strike partner Mario Balotelli chose to shoot, and miss, instead of setting him up. The furious forward stormed to the touchline haranguing his teammates and demanding to be substituted. Mourinho recalled, 'He was very angry and upset as he came at me. He was shouting, "We are champions, I helped a lot to make you champions, now nobody's helping me. I want to go out now. I want to go out!" But I pretended not to understand him. I pretended I couldn't tell what he was saying. I said, "What? What? Do you want a drink, do you want some water?" and I threw him a bottle. I told him, "Here, take a drink and go" and a few minutes later he scored a beautiful goal, one of those backheels of his that he often scores. We won the game and he was the top scorer in the league – twenty-five goals I think. So he was happy in the end.'

Ibra was not so happy after that 2014 quarter-finals clash with Chelsea. PSG won 3–1 in Paris but it was Chelsea who eventually went through, winning 2–0 at Stamford Bridge to squeeze into the semi-finals on the away goals rule after Demba Ba scored a late eighty-seventh-minute winner. Mourinho had come out on top in his dealings with Zlatan once again, but always hoped they'd be back on the same side one day. And so it proved when José's 'he has to play in England … in my team!' became a reality in 2016.

15

RE-UNITED

José continued to be exceptionally good to me, even from afar. For instance, our enduring contact earned me a great scoop when his Inter Milan side were drawn against Manchester United in the knockout stages of the Champions League in early 2009.

I duly jetted off to meet up with him at Inter's training ground where he had just one thing on his mind – and it wasn't United. All he wanted to focus on was Chelsea. Clearly his shock exit in late September of the previous season still hurt him and he spent most of our chat talking about what might have been if he'd stayed at Stamford Bridge. In that 2007–08 season the Londoners had gone on to lose out to United on penalties in the Champions League final, leaving owner Roman Abramovich empty-handed again in his pursuit of a first European crown.

Mourinho being Mourinho, he couldn't resist a bit of a dig about that, claiming he would have won the Champions League for Chelsea and delivered Abramovich his 'holy grail'. José told me, 'While I was at Chelsea we did everything but win the Champions League. We won all the other big, big trophies. There was the first league title for Chelsea in fifty years and the next year we were champions again. We won the first FA Cup at the new Wembley, beating Sir Alex Ferguson and Manchester United. And two Carling Cups. So we'd won absolutely everything apart from the Champions League. But people always want more – and at Chelsea that was the Champions

League. I would have won it with Chelsea. My contract was until 2011, so I would have been there for seven years. It's enough time. And don't forget that as well as winning all those trophies in England, we got to two Champions League semi-finals in my three years. So we were going in that direction. We were very close. Then Chelsea decided to make a change and suddenly it was over. But I don't see it as unfinished business and I don't dwell on it. I had three great years at Chelsea. It was a special moment for me there; there was a special feeling and I had a passion for that club – I still do. I am proud I have left a legacy there that will survive for a long, long time. And I don't regret anything.'

The obvious suggestion was that Abramovich was the one who should have regrets – at letting Mourinho leave – and that things may well have been different if he'd stayed put and been in charge on that fateful night in Moscow instead of Avram Grant; would certainly have been different if he'd been allowed to see out his contract. Maybe he even saw the upcoming game with United as his chance to prove it, in his very first season at his new club.

In any event he decided to fly over to Manchester to watch United host his old club Chelsea at Old Trafford in January 2009. Yes, of course there would be the chance for reunions and remembrances but the main reason for the trip was a reconnaissance mission to try to plot United's downfall. José revealed, 'I go to Old Trafford, where I had some great moments. I go to a Chelsea game where for sure I will find in the stands people that I love and people that I know have a great feeling with me. But my focus is on United and my preparations to meet them.' And he reckoned he wasn't bothered about bumping into Abramovich, revealing they'd kissed and made up long ago. Mourinho continued, 'My relationship with Roman is fantastic. Everything is perfect. He's very friendly and I'm so pleased we managed to maintain relations. Human relationships are very important, that's why I am very, very happy that everything has remained so amicable. It was hard to leave Chelsea, hard to live without Chelsea, but it was better ending it the way we did than going on for two to three more months and falling out forever. It was better for me, better for him, better for everybody. We still talk and text each other – but we don't talk about football all that much. We talk about this and that, whatever is happening with us. I don't ask his opinion about my professional situation and he doesn't ask me for advice with Chelsea.'

Abramovich might have been asking for advice after the United match. A dismal Chelsea lost 3–0, with goals from Nemanja Vidić, Wayne Rooney and Dimitar Berbatov sealing a comfortable victory. Not that Mourinho fared much better when Inter visited Old Trafford in March.

United had dominated the first leg in Italy but had failed to capitalize as the game ended goalless. It was a different story in the return encounter. Sir Alex Ferguson's side were a goal up after just four minutes when Vidić headed home, just like he'd done against Chelsea a couple of months before. José would not have been happy his homework hadn't paid off. Inter did respond, though, and enjoyed plenty of the play and applied plenty of pressure. Zlatan Ibrahimović hit the bar and a host of chances were wasted before Cristiano Ronaldo settled the match just after the interval with a header of his own. Inter were out and United were through to the quarter-finals.

The following season, Inter's tremendous treble-winning campaign, I was back in Italy interviewing Mourinho again, and this was an even bigger deal. This time Inter had been drawn against Chelsea in the last sixteen of the Champions League. José wasted no time getting in touch, tipping me off that he would be returning to Stamford Bridge for the first time on a spying mission ahead of the clash.

He flew in on Monday 28 December 2009 and we met in the Chelsea Sports Club behind the Matthew Harding stand before the Blues took on West London rivals Fulham in a festive derby match. He was in great form. He revealed he wanted 'to come back to England' one day, which of course he did just four years later, rejoining his beloved Blues in 2013. Really we should have known back then, for Mourinho kept repeating over and over his love for Chelsea, his hurt at leaving in 2007 and how he'd deliberately stayed away to let his wounds heal and allow Chelsea to move on.

He explained, 'I left it so long because I didn't want to be a factor disturbing things here. They seemed to be changing coaches every three months and I didn't want to be seen to be interfering or causing problems. I also stayed away because it was painful to return. I had such great times here. I loved it here and I never wanted to leave. Stamford Bridge is my home. I was so very sad when I had to leave.' He stressed how 'happy' he was to be back 'home' among 'so many friends who don't forget what I have done for them'. He promised, 'If we [Inter] win I do nothing; I have a love affair with Chelsea so I will not celebrate. I still love this club.'

He even claimed that it was essentially still *his* Chelsea team, adding, 'This, apart from Nicolas Anelka and Branislav Ivanović, is still my team and they all mean an awful lot to me.'

José also explained the clear-headed thinking behind his early visit to check out the Blues ahead of a European clash that wasn't until the end of February. 'I came to do some homework but also to get the emotion out of the occasion. I wanted to come before the Champions League game because I knew my return was going to be a very strange feeling; a beautiful feeling but very strange. I wanted to come back for the game itself feeling cool, concentrated and relaxed. I wanted just to have a professional feeling, not a human feeling. I wanted to focus on the game, not everything surrounding it.'

Thanks, José. Another great exclusive, another great interview and another great slap in the face for the Italian press. For Mourinho had a fractured relationship with most of the Italian journalists and frequently refused to have any real dialogue with them. During his time at Inter he gave me far more scoops than he did the Italian press, even though I was working in another country and Inter were of little interest to English football fans. I wasn't interested much in Inter either; it was all about Mourinho himself. He was still box office back in Blighty, especially at times like this when he was pitted against English teams. And it was in the build-up to Chelsea's February visit that I experienced first-hand the bitter divide that existed between Mourinho and the local reporters.

I'd gone to Milan to see José in the week before the Chelsea match and stayed on in town to take in a key match in Inter's title tilt. What a match to pick. Inter versus Sampdoria at the San Siro on 20 February 2010. It was explosive. The home side had two men, Walter Samuel and Iván Córdoba, sent off in the first half. Mourinho made his infamous 'handcuffs' gesture to the cameras, which was seized on by the Italian FA and subsequently brought Mourinho a three-match ban.

Remarkably the game ended goalless but Mourinho was still not happy and walked through the press interview zone without making any comment to the throng of newspaper reporters who were machine-gunning questions at him. Until, that is, he saw me at the end of the line. He called me over, out of the pack and beyond the rope, keeping everyone back, and then promptly stood there happily conducting an interview with me in front of all of these incensed Italians.

Mourinho was mischievously making his point: he'd speak to whomever he wanted, whenever he wanted and nobody else. I loved it of course and José didn't care a jot either, but it was all too much for one of Inter's press officers, who came rushing along and urged us to move around the corner out of sight. We did eventually but not until José had dilly-dallied long enough to milk the moment.

It was very amusing and I'd got another big exclusive into the bargain as the Inter boss revealed his thoughts about facing his old club in the Champions League in Milan just four days later. Perfect timing for me to land another scoop, and perfect timing for José to get more of his mind-game messages out in England for his Chelsea old boys to absorb ahead of the trip to face their former manager.

Almost inevitably, in that upcoming Wednesday-night clash, Inter beat Chelsea 2–1 with goals from Diego Milito and Esteban Cambiasso coming either side of a score by Salomon Kalou. They went on to complete the job with Samuel Eto'o securing a 1–0 second-leg result at Stamford Bridge to go through to the quarter-finals. Didier Drogba was sent off late on to compound Chelsea's woes.

It was glory all the way, though, for Inter. One-nil wins home and away against CSKA Moscow then set up a mouth-watering semi-final clash against Barcelona.

Barca were big favourites but this Inter team would not be daunted by the celebrated array of superstars the Spanish giants possessed, and Mourinho was in no mood to be outdone by his arch-rival Pep Guardiola either. The Italians made a massive statement with a 3–1 triumph in the first leg at the San Siro to take control of the tie. They had gone a goal behind after Pedro scored for Barca early on but the Italians powered back with goals from Wesley Sneijder, Maicon and Milito. Most people still suspected that the much-lauded Spaniards could rescue the situation. It was an ill-founded belief, with Barca only able to manage a 1–0 win in the return match at the Camp Nou despite having the extra man for more than an hour in the wake of a red card for Inter's Thiago Motta. Gerard Pique's eighty-fourth-minute goal proved too little, too late as Inter marched into their first European Cup or Champions League final since 1972, a date with destiny at the Bernabéu.

They didn't disappoint in what was to be Mourinho's final match in charge; Bayern Munich were the next 'superclub' to succumb as Inter triumphed 2–0 in the final after a brace from their in-form striker Milito. It was a fabulous final flourish from Mourinho, who'd outwitted his one-time mentor at Barcelona, Louis van Gaal, to claim a second Champions League crown. Then suddenly he was gone, with his work done and his achievement nigh on impossible to surpass. Just days after the final, and his greatest moment, he was back off to the Bernabéu to replace Manuel Pellegrini as Real Madrid boss and chase new dreams and trophies. Oh yes, and spark new controversies and headlines.

16

BROKEN DREAM

Mourinho never did win the Champions League at Stamford Bridge, but Chelsea were crowned European champions on a dramatic night in Munich on Saturday 19 May 2012. José watched the match at home drinking red wine and supporting his beloved Blues.

He celebrated excitedly when Didier Drogba's decisive spot-kick settled a tense penalty shoot-out as the Pride of London overcame favourites Bayern Munich, in their own city, in their own stadium and in front of their own fans. He was genuinely happy for his old club and especially for his former players, even though he'd just missed out on the chance of a third Champions League crown with current club Real Madrid after being beaten by Bayern in the semi-finals.

He recalled, 'I could watch the final without the sad feeling of losing in the semi-finals because it was Chelsea. I watched it at home with my family and everything was perfect. That the last touch to give them the cup was Didier's [Drogba] – it could only have been Didier, Frank [Lampard] or John [Terry] … Okay, so I think it was not the best game, was not the best performance but the holy grail finally came and, so, they made history. I think it was justice. Football justice. Because Chelsea have a semi-final with [Claudio] Ranieri that, to lose against Monaco the way they did, was unbelievable. After that, with me, we lose reaching the final with the "ghost goal" [Luis García's controversial goal for Liverpool at Anfield in the 2005 semi-finals]. After that Chelsea lose the semi-final on penalties [2007 at Anfield again] and then the final on penalties [Manchester United in Moscow 2008]. Then there's the scandal of the 2009 semi-final, one of the biggest scandals [against Barcelona when Norwegian referee Tom Henning Ovrebo turned down four strong Chelsea penalty appeals and the Blues went out to an injury-time strike from Andrés Iniesta]. So everything together, it would have been a disaster if Chelsea doesn't get a Champions League trophy, especially for this generation of players.'

José's only lingering sense of regret on a joyous night was that he'd come so close to meeting the Blues in that final. We had both been convinced that fate was going to bring Real Madrid face-to-face with Chelsea at the Allianz Arena. What a prospect that was and our joint sense of destiny only grew when the draw for the semi-finals had kept the two teams apart and paired Chelsea with Barcelona and Real Madrid with Bayern Munich. Madrid were actually most people's favourites to make it to Munich.

'Los Meringues' were enjoying an imperious season. They were on their way to a record-breaking league title, with Mourinho's men overshadowing Pep Guardiola's great Barcelona side. They would win La Liga with two games to spare and set a host of records in the process. The dream was to add 'La Decima', a record tenth European Cup.

Madrid faced Bayern in Munich on Tuesday 17 April. It was a testing night and Franck Ribéry's powerful finish put the hosts ahead only for Mesut Özil to equalize early in the second half. Right at the death, Bayern striker Mario Gómez grabbed a last-gasp winner for the Germans, to give them the edge and a lead to take to the Bernabéu.

The following night it was Chelsea's turn as they entertained Barca at Stamford Bridge. It was a special night, with Didier Drogba scoring in first-half injury time to stun the Spanish giants. The great Lionel Messi was caught in possession by Chelsea's own hero Frank Lampard. He then released fellow midfielder Ramires and the Brazilian dutifully delivered a perfect cross for Drogba to sweep a left-footed finish beyond Barcelona goalkeeper Victor Valdés. It proved enough to secure a 1–0 win and a precious lead to take to the Camp Nou, although the prospect of Chelsea winning through to the final was undermined by game statistics which showed the visitors had dominated the contest, enjoying 71 per cent of possession. The away leg was going to be a real test of character and resolve.

On Tuesday 24 April Chelsea fans travelled to Barcelona for the return in defiant mood: a mix of hope, trepidation and expectation. The Blues supporters knew their team had a remarkable record against Messi and co. and their last three visits to the Camp Nou had all ended in draws so, maybe, they could pull off another surprise.

It didn't seem likely with Barca 2–0 up after forty-four minutes thanks to goals from Sergio Busquets and Andrés Iniesta. Worse, the Londoners were down to ten men after skipper John Terry had been sent off in the thirty-seventh minute for violent conduct, the Chelsea captain senselessly kneeing Alexis Sánchez from behind in an off-the-ball incident. The score had been 1–1 on aggregate at the time but within seven minutes Iniesta had put Barca in front. Their celebrations did not last long. The ten men of Chelsea stunned the Spaniards, and again Lampard played a key role. It was his through ball that enabled Ramires to break free and chip home a Chelsea equalizer in first-half injury time. It meant the Blues were now level at 2–2 on aggregate and going through on the away goals rule. Guardiola's stars needed to respond.

It didn't take long. Only four minutes had gone in the second half when the game twisted back towards Barcelona. Drogba's trip on Cesc Fàbregas earned the home side a penalty and the mesmerizing Messi was presented with the chance to put Barca back in front, back in control and back on course for Munich. The diminutive Argentinian had already scored 14 goals in the Champions League and 63 in all competitions that season and naturally the world expected to now see numbers 15 and 64. Messi missed. He hit his spot-kick against the crossbar and the Blues were off the hook. Messi also hit a post later but just couldn't find a way through to score his first-ever goal against Chelsea.

Ironically the misfiring Fernando Torres showed him the way to do it as he romped clear to score in injury time to earn his side a fourth successive draw at the Camp Nou and a thrilling 3–2 win overall. I was ecstatic and at 10.30 p.m. I sent my mate Mourinho a cheeky message. It said, 'Over to you José, good luck but sorry – I will be supporting Chelsea in the final!!!!!'

The next evening it was the Special One's turn to try to make it a special night by beating Bayern. They started on fire with Cristiano Ronaldo converting a penalty after five minutes to make it 2–2 on aggregate, but with Madrid having the advantage of an away goal. When Ronaldo swept in a second after thirteen minutes the Spaniards looked irresistible. I was certain it would be Chelsea vs José now, but then Stamford Bridge and Bernabéu old boy Arjen Robben stunned his former boss by firing home a penalty to make it all square after twenty-six minutes.

Neither side could claim the killer goal so Mourinho's hopes of a third Champions League final rested on a penalty shoot-out. David Alaba scored for Bayern, 1–0. Ronaldo missed for Real, 1–0. Mario Gómez scored for Bayern, 2–0. Kaká missed for Real, 2–0. Toni Kroos missed for Bayern, 2–0. Xabi Alonso scored for Real, 2–1. Philip Lahm missed for Bayern, 2–1. Sergio Ramos missed for Real, 2–1. Bastian Schweinsteiger scored for Bayern, 3–1, and Mourinho was out.

I waited until the Thursday evening before sending him a message. I said, 'Can't believe last night ... gutted for you. Would have been the perfect final. But remember you will be celebrating soon – the La Liga title. Loads of love from England, Big hug Rob.' The next day he replied in typical José fashion: defiant, unbowed and looking forward to his next success. He'd even invented a new nickname for himself. 'In one week I'm the Only One ... titles in Spain, Italy, England and Portugal. And a big new contract!!! 12m net ... but didn't sign it ... when I do I tell you.'

I loved it and obviously did a 'José: the Only One' story, a reminder from him of how special he was even if he had just missed out on the chance of a third Champions League crown. Sure enough, a week after the Bayern reverse, Madrid won 3–0 at Athletic Bilbao and were deservedly crowned champions in record-breaking style after outgunning even Guardiola's free-scoring Barcelona.

17
PARK THE BUS

If you're feeling brave and want to provoke an immediate reaction, then just tell José you think he is a negative, defensive coach who always 'parks the bus' and would do anything to win. Then take a step back and prepare for a broadside.

When I raised the subject with him shortly after his return to Chelsea in 2013, he was straight on to the attack. He railed, 'The other ones are the "attacking" managers yet I am the manager with the record of goals! The other ones are the fantastic attacking people, yet I am the one with the record in Spanish football, in English football, in Italian football and in Portuguese football, so I don't know very well where this statement comes from.'

Well, from at least one of those 'other ones' in the shape of Arsenal boss Arsène Wenger, who's been a critic virtually since day one. As early as 2005 Wenger commented, 'I know we live in a world where we have only winners and losers, but once a sport encourages teams who refuse to take the initiative, the sport is in danger.' Then there was Dutch legend and former Barcelona star and coach Johan Cruyff. He laid into José after a 1–1 draw between Barca and Real Madrid at the Bernabéu in April 2011. Cruyff complained, 'This game confirmed that José Mourinho is a negative coach. He only cares about the result and doesn't care much for good football. His decision to play seven defenders and three attackers was kind of extreme. It was also remarkable to see that Barcelona played with eight players who came through the ranks of the club's youth academy, while Madrid fielded only one youth academy product. The different football philosophies of both clubs were very clear to see.' Denmark manager Morten Olsen was even more damning: 'In my world Mourinho is a danger for football. If many try to copy his style, then the game will die. Imagine if everybody played football like Mourinho. Then it would certainly be boring, and I wouldn't watch the matches. I could play so differently … but Mourinho is only able to play defensively. The club has spent so much money on so good players. Hell, use them then!'

Ex-Liverpool manager Brendan Rodgers, a former reserve team coach for Mourinho at Chelsea, went furthest of all. He couldn't contain his contempt in April 2014 when Chelsea won 2–0 at Anfield to ruin the Kop's hopes of winning the Premier League. Afterwards he sneered, 'They parked two buses, rather than one. From the first minute they had ten men behind the ball. We were the team trying to win but we just couldn't make the breakthrough. It was difficult because they virtually played right from the off with a back six. They had a back four, with two wingers back and then the midfield three in front of them. Just putting ten players right on your eighteen-yard box is not difficult to coach, but it is obviously much harder to try and break through it. José is happy to work that way and he will probably shove his CV in front of me and say it works, but it is not my way of working. I like to take the initiative in games, to try to dominate them and let my players express themselves. If a defensive style gets results, great. José has got his result here and he will be happy with that but it is the polar opposite to how we work. We are a team that tried to win the game, in a sporting manner. We tried to initiate play with the ball but it was just not to be.'

Mourinho hears the criticisms but will not accept this sort of portrayal of himself. He admits to being a pragmatic man and a detailed, tactical coach but he rails at talk of him as this arch-enemy of brave and attacking football. He is adamant that such a negative portrayal of him is in complete contrast to the footballing facts and record-breaking statistics he's achieved during a glittering career. He argues it is unfair and he feels slighted, disrespected and derided by such criticism. To counter it, as Liverpool boss Rodgers' CV jibe had hinted, he defiantly demands scrutiny of his unrivalled haul of trophies and long line of successes in four of the world's biggest, toughest and most competitive football leagues: Portugal, England, Italy and Spain. Mourinho believes there has been, and still is, a deliberate rewriting of history, a sustained misrepresentation of his career, his methods and his tactics. It is an open wound that shows no sign of healing.

So what are the facts? Well, in his first season at Porto in Portugal Mourinho won the Primeira Liga with a record 86 points total. He also won the UEFA Cup and the Portuguese Cup. The following season Porto had the league wrapped up again with five weeks of the campaign left and then lifted the ultimate prize, the Champions League trophy, with a thumping 3–0 win over Monaco in the final in Gelsenkirchen, Germany. It was a special moment for the man who, as a European champion, now saw himself as a 'special one'.

In 2015 those remarkable achievements in his homeland were honoured by the Portuguese Football Federation as they celebrated their centenary, presenting José with the 'Coach of the Century' award. Afterwards Mourinho said, 'Obviously the titles that I won with Porto in this context are the most important in my career because they were titles won with a Portuguese team for Portuguese soccer. With Porto it was a unique case because that was winning a Champions League final with nine Portuguese players.' How many of Europe's top flight can boast so many home-grown players these days?

A quick analysis of his first spell at Chelsea, 2004–07, dispels many misconceptions of Mourinho the manager. In his first season, the 2004–05 campaign, the Blues won the league for the first time in fifty years. That was some feat in itself, but a close look at the facts and figures of that triumph make astonishing reading. Chelsea's brilliant season rewrote the football history books back then. They amassed a record 95 points, won a record 29 games, won a record 15 away games, kept a record 25 clean sheets and conceded just 15 goals in 38 games, another record. They didn't concede a goal in their first six games, another record, and only conceded nine goals on their travels to notch another first. What's more, they proved they were the complete team by rattling in 72 goals that season, a total only bettered by runners-up Arsenal, who finished eight points behind. Chelsea's goal difference – that's goals conceded subtracted from goals scored – was an astonishing 57.

It wasn't a one-off fluke. The following season Mourinho's Chelsea were champions again, finishing on 91 points, this time after once more winning 29 matches and scoring 72 goals. No one could better that goals haul or the miserly 22 they conceded as they finished with a goal difference of 50, eight points ahead of runners-up Manchester United.

Even in Mourinho's third season, his least successful, Chelsea finished second on 83 points despite losing fewer games than champions Manchester United. A total of 11 draws had cost them the chance of a third successive triumph but, significantly, only United scored more goals.

In his two years in Italy he won back-to-back Serie A titles with Inter Milan and achieved the treble for the first time in the history of the football-mad country. That's the one Mourinho rates as his greatest-ever achievement. Again the stats are compelling. In 2010 Inter won the Scudetto by two points, were top scorers with 75 goals and boasted a goal difference of 41, by far the best in the division. In his first season at Inter, 2008–09, he'd won the league by 10 points, with his team joint top scorers with AC Milan on 70 but with a goal difference three goals better than their arch-rival's.

José is also immensely proud of his time in Spain where he took on Guardiola's much-lauded Barcelona side, rated by many as the best club side ever. In his second season, 2011–12, Mourinho overcame Barca in imperious style, winning the league in record-breaking form. Real achieved a record 32 wins, a record 16 away wins, reached a record 100 points, and set a new goals record of 121 to finish with the highest ever goal difference, 89. They were nine points ahead of runners-up Barcelona. Yet still Mourinho's time in Spain is deemed a failure and his team dubbed defensive. Not in his eyes. He complained, 'Real Madrid were a defensive team? We scored 121 goals and got 100 points. We were champions against the best Barcelona there ever has been. My teams are great teams. My teams are built to win. You have to be dominant to win so that is what my teams try to be. My teams are the ones with all the goal records. I am the champion of the League of Records. Who is the manager of the best Real Madrid team in history? That's me. I am the one. That is my place in history.'

18

SPYING MISSION

Not everything always goes to plan, even with José Mourinho as your mate. Like in the autumn of 2012 when José was boss at Real Madrid and had just been drawn in the same Champions League group as Manchester City. Group D was immediately dubbed the 'Group of Death' as it was a group containing four champions: Spanish champions Real Madrid, English champions Manchester City, German champions Borussia Dortmund and Dutch champions Ajax. What's more, Real Madrid's first Group D game was at home at the Bernabéu against City.

Obviously I wanted a reaction from José and sent him an email within minutes of the draw being made. 'Man City!!!!! Mancini and Balotelli – some history there!! I know who my money is on!! Good luck, Rob.' He didn't reply until the following lunchtime, 31 August, but his plans for that first match were already in place, even if it wasn't to be played until 18 September. Mourinho replied: 'Eh eh eh eh [José's version of Hee, hee, hee, hee] ... I go to Manchester tomorrow. Top secret ... just for you to know and write ... Mou in Manchester ... I bet this manager is working already.' Clearly he was, and working on the mind games, for a start. A secret visit deliberately leaked to me to show he was already plotting and planning City's downfall.

That was a good start for me and for him. But as a journalist you always want more, you always want better. I told him I was heading to Spain anyway in the week before the City clash to see Cesc Fàbregas to do a feature with the ex-Arsenal star on

Barcelona and their Champions League ambitions. Clearly it was only a short hop on a plane from Barcelona to Madrid, so I pushed hard for the chance to extend my trip so I could pop along and see Mourinho. I asked him could I grab five minutes after his weekly press conference that week? 'Ok mate,' came the reply and I quickly booked up the trip.

The meet with Fàbregas went superbly. I know him pretty well and we had a great chat so I knew I'd got a good piece. Cesc has always been a very straight talker, with firm opinions on football and individuals, which makes matters so much easier. After the chat, which was organized by his sponsors Puma and staged at Barcelona's Olympic Park, we sat and enjoyed some sushi together in the sunshine. It's occasions like that when you really do believe you have the best job in the world: flying off to cities around the world to meet world-famous sportspeople and being paid to sit, chat and eat with them; then just write down what they had to say to you. Simple.

It's fair to say I was feeling pleased with myself as I returned to my hotel and ventured up to the rooftop pool to have a swim as the Spanish sun began to sink in the cloudless sky. The following day I emailed José to confirm I was heading to Madrid to see him the next day. I reminded him that we were happy to pay a fee to a charity of his choice in return for this exclusive interview and I pushed him for the name of the charity. There was no reply but I didn't anticipate that meant there would be a problem. After all, it was all agreed, wasn't it?

Well, apparently not. When I arrived at the Valdebebas training complex I was soon aware that there was a problem. It all started when I said 'hello' to Real Madrid's press officer Juan Camilo Andrade and told him I'd arranged to have a chat with José after the press conference. This was clearly news to him and he was not happy. Why couldn't I ask my questions in the press conference like everyone else? Er … because we wanted something exclusive, not something shared with everyone else. Because we wanted to hold the interview until the day before the game but wouldn't be able to do that or control that if everyone in the media already had the same answers to my questions. Juan didn't care. This was setting a dangerous precedent. The manager had a game away to Seville that weekend and shouldn't be talking about any match beyond that. A 'foreign' journalist shouldn't be getting preferential treatment like this. No journalist should be getting preferential treatment like this. I tried to explain to Juan that the article wouldn't appear until after the Seville game, that everything had been agreed, that I'd flown to Madrid specifically to do this interview. I promised to be discreet and not broadcast to other journalists the reason for my visit, appealing to his better instincts but he was in no mood to let me see José alone afterwards.

Suddenly all the elation from the Fàbregas interview was evaporating fast. Suddenly this was the worst job in the world. You make an arrangement to see someone, you go to fulfil it and then someone threatens to wreck the whole thing. Don't get me wrong, Juan is a top guy, brilliant to work with and was only doing his job, but right then I could have throttled him. This big Mourinho exclusive was in danger of going down in flames, and I'd be the one who'd get the flak from the office for the failure to deliver 'the interview they all wanted'. So I couldn't give up, I had to keep trying, which is why I headed into the press conference room and sat in a prominent position where Mourinho couldn't fail to see me. Hopefully he'd give me the nod to follow him backstage after he'd finished with the formal press conference. But what if he didn't? I'd be right in the mire, that's what.

I desperately needed a plan B, so as José emerged for the presser I got down to it. He saw me and acknowledged me. Okay, fine. Still no guarantees that Juan hadn't ruined my day, my trip and my scoop. So I found myself in the bizarre situation of sending an email to someone who was sitting right in front of me. My thinking was that if I couldn't get to see José in person afterwards, at least I could make sure he had my questions. If he wanted to delay answering them until after the Seville game then fair enough. I could live with that. I couldn't accept getting nothing. So as he sat answering questions from the local press and media I was busy bashing out a few of my own. It was a good job I did. When the press conference was over he was up and away, with Juan making sure there was no way of following José.

So much for Plan A. So I went to Plan B and pushed the button to ping Mourinho my email. It was 17.14 on 14 September and it read:

Hi José,

Juan is very nervous about this – so am emailing some questions just in case.
Please, please try and give your usual special answers!!
If you want to add any ideas of your own, that would be great.
1) You went to Manchester to watch City, what did you learn, which players are the big dangers to Real Madrid and why?
2) How do you compare and contrast Cristiano Ronaldo with his former Manchester United teammate Carlos Tevez? Who is the best?
3) How worried are you that Mario Balotelli will be extra-motivated to try to prove something to you after Inter Milan?
4) Is it easy to manage a team like City, with all that money – you had Roman at Chelsea – or does Roberto

Mancini have a difficult job because of all the pressure
and expectation?
5) What would it mean to you to lead Real Madrid to the
Champions League trophy – a third for you and a tenth
for Real?
6) Can Manchester City ever be as big worldwide as Real
Madrid?
7) If City bid 200m euros for Cristiano Ronaldo – what
would you do and say?
8) What charity do we send the donation to!!!!!!!!?

Cheers

Rob

I packed up my stuff slowly, hanging around and hoping I
still might get the call. Nothing. Reluctantly I sloped off to
reception, ordered a cab and sat and waited, wondered and
worried. I needn't have fretted.

Suddenly there was a ping and there was an email from José.
I frantically opened it up to read it, and lo and behold there
were his answers to all of my questions. Phew, what a relief.
Obviously it was not the same as seeing him personally and
spending time analysing and expanding his answers but it was
a lot better than nothing and far better than any of our rivals
would manage. No one else was going to have a Mourinho
exclusive, were they? And I wasn't going to tell anyone, not
even my boss, that it had all been done by email.

It made a great piece, although his best answer never made
it into the newspaper. It was to question eight and Mourinho's
answer was, 'If we give some money it would be to Mark Halsey
… the ref … cancer foundation.' Brilliant. Mark Halsey was a
top Premier League referee who had beaten throat cancer and

who'd used the publicity around his illness to raise thousands of pounds for cancer charities. I knew Mark and rang him up to tell him he'd be receiving £2,000 from the newspaper and that it was at José's request. He was well pleased and told me José had been in touch with him throughout his ordeal to wish him well. I don't think many people knew that. I don't think many people know a lot of the good work that Mourinho does under the radar and away from the glare of publicity.

City's visit in the Champions League turned out to be a tumultuous night at the Bernabéu as Mancini's men almost pulled off a real upset. However, as so often happened, ex-Manchester United star Cristiano Ronaldo turned up with a late winner to secure a 3–2 victory.

It had all looked so different just three minutes before. City were winning 2–1 and seemed on course to become the first side ever to beat the hosts in their opening home game of a Champions League campaign. Real Madrid boasted 40 wins, two draws and zero defeats. This was looking like a first defeat until a Karim Benzema equalizer in the eighty-seventh minute rescued Real and spread relief around the Bernabéu. When Ronaldo grabbed the winner at the death, the roar of the 67,000 home crowd was deafening and Mourinho raced off the bench to do a crazy knee slide on to the pitch to celebrate, ruining his trousers in the process.

The return match in the group stages came two months later and by then City were in a perilous position. They needed a victory to stay in the competition after failing to win a single game in Group D.

It started to go wrong very quickly, with Karim Benzema scoring in the tenth minute to push City to the brink. Not even a seventy-fourth-minute penalty by Sergio Agüero and the resulting red card for Alvaro Arbeloa could spark a happy ending. Mancini's side finished bottom of the group with just three points and without even a solitary victory. Real Madrid finished second in the group, three points behind winners Borussia Dortmund, who had beaten the Spaniards in Germany in October. The consequence of that was that Real Madrid were drawn to face Manchester United in the last sixteen of the competition, which would see Cristiano Ronaldo return to Manchester for the first time since his move in 2009.

19
SPECIAL SON

Alan Hudson was a Chelsea star of the 1970s. A classy midfielder born in a council house prefab in the shadow of Stamford Bridge. A home-grown talent who hit the big time. He really was one of our own. Let's face it, you can't get more local than a lad who was raised in the streets alongside the stadium and you couldn't get more Chelsea than Hudson either. Well, the Chelsea of that era, anyway.

The swinging Sixties had made London the music and fashion capital of the world and in the 1970s the King's Road, Chelsea, was one of the coolest, most happening places in the capital. It was also where Hudson earned his reputation for being just as at home in the clubs and bars of the district as he was on a football pitch. For 'Huddy' was a player in every sense of the word in a team full of players. He was just like the legendary Peter Osgood, the brilliant striker dubbed the 'King of Stamford Bridge'. They were partners in crime. Mavericks on and off the pitch. Long hair, good-looking, drinkers, womanizers, but both blessed with extraordinary footballing talent. The pair were the scourge of the then Chelsea manager Dave Sexton, who led the Blues to FA Cup and European Cup Winners' Cup glory in 1970 and 1971 respectively. So much so that an exasperated Sexton sold off both of them within weeks of each other, much to the anger and disbelief of fans who adored their swagger and flamboyant style of play and way of life. Hudson joined Stoke

City for a then club record fee of £240,000 in February 1974. Osgood set a new record when he joined Southampton for £275,000 in March 1974. Then, to compound it all, Sexton was sacked in October 1974. Typical Chelsea.

I first met Huddy ten years after he'd left Chelsea. He'd just re-signed for Stoke after five years away playing in the USA. I was working in the Potteries on the local independent radio station, Signal Radio, and was responsible for their coverage of Stoke City. Huddy became my buddy. We got on famously and have kept in touch over the years. Which is how I came to receive an email from his son Anthony in late September 2012. Anthony was out in Bahrain coaching the Bahrain Under-23 team as an assistant to Peter Taylor, who was coaching the Bahrain national side. Anthony was just thirty-one: a bright, ambitious young coach looking to become a top manager. Which is why he wanted me to set up a meeting for him with Mourinho at Real Madrid. He was hoping he could spend a few days watching how one of the world's greatest coaches worked and trained his team. I asked José and he just told me to give Anthony his email address so the pair of them could arrange a visit. José also agreed to do a special article about the Special One and the Special Son with me. A win-win scenario. Helping a friend, gaining a scoop.

It was all duly arranged for the New Year of 2013, but as the date approached both Anthony and I felt sure the trip would be cancelled. Mourinho's third season at the Bernabéu was in desperate trouble. It was his darkest hour in charge of Real Madrid and the vultures were hovering. The Spanish giants were sitting third behind leaders Barcelona and second-placed neighbours Atlético Madrid. What's more, José had enraged Real's fans by dropping iconic captain and goalkeeper Iker Casillas. The word was that if 'Los Blancos' lost to Real Sociedad in their next match then Mourinho would be fired. The man himself admitted to me that he was steeling himself for that very outcome if he failed against Sociedad. So surely Mourinho would pull the plug at this time of crisis; he'd postpone the visit explaining that he needed to concentrate on securing a much-needed win and keeping his job. Not at all. José kept his word and confirmed the trip was still on and we were welcomed with open arms.

I flew out to Madrid on 2 January and the following day met up with Anthony at the training ground, where we both stood on a balcony drinking coffee and eating pastries while watching José put his Real Madrid stars through their paces. All the Galácticos were there: Cristiano Ronaldo, Ángel Di María, Karim Benzema, Luka Modrić, Mesut Özil, Gonzalo Higuaín, Sergio Ramos, Pepe, Casillas. They trained hard, they trained well, and none better than Ronaldo, whose dedication was obvious, even staying on to do drills and free- kick practice on his own.

We were back for more the next day and ended up being invited into José's office afterwards. If we were expecting to meet a man who was bunkered down, fighting for his future and feeling the heat, we couldn't have been more wrong. We had a hug and then a catch up on what was happening for him, for me and for Anthony. He was in top form. He showed me photographs of him looking very small and insignificant alongside the world's tallest man. It was hilarious. He proudly showed me the shot of him with Hollywood star Al Pacino. He put on his glasses and spoke about how working on videos and on Photoshop to prepare for his presentations at team meetings and team talks was ruining his eyes. He posed for pictures with me sitting in his manager's chair. He pointed out a pile of 'Mourinho' books written about him that were on a table. He reckoned most of them were full of lies but said the only people who got rich from taking legal action were the lawyers. I pointed to a photograph on his desk, a young goalkeeper diving full length to make a fantastic save. 'Is that your boy?' I asked, and a beaming smile and nodding head confirmed it was indeed José Jr in action.

Down to business. I put him on the spot about his predicament at Madrid and the speculation about his future even though he'd won three trophies at the Bernabéu since his arrival in 2010. His response was classic Mourinho. He compared himself, his record, to that of arch-rival Arsène Wenger, whose last trophy had come way back in 2005 yet who was still comfortable in his post at Arsenal. I realized it would make a great article to publish on the day of his date with destiny against Real Sociedad that weekend, especially as the Gunners were playing Swansea in the FA Cup that Sunday too. It was a compelling contrast-and-compare analysis of two different managers at two different clubs and their differing philosophies and attitudes.

Needless to say it was a good day and one that was about to get even better for Anthony and me. As I left, José told me to help myself to a bottle of red wine from the long line of 'samples' sent by local vintners who were keen for his custom. Mourinho also allowed Anthony to plug a memory stick into his computer and download all his training schedules and game plays. He explained to me afterwards: 'Anybody can have that. I give them my training methods and programmes but I don't give them my brain.' His point was the schedules were one thing, having the brains to use them to make champions was something completely different. 'Anyway,' he added, 'I change the schedules every year!'

Anthony didn't mind. He was thrilled to have been granted the opportunity. As we chatted later, Hudson said, 'I was sure he would cancel my visit because of the immense pressure he must be under right now. But he didn't. He even took the time to tell me where to stay, where to go. It's incredible really. He's in charge of the biggest club in the world, dealing with the biggest players, and right now the biggest problems. Yet he still has time for someone like myself. That shows true class, huge stature and has left a big impression on me. There have been managers in the first and second divisions who have been "too big" or "too busy" to get back to me. But not the best of the best – and for me it's just another example of why he is the number-one coach in the world. I had already been to see how Sir Alex Ferguson works, to shadow Harry Redknapp, and they were both great, but I have never seen anyone put on a training session like José. They are the best I have ever seen: the attention to detail, the quality and variety of the work is just amazing. It's been a real privilege and it's been an inspiration. It's really boosted my confidence and convinced me that I can go on now and make my own mark in the game.'

And later Anthony sent me a copy of the 'thank you' message he'd sent to José on Saturday 5 January, the day before the do-or-die Real Sociedad clash. It read:

Dear Mr Mourinho,

I just want to say a huge thank you for allowing me to come in and observe, especially during this moment. I learnt a great deal in a short space of time and it's an experience I will never forget. If I can ever be of any assistance in the Middle East or in England, please let me know. All the best tomorrow night! Un abrazo, [an embrace/hug] Anthony.

Four minutes later Mourinho replied:

Happy to give you that chance, happy that you enjoyed
it. We have contact now so we keep in touch.
Good luck
Hug
jm

The speed of the reply blew Anthony away. He emailed me
saying: 'I got a reply from him [Mourinho] today. Look at his
response time below – a day before a game!!!! With three video
meetings, training, picking his team and [the] hotel to deal
with. Unreal!!!!! Legend!!!!!'

I think it's safe to say that José had left a lasting impression.
I'm pretty sure Anthony would have been impressed at any time
but being allowed into the inner sanctum during such bleak
days made Mourinho's welcome and cooperation even more
memorable. The easiest thing for him to have done would have
been to cancel the visit. We would have both understood. The
fact that he didn't spoke volumes to us. It also reminded me
that José knew what it was like to be a young coach fighting
to break through into the cut-throat world of top, professional
football. Early in his career he'd been helped enormously by
the likes of Sir Bobby Robson and Louis van Gaal. Here he was
continuing the tradition for the next generation.

So the next day, Sunday 6 January, I watched nervously on
TV as Real Madrid faced Real Sociedad in a match that could
have been the end for my friend. It was an extraordinary clash,
with Madrid finally winning 4–3 in a thriller, despite having
goalkeeper Antonio Adán sent off in the sixth minute. José
survived the chop and went on to keep his job until the end
of the season before negotiating his way out in the summer so
that he could return to Chelsea and set about completing some
unfinished business.

The following year, August 2014, Anthony Hudson was appointed the international manager for New Zealand, aged just thirty-three.

20
CRIS AND CROSS

I made a second trip to Madrid in that month of January 2013, returning to Valdebebas to do an exclusive interview with Real Madrid and Portugal superstar Cristiano Ronaldo. José had arranged it for me with Jorge Mendes, boss of the influential Gestifute agency in Portugal, who managed the careers of Mourinho and Ronaldo. It was a real coup, as an exclusive Ronaldo interview was a rarity at any time, but this was extra special: his Real Madrid team had just been drawn against his former club Manchester United in the last sixteen of the Champions League, so the timing was absolutely perfect. He was set to play against his old side for the first time on 13 February in the first leg at the Bernabéu and then, on 5 March, make his first return trip to Old Trafford since his £80 million transfer in 2009. It was a great opportunity and I was determined to exploit it to the max, mindful the whole time that it was all due to the loyalty and friendship that José continued to show to me.

As luck would have it, my trip came just a couple of days after Mourinho's fiftieth birthday. I duly emailed José on his big day (Saturday 26 January) to say I was coming over to wish him happy birthday and welcome him into the fifties club, joking that he was 'halfway to 100'. 'F**k 50!!!' was his response. It made me laugh. I already knew what it was like to break through the fifty barrier and to realize that the years were flying past in alarming fashion. At least José still had his hair, although the black locks were by then turning grey to mark the passage of time since we first met.

The following Monday I bought an expensive bottle of champagne, headed to Madrid and looked forward to seeing him for a belated celebration. First I had my big interview with Ronaldo to conduct and, amazingly, my 'only five minutes' with Ronaldo became almost an hour. We got on famously, right from the moment we shook hands and I set him off laughing by asking, 'Don't you ever get bored of scoring hat-tricks?' He loved that. He'd hit a treble the day before in a 4–0 home win over Getafe. It was his third hat-trick of the season and the twentieth of his career. It also saw him surpass 300 club goals, five for Sporting Lisbon, 118 for United and now 179 for Madrid. I then quipped, 'One more and it would have been the perfect birthday present for José ... 5–0 to match him hitting 50!'

Ronaldo was chuckling again. I couldn't have met him at a better moment or in a better mood and he was nothing like I expected. I must admit I was anticipating perhaps a prima donna character, someone who took himself very seriously and might prove hard work to interview. I could not have been more wrong. He was full of fun, self-deprecating, honest and incredibly compassionate and caring. He posed for pictures with me and continued to chat even after the interview had finished. I was well impressed with him and knew I'd come away with not one exclusive piece but half a dozen, which would serve us very well in the build-up to the United matches.

As for Mourinho, he had begun his homework well in advance of the United game, just like he had with City earlier in the season. And, just like against City, the first leg would be in Spain, with United doing well in an entertaining, enthralling contest that lived up to José's billing of it as the match the world wanted to see. Danny Welbeck converted Wayne Rooney's corner to give United the lead after nineteen minutes and set the cat among the pigeons. Just before the half-hour Real responded and it was, almost inevitably, that man Ronaldo. The Portugal international rose above Patrice Evra to head home Ángel Di María's cross.

The match ebbed and flowed from end to end and the Madrid manager was up and down off his bench. United fans bellowed 'Sit down Mourinho' and he acknowledged them with a wry smile and a regal wave, but had to be content with a draw and the prospect of a difficult night ahead in Manchester.

Except in the return leg Mourinho waved United goodbye. A 2–1 win turned Old Trafford into the Theatre of Nightmares, with José enjoying yet another famous victory there. Of course it was Ronaldo scoring the winner against his old club that would grab the headlines on the night, but this triumph was very much a triumph for the lightning fast, tactical brain of Mourinho more than the lightning fast, technical feet of Cristiano.

The match had turned in the fifty-sixth minute. United were in control, leading 1–0 after an own goal by Sergio Ramos early in the second half, but then Turkish referee Cüneyt Çakir sent off United winger Nani for a foul on Arbeloa. It looked a harsh decision. Ferguson was apoplectic, ranting away on the touchline at the referee and officials and trying to rouse the Old Trafford crowd to roar out their own sense of injustice. Amid the mayhem, Mourinho was cool, calm and calculating. He was about to send on striker Karim Benzema in a bid to turn the game. As soon as Nani was dismissed all of that changed, with Mourinho displaying a brilliant, breathtaking piece of decision-making to decide the match. He immediately told Benzema to stand down and summoned midfielder Luka Modrić from the bench instead. With Ferguson's fury in full flow he quietly instructed the Croatian to go out and play in between the lines of Real's attack and midfield and create havoc. He did just that.

Within seven minutes Modrić had scored the equalizer. Within another ten minutes Ronaldo had sent United crashing out. It was cruel on the English side and even Mourinho admitted as much afterwards, confessing that the 'best team lost'. José might have added that the best manager had won, though, for while Fergie ranted and raved he'd plotted and prevailed.

Mourinho survived the next round but for the second successive year he exited in the semi-finals. A 4–1 first-leg defeat at Borussia Dortmund, managed at the time by Jürgen Klopp, was a hammer blow to their chances, and a glut of misses in the 2–0 win at home cost them a place in the final.

Back in Madrid, with the Ronaldo interview concluded and the star man having left, I spoke with Real press officer Juan Camilo Andrade to see if I could now pop in and see José to give him his champagne and have a chat. The trouble was that José was in a meeting just then and it wasn't clear how long it might last. After the marathon interview with Cristiano it seemed like my chances of also seeing José had bombed. So I gave Juan the champers, went to the reception area to call a taxi and headed out to sit in the winter sunshine until the cab arrived. The next thing I heard was some awful singing from just around the corner. I looked over and realized the man responsible for all the noise was none other than José himself. I shouted over and he did a double take. 'What are you doing here?' he asked quizzically. I shook my head and said, 'I told you I was coming. I've just interviewed Cristiano!' He grinned: 'Ah yes, it's good you got Cris.' 'All thanks to you,' I replied, before remembering my gift for him: 'Did Juan give you your champagne?' He went straight-faced for a moment, asking, 'What champagne?' I explained I'd brought him a bottle for his birthday and had given it to his pressman as I didn't think we were going to meet up. He said he would track it down. (He emailed the next day to say he'd finally got his bubbly.)

After the typical opening banter we quickly got to talking about more important matters, starting with his future at Real Madrid and beyond. The build-up to the Getafe game had been dominated by a report in top Spanish sports paper *Marca* that captains Iker Casillas and Sergio Ramos had threatened to leave the club unless Mourinho was sacked. President Florentino Pérez had been forced to call a news conference to dismiss the report as untrue. José gave me a quick guided tour of the superb facilities at Valdebebas while we chatted. At the end of it, I told him: 'It's magnificent, you've got everything here!' His reply was swift and telling. 'Everything but team spirit.' He then admitted he didn't like it at Real Madrid but was not about to quit or be sacked. He said he had a fantastic relationship with the president, who was keen for him to stay, with José having pledged to see out the season. However, he said he would definitely be leaving in the summer after three years in charge. 'Not many managers stay here for three years,' he shrugged, clearly feeling he'd done well to last so long in such a confused and conflicting set of circumstances. He sighed in frustration, an obvious demonstration that the most famous football club in the world was not what he expected. He said it was not a football club, not a sports club; it was a political club full of warring factions and vested interests. The regular elections for the presidency of the club undermine any chance of a sustained, long-term plan.

José then told me a story that served to illustrate the point perfectly. It had been Real Madrid midfielder Michael Essien's thirtieth birthday party in December and the on-loan Chelsea star had invited all his Madrid colleagues to his birthday bash. Only a handful of them turned up and it was left to the Bernabéu boss to console his upset player. He told the Ghana international that it was nothing personal; it was not even that his teammates did not like him and, sadly, it was not because they had anything better to do. Mourinho said it was simply because they were more interested in themselves than anything or anyone else. They had superstar egos to go with their superstar talents. Mourinho was speaking from bitter experience because he had come up against the same attitude himself. Players believing they were bigger than their coach, maybe even bigger than the club.

Finally, as I was about to leave, José told me the most important news: he said he wanted to go back to Chelsea next season and thought it could happen. Wow. This was one hell of a day trip to Spain! The only proviso was that I couldn't quote him and couldn't write the story just yet. It would have been too obvious that he'd tipped me off about his plans if I did the story immediately. I understood and agreed to wait for his okay. I didn't have to wait long.

21

BREAKING NEWS

It was just a week later that I went to print with a big back-page story headlined: 'José – Let Me Save Chelsea!' It was dramatic stuff. Back then Chelsea were out of sorts and out of harmony: dumped out of the Champions League and down into the Europa League after a dismal defence of their 2012 European crown. One of the heroes of Munich 2012, manager Roberto Di Matteo, had been sacked in November after just 262 days in charge, despite winning the Champions League and FA Cup. Worse, the reviled Rafa Benítez, the ex-Liverpool boss, had been brought in as interim manager, to the disgust of many true Blue supporters. So Chelsea needed rescuing and who better than the man who was the club's greatest manager of all time, boasting six trophies in three seasons, including back-to-back league titles in 2005 and 2006.

So my José comeback story definitely lit the blue touchpaper for his eventual return to Stamford Bridge that summer. Straightaway Chelsea fans began singing Mourinho's name at games and there was an absolute clamour for him to come back to the place he loved and where he was loved. Chelsea fans, who'd protested against Benítez right from the beginning, stepped up their campaign. They taunted Rafa even more. During a 1–0 win over West Brom at the beginning of March they held up banners reading 'Divided We Fall #Rafaout' and 'We're just not Inter 'im.' They sang: 'You're not wanted here', 'Stand up if you hate Rafa', 'We don't care about Rafa, he don't care about us', and loudest of all they sang 'José Mourinho!'

Just a couple of days later Mourinho was back in England knocking Manchester United out of the Champions League. It completed a remarkable run for Mourinho and Madrid. In the space of three matches he'd masterminded three incredible results. First he'd won 3–1 against bitter rivals Barcelona at the Camp Nou in the semi-final of the Copa del Rey, then he'd beaten them again in Madrid in La Liga and finally he'd won at United. He played it all down, though, when he gave me yet another exclusive interview afterwards.

The Special One insisted it wasn't his most special run. He reminded the world, and especially Chelsea owner Roman Abramovich, that in Italy he'd won the treble in the space of a fortnight, the first in the history of Italian football. Not a bad time to remind everybody either – just as you're looking for a new job in the summer.

Never one to miss an opportunity, José also sent me a series of photographs of him walking around Manchester City's Etihad Stadium. The background was that City had agreed to let Real train at their stadium on the Monday before the Champions League clash at Old Trafford. José had mischief on his mind. He had Real Madrid photographer Helios de la Rubia take various pictures of him at the stadium and wanted us to reproduce them in the *News of the World* just to plant the seed of what it would look like if he were to take charge at City in the summer. City manager Roberto Mancini may have won the Premier League title the year before but it was believed that he was in dire danger of losing his job if he didn't win the league again. I'm pretty sure City and José had been in touch to discuss the possibility. I am sure it was one of the options he was considering, although not his top choice. I knew he had set his mind on fulfilling his 'unfinished business' at Chelsea, but nevertheless he was not above trying to use the moment to his advantage, to provoke Abramovich into fearing he might go to City instead. So he sent me the pictures. This time, though, his mind games and manoeuvring didn't work. We didn't use the photographs.

José was undeterred. Later that month, he tipped me off that he was coming to England again. Even better, he was coming to London; better still, he was coming to Stamford Bridge for the first time since 2010. Not for a Chelsea game, but for an international match between Brazil and Russia staged at the Bridge. He'd been invited by the Brazilian FA so it had absolutely nothing to do with the Blues. However, he knew he could exploit the situation just by being there. Especially if I highlighted it in the newspaper. He even told me where he would be during the day so we could go and picture him back in the capital. He revealed: 'Easy to find me during the day ... Monday shopping at Harrods [and] Sloane Street. Sunday lunch or dinner at La Famiglia [his favourite restaurant] for sure. I don't speak but you can have [the pictures] if you want. Last time I was at Stamford Bridge was Chelsea v Inter 2010.'

Talk about being spoon-fed. Obviously he was using me and the newspaper to make sure he was able to fulfil his dream of returning to the club he loved, Chelsea, but I was unperturbed. I didn't feel used and abused. I just felt delighted he trusted me with the information and that I would do a good job with it. It was very much a quid pro quo scenario. He scratched my back, I scratched his! A win-win arrangement that worked brilliantly for both of us.

On 25 March I did the story of his return. It was on the back page headlined 'José Back at Chelsea', with a smaller sub-header underneath saying, 'But Rafa has no need to panic ... yet!'

On 27 March José went even further, and I wrote an article headed 'I LOVE CHELSEA', with a big blue heart in place of the word 'LOVE'. Mourinho was at his mischievous best in the piece. He was shamelessly touting himself for a return, as he gushed, 'I have big emotional connections with Chelsea. One day, naturally, I have to come back to English football to Chelsea or another club. Of course Chelsea means [something] different for me than the other clubs. Chelsea is in my heart as Inter is. So one day I have to be back.' He then turned his eyes north to Manchester, and the possibility of bossing United or City, saying, 'I think Manchester is Sir Alex's kingdom and I would love that job to be his job forever. Of course it cannot be forever but I would love it to be for many, many more years. And in the other chair in Manchester is Roberto Mancini with a contract. He was a champion last year so I don't think there is a move there.'

Hilariously Mourinho went on to blame all the current speculation over his future, including a possible return to Chelsea, on him innocently spending a long weekend in London during the international break. I was chuckling because he'd blatantly used me to highlight his trip for that very reason. He claimed, 'I'm in London, we have a house here, we love it here. Our daughter is coming to study in London so being in London has to be seen as a very normal thing for us. Yet every time I come, every time people see me walking around or shopping, people start immediately making connections to a return.' Then he confessed to something I already knew: 'I feed it a little bit because I say every day when I have the chance that I love it here, that I spent a fantastic time here, that I will return one day. So to be fair I give a little contribution to that speculation but just because I love it.'

He even revealed his timeline for any switch by saying, 'Movements have to be done in the summer so let's wait to see what happens. I have a contract with Real and I am very, very committed [to] the ambitions of the club for the rest of the season. So in this moment I only think about Real.'

The truth is he was thinking almost as much about his Chelsea return. He was studying recordings of Chelsea's games and analysing the playing squad, deciding who he'd like to keep and who he'd like to kick out. Although he was in charge at Madrid he was growing impatient, keen to seal the Chelsea deal.

That impatience led to another exclusive on the subject on 7 April. The headline was 'Hurry Up' and the subtitle read: 'Grab José now Rom or lose out'. What few people knew was that he had been considering his options for months. We'd chatted when the rumour mill was in overdrive about a switch to Manchester City. He revealed then, 'Not sure what's going to happen. I want Chelsea but really Real Madrid, PSG and City are pushing hard. I wait because I want Chelsea but not too long.' In the article I quoted a close friend of Mourinho saying, 'José wants to go back to Chelsea. It's where he wants to be. Every time Chelsea fans sing his name it makes him want to go back even more.' The source of the story even let it be known that Mourinho wasn't looking for a pay rise either, adding, 'He'll sign for the same money he's on at Real, even though he's sure he could earn more elsewhere like City or PSG. José could even remain at Madrid but he is clear about where he'd like to go; it's now down to if Roman Abramovich wants the same.'

Manchester United suddenly entered the discussions. Sir Alex Ferguson had by then tipped off his friend that he would be quitting Old Trafford in the summer. In return Mourinho had confided to Fergie that he would be leaving Real Madrid at the end of the season. It all seemed a very convenient coincidence. Things accelerated quickly. So fast in fact that Mourinho thought he had the United job in the bag that April, only for it to turn to dust. It was a setback that shocked and rocked him. He couldn't quite believe what had transpired, telling friends 'you can't imagine what happened'. But despite the disappointment of that moment he still never lost the burning ambition to manage the mighty Manchester United one day.

Finally, on 3 May, I went all-out for it and announced José would start back as Chelsea manager in July. It was a front-page world exclusive alongside the headline: 'Back for Mour'. I followed it up the next day with the news that José wanted to keep legends Frank Lampard and John Terry at the club. They both stayed. Then I revealed he wanted £50 million flop Fernando Torres out, something it actually took him a year to achieve. I was on a roll thanks to my man in Madrid. The scoops kept coming.

On the morning of 20 May, José told me, 'I am free now. I have agreement to leave RM at the end of the season – mutual agreement … no money … free to go.' The next day Real Madrid president Pérez confirmed Mourinho was leaving by 'mutual consent' at the end of the season, meaning Chelsea wouldn't have to pay any compensation for their man, who still had three years of his contract to run.

A deal was agonizingly close to completion now and when José tipped me off that he was flying into London with his trusted right-hand man Rui Faria for the Championship play-off final between Crystal Palace and Watford, I sensed there was a more compelling reason for his visit to the capital. The sports desk duly arranged to photograph the pair of them at the game for another exclusive, announcing José's back-room team ahead of his impending return. Of course I also told him of my suspicions over the real reason for his trip but agreed not to write anything until he said so. The next day I got the nod. 'Signed last night, now official – a Chelsea man!'

On Thursday 30 May 2013 I broke the news, with the back page of the newspaper screaming out another exclusive: 'José Signs', informing the world that Mourinho had put pen to paper on a four-year contract at Chelsea. On 3 June 2013 Chelsea

Football Club officially announced that José Mourinho had returned to manage the club on a four-year deal. It was a month after I'd announced it to the world and four months since my first story on 4 February, 'José – Let Me Save Chelsea!' Now he finally had the chance.

22

SHOW ME THE MONEY!

Mourinho isn't motivated by money, but he has a keen sense of his own worth. I know because several times I've tried to do a deal with him and every time I've walked away empty-handed. Once I even tried to do two deals with him in one day and got a double whammy of a knock-back.

It was in September 2009 when he was coach at Inter Milan, but for the first time in fifteen years I was on the move. I was about to leave one newspaper and switch to another. The funny thing was that both newspapers wanted me to make contact with Mourinho and offer him a deal to do a column for them during the upcoming 2010 World Cup finals in South Africa. My existing boss, who had no idea I would soon be leaving, packed me off on a plane to Italy with a personal letter to José.

Honestly, it was a silly letter, a poor attempt at banter with someone he didn't even know. It hoped the 'nasty' Italian journalists were not giving him a rough time and asked that he hurry back to the Premier League. I cringed when I first read it. What was even worse was that the money he was offering was even poorer than his badinage. The deal was between five and six thousand pounds each for five to six columns beginning a week before the actual finals and going through to 11 July and the final. Somewhere between £25,000 and £36,000 in total then, which is decent money for an ordinary bloke like me but a couple of days' pay to someone like Mourinho. No problem, I didn't really care. I was leaving.

When my soon-to-be new boss found out I was off to Milan to see José, he asked me to make an offer to him, too. I was happy to oblige as obviously I would much prefer for my new paper to do the deal, as I would be the one speaking with José and writing the column.

Their offer was considerably better. It was slick, super professional, full of detail and offered serious money, in newspaper terms, dwarfing what my current employers were putting on the table. My dilemma was how was I going to pull it off? How could I possibly present both offers to Mourinho in one meeting? After deliberating over it for a while I decided the best way was to be honest with him about it, to make light of the whole scenario. I felt I knew him well enough to have a bit of fun about it all without embarrassing myself or him. So off I set with two letters from two different newspapers to make the offers to José.

On arrival at Milan airport I jumped in a cab and headed straight off to Inter's training ground where the Inter boss was doing a press conference. Afterwards, José came over, shook hands and in no time at all we were chatting away and, sure enough, he invited me to follow him out of the pressroom for a more private conversation. What had I got for him? What did we want him to do? What was the offer? The expected stuff, except this was an unusual occurrence as I actually had two offers to put before him. Now, you might think that was pretty shameless, but I did try to act as appropriately as possible in the circumstances. I thought it only right and proper to go through the deal on offer from my current employers first. After all, they were the ones paying for the trip! It didn't take much time, as the offer itself was so basic: the letter was only thirteen lines in length. It's fair to say it left him completely underwhelmed and it became quickly apparent that there wasn't any hope of him putting pen to paper this time.

Time to own up and go for plan B. José just smiled as I

explained my unique circumstances. He wasn't bothered. He just wanted to know what the second offer entailed. I went for it and thankfully this time I had more than a soppy letter to work with. I had a detailed, professional proposal and we went through it all thoroughly, the number of columns, a TV advert to promote the column, an exclusive photo shoot, including shots of José reading the newspaper. This was more like it. The paper was treating him like a superstar, giving him a showbiz-style platform, making it clear how much they valued him and how excited they were to work with him.

It succeeded. He was interested; I even got the feeling it could happen, but he didn't think the money was good enough. To make the point he took my pen and flipped over the offer letter. He scribbled his Inter email at the top and then scrawled a huge £ sign below it and pushed it back at me. The message was clear: show me the money! I laughed, we shook hands and I promised to do my best. The trouble was there was no more money to be had and José wasn't going to sell himself cheap, so in the end neither newspaper managed to seal a deal.

I duly switched newspapers and almost four years later I was chasing José again. It was 20 May 2013, a landmark day in Mourinho's career, and once more he gave me the inside track, beginning with that email from José saying he was 'free now. I have agreement to leave RM at the end of the season.' I quickly fired one back asking, 'Have you agreed with Chelsea too?' To which he immediately replied, 'CFC I will meet at the end of season. I have 2 matches [left] but will all be fine.'

That was great news of course and meant I already had a scoop in my hands by 08.47 in the morning. However, I was greedy. I wanted more, which is probably why I lasted thirty years at the top of journalism in the cut-throat world of Fleet Street. So I went straight in with a new offer for him to link up with the newspaper.

I replied, 'Brilliant news, especially for me as a Chelsea fan!

Can't wait for the announcement. Can't wait to see you back where you belong. I also have some big proposals for you from the Sun. They will pay you a lot of money to officially link up with you now. Things like: First exclusive picture of you in a Chelsea shirt or tracksuit. First exclusive interview. A video interview of you talking about you and your football philosophy. A television advert. A regular column in the newspaper. A World Cup column next summer. A book deal with HarperCollins. We could also work together on the definitive Mourinho book and a DVD film charting your career or simply a video diary through the season charting your return to Chelsea. There are so many opportunities to be exploited. I really think we should do this. I can come to Madrid to show you in detail the ideas and the figures. I was going to Spain for a few days later this week anyway; a quick diversion to Madrid to go through all of this would be no problem if you have half an hour for a chat. Let me know. Cheers Rob.'

It was a bid to get in first and seal a deal even before the news of his return to Chelsea was confirmed. My previous experience told me not to expect a quick response from José or his people regarding this latest business proposal but at least I felt I was in there fighting. I felt even better when I received an immediate reply from Mourinho. It told me all I needed to know. He simply wrote, 'Not sure about what I can and can't do but for sure we are friends and I am a good friend.'

In the end, friends or not, the only part of that 2013 proposal that was pursued by Mourinho and his agent Luis Correia was for a World Cup 2014 column. I guess the logic was that it would not impact on his role as manager of Chelsea as it was international football and taking place during the close season. The main difficulty was that José, who was now back managing Chelsea, wasn't actually going to be there for the World Cup finals. He was off on a trip to Africa in his role as a United

Nations ambassador for the World Food Programme, a global scheme to feed the millions of starving people on the planet. That posed an immediate problem. How were we going to do a column with him when he was so far away? Naturally I wasn't keen on missing five weeks of covering the World Cup finals in the land of carnival to go to Africa just to do a José column. I love the guy but not that much!

So I proposed I would do it via Skype, or by phone or email. Negotiations seemed to be going well. The one worry for me again was that obviously Mourinho doesn't need the money, and while £200,000, the figure we offered him, may be a fabulous fee for a newspaper to pay out, it was still no great shakes in the money-laden world of football. It was a top manager's weekly wage. So I had to think of another way of selling it to him in an effort to entice him into doing it. I told José, 'It's great money, it's £30,000 a phone call. Imagine if you got thirty grand every time you made a phone call!' I added, 'It will buy you an Aston Martin, a Ferrari, a Lamborghini. Buy something with it for your wife, make it a memorable gift which you and Matilde will always remember.'

The discussions went to and fro with José and his agent. This was progressing, we were much further down the road than ever before, and then we were completely blown out of the water. Internet giants Yahoo came in and offered him an exclusive worldwide deal to be their World Cup expert and were offering a cool £1 million. You can buy a few Aston Martins with that. I still tried to make it work. I promised José our columns would not clash with his articles for Yahoo. We could just concentrate on the England matches, the England players and the performances of the big-name Premier League stars with their individual countries. I argued that this way we wouldn't compromise or conflict with the expansive overview of the finals he was expected to deliver for Yahoo. It was discussed, it was considered, but ultimately it was rejected. No, it was Yahoo putting the big money on the table, and José and his people weren't going to do anything that might jeopardize such a windfall.

It all reminded me of a saying my mum used to come out with: money goes to money. Here he was, already fabulously wealthy through his football contracts, and still there were people falling over themselves to give him even more money just to be associated with him. Major brands like Yahoo, Jaguar, Hublot, Adidas, MasterCard. Too big, too powerful, too global for even a top-selling newspaper to compete with. I sensed we were only ever in the ball game because José wanted to do me a favour if he could. Unfortunately it just didn't make financial sense for him, so we were rebuffed once again.

Yet, as a 'thank you for your interest' gesture José did offer to do a big exclusive interview with me for free at the end of the football season. And he went on to prove what a good friend he really was by going on to give me chapter and verse on pretty much everything he was planning at Chelsea from that moment on; virtually up until the day he left in December 2015. All of it for free, when he could have been on the payroll to the tune of £200,000. Now that's what you call a mate!

23
PEP TALK

José gifting me the inside track on his plans to return to Chelsea had guaranteed me scoop after scoop from early 2013 through to the summer. It also guaranteed a string of 'herograms' from the office. There was one huge exception to this triumphant run of success.

In mid-January 2013 I wrote a big back-page story announcing to the world that Pep Guardiola would be the next manager of Manchester City, succeeding current coach Roberto Mancini at the end of the season. Just days later, on Wednesday 16 January 2013, it was officially announced Guardiola would be the new boss of Bayern Munich. It was the biggest failure of my journalistic career. I was utterly stunned. To this day I can still remember exactly where I was and what I was doing when I got the call saying the Spaniard was not going to City at all, but was off to Germany.

I was sitting at the bar in Selfridges in London's Oxford Street having a lunchtime drink with a friend and fellow Chelsea fan, Deborah Leatherdale. She was drinking red wine; I was on the champagne. The bubbly quickly lost its sparkle, though, when I answered a call on my mobile phone. It was my boss, Head of Sport Mike Dunn, and the conversation went pretty much like this: 'Beas, it's just been announced that Guardiola is going to Bayern Munich.'

I laughed and said, 'Yeah, good one, what's up?', thinking it was all a wind-up and there was another, more serious reason for the call.

Dunn wasn't laughing. He just replied, 'I'm not joking, Guardiola's going to Bayern.' Suddenly I wasn't so sure it was a wind-up at all and my heart began to sink.

'You're kidding me?' I managed to say, still incredulous.

'No, it's just been announced ... this is an almighty cock-up! How have we got it so wrong?' It was a rhetorical question. We both already knew the answer: it was all José Mourinho's fault!

It had all started innocently enough. On Friday 11 January I had emailed José some photographs from my visit to Real Madrid's training ground complex the previous week and asked him if he was still planning to fly in to watch Manchester United face Liverpool at Old Trafford on the Sunday, 13 January. It was a good story as United had been drawn against Mourinho's Real Madrid in the Champions League knockout stages and the Bernabéu boss had tipped me off that he was coming with his son José Jr on a spying mission. Sure enough his reply confirmed the cloak-and-dagger visit was on. 'Hi mate ... yes I go to Old Trafford. Thanks for the pics', and then totally unsolicited he added, 'Don't write Guardiola to CFC [Chelsea] because he goes 100 per cent to [Manchester] City and when I say 100 per cent it's 100 per cent not 99. Hug.'

Now that got my immediate interest and I responded by asking, 'So Pep will take over for Mancini in the summer? Or sooner???' and moments later José confirmed: 'summer'. What a tip-off, and obviously I was chuffed. I told José: 'Brilliant – that's a bottle of red I owe you!!!!'

Next, I was straight on the phone to the office with the good news. Every journalist loves a tip-off like that, although normally we were expected to provide two sources for such a big story as this. So, even if you had a top tip-off from a contact, you still had to find someone else who could verify their information. Sometimes it is easy and straightforward. Other times it's a real pain. You are convinced that what you have been told is true but you just can't find that all-important second source to give you the necessary confirmation. As a result, sometimes the story never comes out at all. Even worse, there are times when the story comes out officially before you have managed to obtain the verification needed to go into print. That's incredibly frustrating, but the bottom line is that demanding a second source is a very good way of ensuring that you don't rush to publish and then find out you've got the story dramatically wrong. If only we'd kept to the rules with this Mourinho tip-off.

Instead, we messed up big-time. We were all guilty of becoming a bit complacent because of the identity of the source for this particular tale. With good reason, because José's track record on stories up to this point had been 100 per cent on the button – twenty-four-carat gold. I was expecting this to be the same, so I was pretty bullish when I told the boss about my latest exchange with José. I even forwarded the relevant emails to the sports desk to convince them of the authenticity of my information. Inevitably there was a lot of toing and froing. I think even the editor became involved in the discussions and deliberations over whether to go with the story or not. I was keen, of course, but it was never my decision to make. Guys higher up the News International food chain had that responsibility. In the final analysis the emails proved to be the clincher for the powers-that-be to ultimately give the go ahead. After all, there it was in black and white from José Mourinho himself from his Real Madrid email address. And remember, he was so convinced about the information he was passing on that he'd insisted: 'when I say 100 per cent it's 100 per cent not 99'. So we went for it. We splashed the news all over the back page and sat back to await the glory that would surely follow.

Except there was to be no such glory, only cringing embarrassment. The story was 100 per cent, all right; unfortunately it was 100 per cent wrong and it had my name on it! I couldn't believe it, the office couldn't believe it and José couldn't believe it. After the story had broken I sent him a quick message saying, 'Pep to Bayern – that's a shock!' I didn't know what else to say. I knew José wouldn't have deliberately dropped me in it but it was clear something had gone badly wrong somewhere. I needed to know what had happened, how such a blunder had occurred so I had to say something. I had to get an explanation. Credit to Mourinho, it didn't take long to find out, with José quick to take the blame and apologize.

It turned out to be an excruciating tale of assumption, misinterpretation and misinformation which, it was claimed, had initially emanated from Guardiola himself. The ex-Barcelona boss had supposedly contacted a fitness coach who was friends with one of Mourinho's assistants, and offered him a job. The coach was keen and believed he was coming to England to work, although oddly he didn't know which club. José was convinced the job wasn't at Chelsea and wasn't at Manchester United so deduced it must therefore be City. He wrote, 'Pep spoke to a fitness coach close to my assistant. Pep invite him to go with him, offered him money to go, wanted an answer from him. He [the coach] said, "Yes, happy to go" and asked him "Where?" Pep told him he has a signed contract in an English club ... all done. We knew not Chelsea or Man Utd so only could be City. Even the fitness coach thought that ... but it was Bayern. Unbelievable. I am so sorry about wrong info. I will never say a thing to you again. So sorry.'

I was horrified by the explanation. A former editor had once told me, 'Never assume anything because it makes an ASS out of U and ME.' It's an old-school journalistic saying teaching you to deal in facts not speculation unless you want to look like an ASS. At journalism college I'd also been taught the mantra 'if in doubt, leave it out!' Yet here I was guilty of forgetting two of a reporter's golden rules. On this rare occasion our absolute belief in our source allied to the thrill of breaking such a big exclusive story had made us forget the essentials of journalism: check your facts and then check them again. It's all so obvious in hindsight, isn't it? Let's be honest, just because someone has been right in the past is absolutely no guarantee that they are right this time or will be in the future. Each case has to be judged on its own merit and double-checked, double-sourced every time. So now I think about it again, it actually wasn't José's fault at all. Yes he'd got his wires crossed and arrived at a fundamentally flawed conclusion from the information he'd been told. However, it was my duty to validate his claims and I completely failed to do so. Which is why I got straight on to José after receiving his apology. In pretty clumsy English I told him, 'Don't you dare not say anything to me in the future. This is a cock-up and it's embarrassing and hurtful but these things happen. You've given us lots of great stories too so keep them coming.' Thankfully he did and happily they were all 100 per cent right. I know because I checked them!

I still had to face my peers, though, and the folk at Manchester City. Soon afterwards I was at Eastlands for a City game and the club's Head of Communications Vikki Kloss and Head of Media Relations Simon Heggie both battered me. I tried to pre-empt it as I saw them approaching me in a packed press box, with all my fellow hacks watching on. I stood up smiling, raised my hands as if in surrender and said, 'I know, I know, I know ... come on, give it to me.' They sure did and I just had to take it. I deserved it; I knew it, they knew it, everyone there knew it. They're both good guys and good people, but they weren't going to let slip the opportunity to give me a right kicking. Trust me, I've been beating myself up over it ever since. A stupid schoolboy error by an experienced, seasoned, award-winning professional. I've never liked Guardiola since!

24
HAPPY DAYS!

On 3 June 2013 Chelsea Football Club officially announced that José Mourinho had returned to manage the club on a four-year deal, a month after I'd 'officially' announced the news to the world.

It was a monumental day for him, six years in the waiting, five months in the planning. Remember way back in September 2007, just after he'd left the Blues for the first time, he'd told me he'd be back as boss one day. Then in January 2013, five months before the big announcement, he'd whispered to me that he was ready to return. Ultimately, on 10 June 2013, José was unveiled at a packed Stamford Bridge press conference which, this time, was hosted in the spacious Bobby Tambling suite rather than the confines of the pressroom. It was there that he finally fulfilled his promise of 2007 that he would one day return to the club he loved.

Mourinho couldn't have been more content. He told the world he was now the 'Happy One', declaring with a smile, 'If I have to choose a nickname for this period, I would choose "the Happy One" because I am very happy.' He proclaimed, 'I am where I want to be. Chelsea is the job I want and I accepted it immediately. It was an easy decision. I met the boss, the owner [Roman Abramovich] and I think in five minutes after a couple of very short but pragmatic questions we decided straight away. I asked the boss, "Do you want me back?" and the boss asked me, "Do you want to come back?" I think in a couple of minutes the decision was made.'

He also made light of reports that his first spell at Chelsea had ended so abruptly because he'd fallen out with Abramovich. José clarified, 'I read and I kept listening I was fired, I was sacked, we had a complete break of relationships. That was not true. Many people didn't believe in that, but it was mutual agreement. At the time we thought it was best for both of us, me and the club. It was a sad moment. Of course it was a sad moment, but I don't regret that decision.'

In contrast, his triumphant return now was a glad moment and he confessed it was also a unique sensation for him, explaining, 'It is the first time I arrive in a club where I already love the club. Before I had to build an emotional relationship and I only came to love the club a little later.'

Obviously I was thrilled too, on a professional and personal level. My big interview with José on his departure in 2007 and my scoop of his wish to return in February 2013 had both been utterly vindicated. I'd set the agenda and beaten the rest of the Fleet Street pack to a huge story. The added bonus was that a man who called me his friend was back in charge of my favourite football team. As a reporter it was wonderful to have that close a relationship with one of the biggest names in the game; a man who was in charge of one of England's biggest clubs. There would surely be more scoops ahead. As a Chelsea supporter it was marvellous that the greatest manager in the club's history was back at the helm – and with Mourinho that usually means trophies.

I must admit, though, that I had initially been nervous of José's return, worried that he was risking his incredible legacy at the club. It was something I raised with him in the early days as he told me of his plans to return. I reminded him of the saying 'you should never go back' because it can't be the same the second time around. I told him 'it's like suddenly seeing an old girlfriend again. You immediately recognize all the amazing things that attracted you to her in the first place, but forget about all the awful things that eventually drove you apart.' I was concerned that the old wounds and scars from before would reopen again, and maybe far sooner than first time around. I was also acutely conscious of José's comments to me in 2011 when he was unsettled and unhappy after a disappointing first season at Real Madrid and was looking over at England for a possible escape route.

I had emailed Mourinho on Sunday 22 May 2011 to tell him that manager Carlo Ancelotti had been sacked by Chelsea and asked him, 'Are you coming back?' He replied, 'No mate, not going. Seems to me that the club is the same ... Marina [Granovskaia], [Guus] Hiddink advisor, agents around, favourite players.' Two years down the line it struck me that nothing much had changed. In fact, Marina Granovskaia, a senior adviser to owner Roman Abramovich, was even more powerful and set to go on to assume most of chief executive Ron Gourlay's duties when he left in 2014; Hiddink was still on the scene and would later replace José when he was sacked in 2015, and the favoured few agents and stars still got the special treatment. José's attitude, though, was that his relationship with Abramovich was all that mattered; they'd stayed close over the years after his 2007 departure and he was putting his faith in that.

He was also bullish when I expressed my concern over his legacy being at risk. Of course he was. While I worried he might not be as successful second time around, he was full of confidence and convinced that there would be more good times ahead. In any event, he was adamant that, whatever happened, his glorious first chapter at the club could never be ignored or forgotten. So Mourinho shot me down in flames, insisting, 'What you did, you did. Nobody can delete, nobody can take away that history for me at Chelsea. I want to be seen as a new manager of Chelsea, to be analysed on what I do now. And I know Chelsea people's mentality, they will never forget what I did before. They will never forget that I give everything to this club. My career is very rich and I won lots of things in different places. I have won every competition that I would love to win; I have won it so I don't feel the pressure that a manager without a CV would feel. The pressure I feel now is fighting for your own club. Chelsea means more than being the manager of another club. It means more because of what I did; it means more because I always want Chelsea to win. So if I wanted Chelsea to win in the last five years with ten different managers in charge, well now I'm there I can do actually something, which clearly I couldn't for the last five years. It's like if someone tells a Chelsea supporter that for this match you are Chelsea manager; that person would feel a big responsibility on his shoulders.'

José had endeared himself even more with Chelsea fans by declaring he was now 'one of them', a supporter just as much as he was the manager. He knew he would receive a tumultuous reception when he stepped out for his first match back in charge on 18 August, conveniently enough a home game at Stamford Bridge and against lesser opposition, Hull City. However, Mourinho wasn't in the mood to bask in all the glory or risk it deflecting his players' attention away from the match itself. Therefore he was quick to stress that he didn't want his return to overshadow the most important aim of the day: a winning start to the campaign and three points in the bag.

We spoke about it in Washington DC at the end of Chelsea's pre-season tour in the USA, with his first Premier League match just over a week away. He used the interview as an opportunity to get his thoughts over to the expectant Chelsea fans, saying he would be happy and honoured to receive their salute for a few short moments before kick-off but not over a prolonged period into the match. He reasoned, 'I'm Chelsea so when I go there and stand in that dugout I'm Chelsea not José Mourinho. I want them to support us. If the fans want to praise me for a couple of minutes to show me how happy they are, I have to stand up and say "thanks" to everyone but I won't be happy if that goes on and on because I want the players to be supported and I want Chelsea to be the Chelsea of everyone.'

José just couldn't wait to get started at putting things right. I asked him how he imagined he'd feel in the moments before kick-off and he admitted he knew he'd struggle to control his emotions. He said, 'Five minutes before the match I would say I want to go and play. I can't control any more the feeling. Your levels of adrenaline are coming up and I want very much to go and enjoy the Premier League again and to enjoy playing on the Chelsea side.' Later he'd declare, 'It's my dugout, my stadium, my people,' and so it proved on the day.

Everything went pretty much as he'd planned and predicted. A huge reception from supporters, lots of noise and support for him and the team throughout, and a 2–0 victory. There was one hiccup when Frank Lampard saw an early penalty kick saved but then Oscar gave Chelsea the lead and 'Super Frankie' Lampard made it 2–0 with a trademark free kick. Three points, job done. Mourinho was back.

25

DEAD MAN WALKING

Chelsea's £50 million striker Fernando Torres was a dead man walking even before José Mourinho's dramatic return to Stamford Bridge in the summer of 2013. Mourinho had it in for the Spanish international long before then. José was Real Madrid manager at the time but remained an avid supporter of his beloved former club Chelsea. He even had Chelsea TV so he could keep in touch with everything that was happening at Stamford Bridge and he watched in dismay and anger as Torres endured a torrid and tormented time in the English capital.

The ex-Liverpool star had joined the Blues for a British record transfer fee in January 2011 after a prolific time with the Merseyside club, where he'd scored an impressive 81 goals in 142 appearances. In the season he signed for Chelsea he'd already notched nine goals for the Kop club when he made his big-money move to London at the end of January, but inexplicably the goals dried up immediately.

A goal-shy Torres fired blanks in his first 13 games for Chelsea, eventually managing just one goal in the 18 games that were left in that 2010–11 season. For the record, it came in a 3–0 home win over West Ham on Saturday 23 April, with only four games of the campaign left. The Chelsea fans' loud cheers were a mixture of joy, relief and irony. Manager Carlo Ancelotti sent Torres on as a seventy-sixth-minute substitute for first-choice frontman Didier Drogba and the Spaniard scored eight minutes later to put Chelsea 2–0 in front. It was all too little, too late, though, and did nothing to revive his already wrecked reputation. By then the player previously nicknamed 'El Niño' (the Christ Child) had earned a new, far less flattering moniker, the '£50 Million Flop'. What Mourinho called him was a lot worse than that.

His opinion of the Chelsea number 9 was damning. 'Torres is a disgrace and has to leave ... but where?? Who wants him??' That was in May 2013 as Mourinho prepared for his second coming at the Bridge. It wasn't the first time he'd complained to me about the faltering forward. Earlier, in February, when Mourinho was already discussing a Chelsea return, he was just as scathing. He'd watched Chelsea get out of jail against Sparta Prague in the Europa League the previous night, courtesy of an injury-time goal from Eden Hazard, which salvaged a 1–1 draw. The result saw a fortunate Chelsea edge though into the last sixteen of the competition but the most notable feature of the game was the clutch of chances that Torres had squandered.

It was too much for Mourinho to tolerate, especially with Chelsea facing second-in-the-table Manchester City just a few days later. José admitted to me that he was far from optimistic that 'our' Chelsea would win if Torres was selected. 'Let's see our CFC against City. If Torres doesn't play we play with 11, with him we play with 10 and [our] opponents with 12.' Chelsea lost, City winning 2–0 after goals from Yaya Toure and Carlos Tevez. Torres did play, but only after coming on as an eighty-first-minute substitute for John Obi Mikel, so on this occasion not even José could blame him for the reverse.

Even so, Torres was already toast in Mourinho's eyes and getting him out was a top priority when the Portuguese coach duly resumed his duties at Chelsea in July that year. His idea was to sell the Spaniard as soon as possible and bring in a new frontman who would fire the goals to make Chelsea competitive again at home and abroad. It didn't happen, though; selling

'Nando', as Chelsea teammates called Torres, was unfortunately far easier said than done.

First of all the man himself had a lucrative £150,000 per week contract with Chelsea until 2016 on terms and conditions befitting a British record signing. Unsurprisingly, the striker was in no mood to jettison such a generous package without a fight. Just as unsurprisingly, there were no immediate takers for the misfiring misfit, either in the Premier League or in Europe. So it was a stagnating, stalemate scenario, the vanity project of Chelsea owner Roman Abramovich proving an even bigger financial disaster than his £30 million recruitment of Andriy Shevchenko in 2006.

So in the end Mourinho found himself in the unenviable and unpleasant position of having to work with a player he had absolutely no faith in and no desire to have in his side. Consequently Torres was a bit-part player for José that season, scoring 11 goals in 41 appearances, albeit many of those outings coming from the bench. It was nowhere near enough for Mourinho who, at the end of the season, tried hard once again to give the £50 million flop the chop.

This time he succeeded. Torres finally left SW6 in August 2014 after agreeing a two-year loan deal with Italian giants AC Milan. Then the following January, just as the loan deal to Milan was poised to be made permanent, Torres was suddenly on the move again, understandably preferring to make an emotional return to his former club Atlético Madrid in Spain. It was where he'd first shot to stardom and so for him was a welcome homecoming.

Finally Fernando was happy again, but Chelsea were far from content. They were left counting the cost of one of the biggest, most expensive transfer blunders in English football history. On top of the £50 million transfer fee, the Blues had subsequently splashed out another £26 million in wages and bonuses, then finally handed Torres a £6 million 'loyalty payment' to help pave the way for his switch to Serie A. That adds up to an astonishing £82 million in all. For that they were 'rewarded' with just 46 goals in 172 appearances. That's about £1.6 million a goal and £426,000 a game, and 55 of those outings were as a substitute.

One of those goals is now part of Chelsea history, however. It was the dramatic, injury-time winner in the Champions League semi-final victory over Barcelona at the Camp Nou in 2012.

Chelsea's slender 1–0 triumph from the first leg was quickly wiped out as Barca cruised into a 2–0 lead. Amazingly, though, ten-man Chelsea fought back brilliantly to knock out Pep Guardiola's great team. It was a delicious chip over Barcelona goalkeeper Victor Valdés by Chelsea midfielder Ramires that had made it 2–1 on the night but crucially 2–2 on aggregate.

Nevertheless Torres must not be denied due recognition for his most memorable moment for Chelsea, which came so famously on that 24 April night in Spain. It was injury time and Barcelona had thrown everyone forward in a bid to rescue themselves. Suddenly Torres broke from deep to race free on to a long clearance from inside the Chelsea penalty area. He had only Valdés to beat but yards to run and plenty of time to think of the consequences, good or bad. A watching world held its collective breath and wondered, but Torres, whose many, many misses had defined his career in Chelsea blue, suddenly rediscovered his ice-cool nerve and glorious finishing touch. The Spaniard masterfully took the ball around the diving keeper and then nonchalantly stroked the ball into the back of the net to complete the Blues' road to Munich.

It was a flashback to the 'goalden' days of the golden-haired forward. A classic Torres goal. TV pundit and former England international Gary Neville screamed, 'Eighteen months forgotten in two seconds!' as if the score wiped out everything that had gone before. It did nothing of the sort. One glorious goal couldn't atone for all the profligacy that had gone before or was to follow afterwards. Neither could Fernando's impressive haul of winners' medals at Chelsea, where he won the Champions League, Europa League and FA Cup. Ultimately the most telling stat of all was the maths, not the mementos. Chelsea had paid out £82 million, and recouped just £4 million to finish a staggering £78 million down on the deal. Now that's what you call a disgrace.

26

STRIKE THREAT

Fernando Torres was not the only player José Mourinho wanted out as he returned to Chelsea in the summer of 2013. Although he'd announced himself as the 'Happy One' in his first press conference back at the Bridge, he was actually far from happy with the players he had inherited. Mourinho didn't think the squad was anywhere near good enough. Chelsea may have just won the Europa League and finished third in the Premier League, but Mourinho's ambitions for the club were much bigger than that. He wanted the Champions League and the league title and was convinced Chelsea did not have the players to match his ambitions. His first move was to ring-fence the ones that did: John Terry and Frank Lampard.

Both had endured a torrid time under departing interim Chelsea boss Rafa Benítez, who seemed determined on dismantling the 'old guard' at the Bridge. Chelsea fans feared the legendary pair were both on their way out of the club, but Mourinho insisted he wanted both to stay; and they did. A soon-to-be out-of-contract Lampard promptly signed a new one-year deal in May as Mourinho began to assert his influence, albeit from abroad. Terry also felt the love, receiving a pep talk from Mourinho from Madrid. Chelsea's captain, leader and legend later revealed details of the phone call, saying, 'When he came back this time, I got that little phone call saying, "I need you to hit the ground running. People have written you off." He knows what buttons to press. He knows what makes me tick.'

Mourinho also had faith in his former Chelsea champions' goalkeeper Petr Cech and defender Ashley Cole and was happy for loyal midfielder Michael Essien to return to London from his loan spell with him at Madrid. José was prepared to give £7 million frontman Demba Ba the benefit of the doubt, deciding he was 'okay' to keep as a second- or third-choice striker. The Senegal international's place in the pecking order was set to be decided by the promise of Romelu Lukaku in pre-season. Mourinho was a fan of Lukaku from afar, encouraged by some rave reviews from West Bromwich Albion boss and friend Steve Clarke. Clarke had been José's right-hand man during his first spell at Chelsea and he'd had the big Belgian on loan at the Hawthorns the previous season. Mourinho's opinion at the time was upbeat, enthusiastically expressing how he liked 'Lukaku very much' and how he had 'already told some Premier League managers "no way he goes on loan"'.

The incoming Chelsea coach wasn't convinced about many of the others, though – not even fans' favourites like Juan Mata, David Luiz, Oscar and even Eden Hazard. His gut feeling was that he needed a clear-out in order to make room, and raise funds, for at least three new star names who he knew could do the job he wanted.

The master plan was to strengthen each part of the team – in attack, midfield and defence. Mourinho had already decided on a 4-2-3-1 style of play for Chelsea and needed the 'new blood' to make it click. He wanted a team with playmakers in every section of his side: a footballing centre half capable of building play from the back; a deep-lying 'quarterback' to be the creative force linking defence and attack, and a striker who could be the cutting edge up front, making and scoring goals. Incredibly, he began working on his Chelsea recruitment while he was still in charge at Real Madrid. In fact two of his main targets were playing for him at the Bernabéu at the time. None other than midfielder Luka Modrić and defender Raphaël Varane.

Mourinho's first priority and first move, though, was for a top-quality striker. He knew it wouldn't be easy. He knew it would be expensive. The world's very best strikers are in big demand but short supply. They consequently command huge fees and pocket bumper pay packets. Now, in the summer of 2013, three of the biggest and best had revealed they had itchy feet. They were Borussia Dortmund's Robert Lewandowski, Atlético Madrid's Radamel Falcao and Napoli's Edinson Cavani. Mourinho was a fan of all three but the futures of two of the three were already as good as sealed. Lewandowski was swapping Dortmund for Bayern Munich straight after that summer's Champions League final, while Falcao was quitting Atlético for Monaco.

Which all meant that the man at the head of José's shopping list was Edinson Cavani. Why not? The prolific Uruguayan ace was arguably the pick of the three and he'd made it clear he was leaving Napoli after three goal-laden seasons, which had brought an astonishing 78 strikes in 97 Serie A starts and 7 outings from the bench. He was twenty-six years old, in his prime and seemingly destined to become one of the world's greatest forwards. All the big European clubs were on alert but José acted quickly, Chelsea making contact in mid-May in an effort to try to steal a march on rival clubs.

The problem was Cavani was in no rush. He knew he was a man in demand, with Mourinho's current club Real Madrid also in the hunt along with mega-money Manchester City, fuelled by the petro-dollars of Abu Dhabi's Sheikh Mansour, and Paris St Germain, who are bankrolled by the oil-rich Qataris. He could wait and take the best offer available. In any event, the early discussions made it clear very quickly that even Chelsea, and the riches of billionaire owner Roman Abramovich, would not be enough in this particular chase. The Russian was the poor relation here, significantly so, and as a result there was absolutely no desire at the Bridge for the club to become embroiled in a bidding war in such affluent company. By 24 May Chelsea were out of the race with Mourinho moaning at the time: 'Cavani ... we can't compete with the money.' Sure enough, the Uruguay striker signed for PSG in July for £55 million, a Ligue 1 record, and with wages to match.

José's mood was not improved when almost simultaneously a deal for Varane was dismissed out of hand by Real Madrid president Florentino Pérez. Mourinho has a reputation for repeatedly ignoring youth in favour of top-name stars but he, with the help of Madrid and France legend Zinedine Zidane, had signed Varane from Ligue 1 outfit Lens in 2011 when the centre half was only eighteen years of age. José then gave the exciting youngster his first-team debut soon afterwards and the teenager went on to establish himself at the club, challenging top stars Pepe and Sergio Ramos for a centre back berth at the Bernabéu. He already looked a class act. He was composed on the ball, strong and quick, good in the air and a fine tactical reader of the game with a mature attitude and approach belying his years.

Which is why he was one of only two Madrid stars Mourinho would contemplate taking with him to London. Significantly, neither of them were 'Galácticos', the term given to Real's array of expensive, world-famous superstars. No, Mourinho had stomached enough of their ego-driven demands, behaviour and attitude over the last three seasons. He'd grown weary of the likes of Cristiano Ronaldo, Ramos, Pepe and Iker Casillas. There was absolutely no meeting of minds with those great players but he was on the same wavelength as Varane and Modrić. They were both top-class players but also honest, hungry professionals who were happy to listen and eager to succeed. The sort of players José loves. So the outgoing Madrid boss tried to use all his charms and his 'special' relationship with Varane in a bid to persuade his young charge to follow him to England.

Unfortunately for Mou, as Mourinho often calls himself, his early and ongoing belief in Varane proved something of an own goal when it came to his bid to sign him for a second time. The six-year contract the French prospect had signed in 2011 still had four years to run, making it impossible even for mentor Mourinho to manufacture a way out, regardless of any amount of money slapped on the table. He might have given Varane his chance at Madrid but the youngster had responded so superbly that he was now viewed as a Real star for the future and considered far too good to let go. The other obstacle was that Madrid didn't need the money. It was therefore another bitter blow for Mourinho and his rebuilding ambitions.

There was seemingly better news in the hunt for a midfielder, though. José encouraged Chelsea to make a move for Modrić to fill his 'quarterback' position after receiving positive encouragement from club and player. Mourinho saw the ex-Tottenham man as the perfect foil to play just ahead of the back four alongside a more traditional, defensive midfielder. The Croatian star was a player who could press the ball, make challenges, cover ground and defend responsibly and determinedly. In addition Modrić was a player who, when in possession, had the ability and flair to turn defence into attack in devastating fashion. A player who could hold the ball, move the ball, dribble with the ball and create with the ball. Mourinho was far more confident with this one and believed he could get Modrić for around £30 million. That was the figure Madrid had paid Tottenham for the tenacious but creative midfielder in 2012 and José's inside knowledge of Madrid had encouraged him into thinking that Real would do a deal at around the same price. He was dismayed when they wouldn't and, yet again, a key transfer failed to materialize. Three signings that Mourinho was convinced would catapult Chelsea back among Europe's elite, all slipping frustratingly through his fingers. Of course, the total cost would have been over £100 million, but Mourinho was adamant the trio would have proved priceless to the Blues in the long run. He had excitedly imagined Varane striding out of defence with the ball, linking beautifully with Modrić just ahead and then on and up through the transitions towards Hazard, Mata and Oscar and finally the swashbuckling Cavani in attack. It would have been a side with a licence to thrill from back to front, his Chelsea dream team.

Unfortunately it all turned into a nightmare experience and those early May setbacks, which came before he'd even signed on again at Chelsea, went on to haunt him throughout the summer and on into his first campaign back with the Blues.

27

OVER TO ROO

Wayne Rooney now became Mourinho's sole focus. The Manchester United and England star had seemingly reached a crossroads in his career at Old Trafford. Sir Alex Ferguson had finally quit as United manager in 2013 and been replaced by David Moyes from Everton. Moyes and Rooney had 'previous'. They'd worked together for three years at Goodison, as a teenage Rooney took the football world by storm. It ended in acrimony and eventually in the High Court, Moyes suing his former player for libel after the publication of his book *Wayne Rooney: My Story So Far* in July 2006. In it Rooney had accused Moyes of leaking a private conversation to the press around the time of his £30 million transfer to Manchester United in 2004.

The unfounded allegation cost Rooney dear. He was forced to pay his former manager 'substantial' damages and foot the bill for his legal costs, which were estimated at £500,000. Rooney's lawyers also told the court the striker had 'sincerely apologized' for any distress and embarrassment caused by his comments.

Suddenly they were reunited at United. And matters became worse when Moyes went on to twist the knife by declaring that deadly Dutchman Robin van Persie was to be his first-choice striker for the coming 2013–14 season. Rooney's world was abruptly thrown into turmoil and Mourinho was ready to exploit the situation to the maximum to try to land the man he felt would end his striker woes.

José had been a long-time admirer of Rooney and three years earlier had expressed an interest in signing him for Real Madrid. That was in October 2010 when Rooney had angrily pulled out of contract talks with United, complaining that he had not received 'any of the assurances' he was seeking about 'the future squad'. Mourinho responded from Spain, saying, 'If Rooney wants to leave – give me a call.' No phone call was forthcoming, as Rooney quickly reconsidered his situation and signed a new five-year contract within days of his outburst.

This time around, Mourinho sensed it could be different and set about making sure it was. He knew Rooney had been unsettled at United even before the appointment of Moyes. Sir Alex Ferguson had revealed as much at the end of the previous season. After a 2–1 win over Swansea in mid-May, in which Rooney was conspicuous by his absence, the outgoing United boss had explained, 'I don't think Wayne was keen to play, simply because he has asked for a transfer. I think maybe he is a bit frustrated. He has been taken off once or twice in the past couple of weeks.' Rooney, who had two years of his contract still to run, later denied putting in a request, revealing, 'I went in to see him [Ferguson] and just said, "If you're not going to play me it might be better if I moved on," then all of a sudden it's all over the press I put in a transfer request, which I never did.' It was clear that Rooney was unhappy and unsettled, though, and that's all Mourinho needed to know. His subsequent pursuit of the then twenty-seven-year-old throughout the summer of 2013 was relentless.

As early as June, Mourinho had said, 'I like him, he is at a fantastic age. He has maturity and big experience.' On 7 July he was turning up the heat, hinting Rooney's unhappiness at United could affect England. 'If Wayne is a second choice for Manchester United, the national team will be affected.' Just a few days later he was back at it, adding, 'I can't speak about players from other teams but you know me, I have always said what I think and I like the player very much.'

When Chelsea arrived in Thailand on 12 July to begin their pre-season tour, the drama was about to go into overdrive. I was on the tour and staying in the team hotel, the Shangri-La on the banks of the Chao Phraya river in Bangkok. José was preparing for his first game back as Chelsea boss, against the Singha All Stars in the busy, bustling city on 17 July, but he and Chelsea chief executive Ron Gourlay were far more concerned with plotting the capture of Rooney. Canny Scot Gourlay was 'Mr Poker Face', staying tight-lipped, often hiding his eyes behind his designer sunglasses and giving nothing away when I pushed him on the subject.

Mourinho was not so guarded and his bubbly demeanour seemed to indicate he was in a very confident mood. So confident that he marked that first game back – a 1–0 win courtesy of a Romelu Lukaku penalty – by making a £20 million bid for Rooney. I knew all about it and the next day enjoyed a back-page exclusive revealing the '£20m Roo Bid' and a two-page inside spread, with Mourinho saying how 'Roo will be my Special One' and would not play second fiddle to anyone.

Now it was finally all out in the open it allowed Mourinho to send not-so-subtle messages to Rooney and United via me and the rest of the media. Mourinho declared, 'We want the player, we are interested in the player, we made the bid. This situation is clear now because nothing is a secret any more. United knows we want the player and he has to know we made a bid for him. We are happy with our behaviour. It was clean. Now they accept or they don't.' Asked if Chelsea had bid for anyone else, the Special One replied, 'No. And we won't.' Then, put on the spot over whether it was Rooney or bust, he confessed it was. Mourinho then took a vow of silence, saying, 'Now we've nothing more to say. You have to respect United. So from now on, I won't say one more word about Wayne Rooney because you all know we want him.'

United flatly rejected Chelsea's opening offer but Mourinho was not giving up. His response was to speak about how important it was to be 'happy' in your workplace; how players with international ambitions needed to be first choices at their clubs, and how the coming season was a vital one with the World Cup finals in Brazil taking place the following summer. True to his word, he hadn't mentioned Rooney's name once. But there was absolutely no mistaking who his comments were aimed at.

Mourinho mused, 'The most important thing in football, for players and managers, is the passion, happiness and feeling we have for the club. If you can execute your mission, not just because you're paid for it or because it's your work but because you can do it with happiness and passion, that's the most important thing. For me, in the second part of my career, after fifty [years of age] the most important thing is the deep feeling that I'm at a really special football club. Chelsea became a special club for me and can be a special club for anybody else.' Then came a quick change of tack as he said, 'Players who want to go to their national team and play for their country, normally they must be first-choice players for their clubs and be playing regularly. That's the big motivation if you are thinking about playing at the World Cup. If they want to go to the World Cup and they're second choice at their club, then they're in trouble. I think it's a crucial year for them. I know many national team coaches are worried because they want players to play regularly for their clubs.' Point made and that's where Mourinho left it, leaving United to sweat and Rooney to stew.

Chelsea had moved on to Malaysia for a match in Kuala Lumpur when they made their next move, edging the bid up to £24 million on 20 July, with United once again reacting by insisting Rooney was 'not for sale'. A week later Mourinho was still trying to work his magic and gave out big hints that Roo was on his way. 'The club is in a very good balance with salaries, income, outcome. So not to break the balance in our numbers and to still invest in a player that costs £20 million, £25 million, £30 million; the club is ready for that. Do we need to sell first? No, no, no, we don't need to sell.' Again Mourinho didn't mention Rooney by name but he had repeatedly made it clear he only had the one transfer target that summer and that was Rooney. So when asked if Chelsea could afford to splash £50 million on a forward, he replied cryptically, 'The striker I want doesn't cost £50 million, doesn't cost £40 million.' Quizzed over whether he would still be ready to do business as late as transfer deadline day, he added, 'That's why it is open. I don't think any manager likes it, but it's open.' Mourinho defiantly declared he was prepared to play a long-ball game to get his man, even if it went all the way to the wire. Knowing José well, I'm convinced he wouldn't have done so without some sort of encouragement from the other side, from Rooney or his agent Paul Stretford.

Mourinho was certainly ultra-confident of success by the time Chelsea arrived in the USA for the second leg of their pre-season preparations at the end of July. It was clear that the Blues were now ready to go to £30 million to sign Rooney, the magic figure they believed would seal the deal. Spirits were high. I remember sitting in the lounge of the Mandarin Oriental Hotel in Washington DC having dinner with my son Joshua one evening when José sauntered over for a chat. Josh, who's a huge Chelsea fan, was sitting in an armchair with his back to José as the Blues boss approached. The next thing my twelve-year-old lad realized was that the Chelsea manager was pushing him along to squeeze into the chair with him. José's opening line was a corker. 'What do you think of us trying to sign the Fat Boy?'

Josh was caught out for a second, a bit confused by Mourinho's sudden appearance, as well as with sharing the same chair with one of his heroes, so he didn't cotton on to the 'Fat Boy' joke at first. I started laughing and told him, 'He means Rooney – the Fat Boy is Rooney.' The penny dropped and all three of us were chuckling now, with Josh enthusiastically encouraging José that Rooney would indeed be a brilliant signing for Chelsea. For all his joking, José was a huge fan of the United striker and desperately wanted to sign him up.

On 4 August the deal seemed imminent. I flew into New York from Washington DC ready for the match with AC Milan that night. On the long and expensive cab ride from JFK airport to the MetLife Stadium in New Jersey, I called Rooney's agent Paul Stretford. I'd known him for years and we had a decent relationship. We had a long transatlantic chat about the Rooney situation and he encouraged me to believe that his man would be leaving Manchester United. It seemed to me to be the final confirmation. It wasn't. In fact, it was far from it. It turned out there was still plenty more mileage left in Mourinho's pursuit of the United star.

Chelsea's four-match trip to the States was over and done with by 8 August and there was still no breakthrough. There was now a Mexican stand-off. The Blues were waiting for Rooney to hand in an official transfer request, something he seemed reluctant to do. That reticence from Rooney made the Blues edgy and uncertain for the first time. What was the problem if the player really wanted to come? Memories flashed back to 2010 when Rooney had also threatened to leave United and then happily signed a new lucrative, long-term deal. Rooney, meanwhile, seemed to be waiting for Chelsea to table their £30 million bid in the belief United would accept it, making any transfer request irrelevant. He probably stood to lose a sizeable signing on fee or loyalty bonus if he'd gone down the official route, although it's pretty safe to assume Chelsea would have covered any potential 'loss' he incurred in demanding a move.

The saga continued to drag on and on, even tumbling into the new season. Eventually all eyes were on the Monday-night clash between United and Chelsea at Old Trafford on 26 August. Would Rooney play or would he be left out altogether? He played in the red of United and received a rapturous welcome from the home fans in a clear show of support for their hero on the occasion of Moyes's first home match as United boss. Rooney responded with a superb performance against Mourinho's men, the main feature of an otherwise underwhelming match, which ended goalless. An intriguing sub-plot was that Mourinho had played without a recognized striker. Torres and Lukaku were substitutes for the match, a clear indication that neither was trusted by the Chelsea boss. Instead he played newcomer André Schürrle as a phantom number 9. It didn't work but aptly demonstrated why he was so desperate to sign United's England star to solve his centre-forward crisis.

Sure enough, after the match Mourinho played his final card, saying, 'One way or another, he has to say "I want to leave" or "I want to stay". The person that started the story has to finish the story. For the good of everyone, it is time to finish the story.' Rooney never did say 'I want to leave' that summer and the deal duly collapsed. Mourinho was left in the lurch. He'd put all his eggs in one basket and had been left shell-shocked. Worse, he only had until transfer deadline day on Monday 2 September to make amends. On 28 August Chelsea paid £30 million, the amount they'd put aside for Rooney, to beat Tottenham to the signature of Brazilian midfielder Willian. He joined along with veteran striker Samuel Eto'o from Russian side Anzhi Makhachkala, with the Cameroon forward joining up again with José after their successful time together with Inter in Italy. Finally, on transfer deadline day Lukaku was loaned out to Everton for the season. The Belgian had looked good on tour against the assorted All Stars of the Far East but was very ordinary against the likes of Inter, AC Milan and Real Madrid in the USA. Mourinho was not impressed.

All his efforts to capture his top targets had ended in failure. His dreams of Cavani, Modrić and Varane had all evaporated early on, then he was embarrassingly strung along during the epic Rooney saga. No new ball-playing centre back, no 'quarterback' midfielder and no star striker to make the difference. Torres, Ba and Eto'o. José was underwhelmed. The Happy One was not so happy now, but he was still expected to work his magic.

Arguably that was the one redeeming factor for Chelsea: the best summer signing any Chelsea fan could surely have wished for was to have Mourinho back in charge. What could possibly go wrong?

28
ON THE DECK

I was heading for the Executive Club Lounge at the salubrious Mandarin Oriental Hotel in Washington DC while still following Chelsea's pre-season tour when I stumbled on a most remarkable scene. As I turned a corner of the corridor I literally bumped into the club's assistant coach José Morais.

He was someone I knew reasonably well: I'd first met him when Mourinho was in Milan and got to know him even better during their time together at Madrid. His reaction to seeing me on this occasion, though, was one of surprise and then horror. I swerved away from the collision and was shocked as he then tried to grab me and block me from turning the corner. I thought he was messing about, although he certainly didn't look as if he was joking. I said light-heartedly, 'Hey, José – that's a yellow card, what are you doing?'

Then my attention was drawn to events further down the corridor. There, lying face down and stretched out on the floor was José Mourinho. Chelsea doctor Eva Carneiro was attending to him along with Chelsea's player liaison officer Gary Staker. Now I understood why Morais had tried to block my path and stop me turning the corner. He didn't want me to witness what was going on with his boss.

Once I'd seen the situation he had absolutely no chance of stopping me. I immediately strode down towards the prostrate Chelsea manager and called out, 'Wow, what a great story this is!' The look of shock on the faces of Carneiro and Staker was priceless. They were speechless but then I heard the weak, muffled hoarse voice of Mourinho saying, 'No, no story, no story. I'm fine.' He didn't look fine or sound fine at all but the doctor was with him and it was very obvious from the reaction of all around that I was a very unwelcome figure in proceedings. For all the drama, it was clearly not a life-and-death scenario and I certainly didn't want to get in the way as José was being treated, so I stepped around the sprawled Mourinho and headed on towards the Exec Lounge and left them to it.

As I sat in the lounge sipping my afternoon gin and tonic and tucking into the complimentary snacks and goodies, I inevitably analysed what I'd just seen and what to do next. As a friend I was concerned about what I'd witnessed; as a journalist I was on red alert given what I'd seen. Either way, I was anxious for an update. Clearly Mourinho collapsing in the corridor of the team hotel while on Chelsea's pre-season tour was not a sports story for the back pages of the newspaper; no, it was a news story for the front pages, maybe even the front page itself. After all, he'd only just returned as Chelsea boss and here he was flat out on the deck, groggy and weak. How serious was this? What were the long-term implications for him and his job? There was a lot to consider here. As with the Ashley Cole 'tapping up' scandal of 2005, I knew some stories are too big to ignore, no matter how close you are to the people involved.

The good news was that I didn't need to decide immediately. The time difference between DC and London meant that the day's paper was already printed and published so it was a story for tomorrow, depending on what I found out and what I ultimately decided. If it was a serious health problem it would be a story that was impossible to ignore. If it wasn't so serious it might be more advantageous not to write the story; keep it as a 'what goes on tour, stays on tour' incident that would be very much appreciated by Mourinho, by his staff and by Chelsea.

You see, as a journalist there is a balancing act between writing everything you see and know and trying to forge a long and productive relationship with a manager like Mourinho and a club like Chelsea. Sometimes being discreet with what you know can pay massive dividends down the line. You become a trusted individual within the group, within the club, and people become far more honest and open with you. So much so that when they want something pushed out into the press and media, you are the first point of call. I had a close relationship with Mourinho already and I didn't want to damage that unnecessarily or risk the flow of information from the man himself. However, just as with the Ashley Cole saga, if the story was big enough and important enough there was no way I would or could turn a blind eye. So what to do? Have another gin and tonic and sleep on it was the obvious call.

Except that matters quickly accelerated long before bedtime. As I slurped G&T number two, I was approached by Chelsea's Head of Communications Steve Atkins. He came straight to the point. He knew what I'd seen but didn't want me to write anything. He said José didn't want me to write anything either. He said Mourinho was fine, it was nothing serious and hoped that could be the end of it.

Well it might have been, except I've never liked being told what to do and what not to do. I like to make my own mind up, not be cajoled or bullied into a decision by anyone else. In fairness, Atkins was only doing his job, a damage-limitation exercise to keep the lid on José's collapse. So I feigned mock indignation. 'How long has José known me? How long have you known me? Do you think I'd write a story like that without checking the facts with José and with you? Of course I wouldn't.' Then I told him, 'As it stands, I'm not writing anything. The paper has gone for the day so there's nothing to worry about.' But I added, 'I'll speak to José about it.'

I didn't need to hunt Mourinho down. He found me. He came across smiling but looking a little bit sheepish and embarrassed. I can't remember the exact words but the gist of his explanation was this. What you saw was nothing serious. I went all dizzy and fell to the floor as I was walking to my room but everything is okay. What's happened is a mix-up. I have been taking some pills for a bad back. Then on tour I've started losing my voice because I have been doing so much shouting and organizing in training. I saw the doctor and was given some drugs to treat my throat. Unfortunately the pills for my back and the drugs for my throat have reacted to each other and made me disoriented. It's all been sorted out now and I'm fine.

Great, mystery solved, leaving me with an easy decision, which was simply to ignore the incident as if it had never happened. Yes, it could still have made a good, one-off news story. No doubt about it. The paper would have run it big. However, my focus is always on the long-ball game with manager and club. A one-off hit is no compensation if the characters concerned make sure it is your last hit; if they decide you can never be trusted again, you will never get their help and assistance again. That's the greatest own goal a reporter can score. So I was happy to let this particular story slide by in the belief that I would be rewarded, maybe more than once or twice, further down the line.

And so it proved. When I asked Atkins if I could do an exclusive video interview with Frank Lampard about the return of Mourinho and the new season ahead, he readily agreed. Lamps was brilliant: twenty minutes on camera to create a video for the website, which also made a big spread in the newspaper. Top man, Steve, thanks. Then, when I asked Atkins if I could do the same with Mourinho, he readily agreed again, albeit asking me to wait until the end of the tour as José had already committed to a number of TV interviews with broadcasters in the US and

UK. Steve's point was that he was trying to keep everyone in the media happy but I would get my chance in the end.

So I bided my time, waited my turn and, sure enough, right at the end of the tour and with the new season just days away, I got my own exclusive face-to-face with Mourinho. It was superb. Half an hour of vintage José talking in depth about fame, fortune, family and football. It was so long, and so good, that we cut it into three parts and used it over the course of a week on the website and in the newspaper. The long-ball game had paid off for all of us – Steve was as good as his word and had managed a difficult scenario superbly and José delivered in spades, ensuring the focus was on matters other than his health, and I got a belter of an interview that had my boss back home singing my praises for weeks afterwards.

I'm not sure I ever told Head of Sport Mike Dunn about the José-collapsing-in-the-corridor episode but I reckon he'd agree I made the right decision. I certainly know I did.

29
ONE OUT OF FIVE

Mourinho had big decisions of his own to make in the summer of 2013. He wasn't just focusing on trying to bring in new stars to reinvigorate Chelsea; he was also trying to galvanize his current squad, and so the mind games began.

In June he delivered a damning verdict on the club's league form over the last two seasons, saying it had not been good enough and insisting the players would have to improve. That was him laying down his marker for what he expected in the season ahead: a strong league campaign as well as successful runs in Europe and the domestic cups.

In July I had joined him in Thailand where he'd kicked off pre-season training in preparation for his first game back in charge, against the Singha All Stars in Bangkok. He seized the moment to eulogize his old guard, declaring that veterans Frank Lampard, John Terry and Ashley Cole had set the pace and the standard in training to leave the young starlets in the squad gasping. Mourinho gushed, 'The good thing with my previous players is that what I see makes me very happy. They know me. They know that I'm not going to make their lives easy, that I'm going to give them absolutely nothing and, because they know me, from the first day they never questioned that situation and worked hard. I honestly don't see them any different to before and when I see Terry, Cole, Lampard, the way they are working at thirty-two, thirty-two and thirty-five years old, it's easy for me to demand the same from the other guys. I can say, "Look at them. They don't miss one minute; they are training like animals so you, who are eighteen, nineteen, twenty-one, don't tell me you can't do it.'" Clearly José was throwing down the gauntlet to his younger players to raise their game and match the intensity, enthusiasm and dedication of the senior pros.

Not that he didn't tweak the tails of those senior pros, too. For the Chelsea manager evidently didn't see any contradiction at all when, a few days later, he warned the very same 'old guard' not to expect any preferential treatment from him on the basis that they'd played for him before and won titles with him before. Mourinho insisted those players he'd announced were his 'untouchables' during his first reign at the Bridge were not 'untouchables' any more. That meant Lampard, Terry, Cole and goalkeeper Petr Cech. It was classic Mourinho, focusing the minds of all his players, be they young or old, on what was expected of them and what was in store for them in the new season ahead. He was challenging them all to compete for the right to play and, when they were selected, to deliver.

José was also specific in what he expected from certain players, including Juan Mata, David Luiz and Eden Hazard.

Mata had been Chelsea's top scorer in the previous season, with a host of assists, too. There were doubts, though, as to whether he was a Mourinho type of player, someone who was just as happy to track back and work hard as he was to go forward and attack. So, remarkably, when we discussed Mata, it was partly on the basis of whether he had a future at the club. Mourinho was diplomatic and replied, 'Juan Mata won both the fans' and his colleagues' player of the year, so that means a lot. They all love the work he did for the team. Of course he fits into my plans. I know him quite well. I have my idea about where and how he produces better but we are here to try and keep him performing and to try and help him to perform better in the situations where he finds it a bit more difficult. I like wingers coming in on the inside for the pass or the shot and Juan is the only player we have to do that on the right side but I also think that he's very comfortable playing as a number ten.' It made me smile. It was the classic veneered-praise approach: give them some praise first, then tell them they aren't quite right, then give them some more praise to finish off.

The inconsistent form of Brazilian centre back David Luiz was another matter for open discussion in those early days. Luiz was full of talent and capable of displaying great skill but he always seemed to be equally capable of at least one major mistake in every match. Mourinho was already up to speed on that, explaining, 'I like central defenders to be able to play. It is a question of making the right decision. You're free to dribble from the back when you have the right conditions. You have to measure the risk. If you see players supporting you, then build short. If you see that somebody gives you the ball and you have no point of support, then it is the long ball. It is about reading the game. I can't read it for them. I can only do that for them before and after the game. So they have to make decisions on the pitch. For David Luiz, that is the important thing, to make the right decision. When a player is different and has more potential than others, he has to use his talent in a good way.'

However, Mourinho declared he was prepared to grant exciting young midfielder Eden Hazard a licence to thrill at the club. 'I think the kid has a lot of talent but he has to make the next movement. Football is about numbers and he has to transform his great talent into great numbers. These are things like how many goals, how many assists, how many winning goals, how many goals in big matches? I'm ready to help him, I'm ready to work with him. He must be ready, too. He has to listen. I always say to creative players, "If you have more than the others, you have to do more than the others. If you have this ability, you have to use this ability." If you do that to score goals, or to create goals, then do it. If you lose the ball, it is no problem, because you had a good objective in mind but when you do this for fun, or lose the ball and then don't defend and the team concede a goal, that's a problem. Because these players can make the difference, I never tell them "you cannot do this, you cannot do that". You can do anything because you have more talent than the others, so go for it but go to score, go to produce, not for fun, to humiliate the opponent, or put the ball through their legs. With me, he will always feel these objectives. He can get the ball and try to dribble past one or two players and go in the direction of the area. With me he will have this freedom.'

The approach here was to say, yes you are good but you are capable of much more and now I want to see it. I don't want a show pony, a circus act doing tricks for the sake of it. I want someone who uses their skill to score goals and to make goals, to make the difference for the team and not just play for their own fun and enjoyment.

Mourinho was also excited by another of Chelsea's flying young attackers, Kevin De Bruyne, who had been in sparkling form on the pre-season tour to the Far East, until being stretchered off after scoring a great volleyed goal against a Malaysian XI. It was initially anticipated that De Bruyne would be sent out on loan to gain more experience and continue his development but Mourinho changed all of that, insisting he wanted him to stay put as part of his first-team squad.

He said, 'The kid is a fantastic player and showing match after match, and in training, that he's going to be a key man on the pitch.' However, while Mourinho built up his expectations of Hazard and De Bruyne, he was careful not to add to the hype over Chelsea's raw young striker Romelu Lukaku. José explained, 'People compare him to Didier Drogba but we have to respect Didier, because he is unique in Chelsea's history, and we have to respect Lukaku. The best way to do that is not compare him to a legend in Chelsea's history. Leave Didier where he is, at the top of Chelsea's history, and leave Lukaku to work hard. The kid is good.'

They were all 'good' players, but the harsh fact of life under Mourinho was that just one year later only Hazard remained at Chelsea; Mata and De Bruyne were sold off within six months, Lukaku was loaned to Everton for that 2013–14 season and signed for them at the end of the campaign, while Luiz joined Paris St Germain in the summer of 2014. Four out of the famous five had failed to live up to José's demands and expectations and were gone. They were controversial decisions which were queried by some of the fans back then and subsequently, but José would argue they were all more than justified in the following 2014–15 season when Chelsea returned to their brilliant best at last and Hazard was imperious, winning the PFA's Player of the Year award and the Football Writers' Footballer of the Year award.

30
THE LITTLE HORSE

A rare trophy-less season was the reason for such a dramatic cull of such young talent. Chelsea had gone close but not close enough for José. Early exits in the two domestic cups were one thing; losing the league from a winning position and blowing the chance of another Champions League final were far more serious lapses.

His new team had crumbled when the pressure was on. It was most unlike a Mourinho team and he knew changes had to be made. The truth is that he was already plotting for a summer revamp as early as February and top of his list was still a top-quality striker, plus a new left back. The lack of a goal-scoring forward was the main problem. Although Chelsea were the third-highest scorers that season, with 71 goals netted, they lagged far behind Manchester City's 102 and Liverpool's 101. Missing out on Cavani and Rooney had come home to roost. Not even Eden Hazard's 14 league goals and 7 assists from midfield could make up for the lack of such a player.

It had all looked so promising at the halfway stage. After nineteen games Chelsea were third in the table, a point behind Manchester City and two behind leaders Arsenal. The Blues then made their push for the top. On Monday 3 February a Mourinho masterclass in tactics and counter-attack saw Chelsea become the first side to win at City that season, completing the double over Manuel Pellegrini's side in the process, and suddenly everyone was tipping them for the title again. Everyone except José.

When he was asked after the game if it was now a three-horse race for the finish line, he quipped, 'Two horses and a little horse. A little horse that still needs milk and to learn how to jump. A horse that next season can race.' (How prophetic those words would prove to be, given what would happen over the next fifteen months.) Mourinho then went on to highlight how his side had once again raised their game for the big occasion against a big team, adding, 'We love the big games. Obviously when you love it maybe you feel extra motivated for that and I keep saying, the best thing for the evolution of this team is not to play Europa League, not to be fifteen to twenty points behind the leader but with pressure to be there, to be close to the leaders.' The very next week, on 8 February, Chelsea were the leaders thanks to a thumping 3–0 home win over Newcastle, which put them a point clear of Arsenal at the top of the table.

The problem was that this Mourinho team had an Achilles' heel. Yes, they were good at motivating themselves for the big matches but they had a nasty and costly habit of slipping up against the also-rans and strugglers. After going top they promptly drew at West Bromwich Albion and in March they lost at lowly Aston Villa, where midfielder Ramires and Mourinho were sent off late on. Another damaging defeat followed at Crystal Palace. It was baffling. This was the same side who had beaten Tottenham 4–0, title rivals Arsenal 6–0 and Stoke 3–0 at around the same time. Then on Saturday 19 April the unthinkable happened: Mourinho lost at home in the league for the first time ever as Chelsea manager. A run of seventy-seven games unbeaten at Stamford Bridge during two spells at the club had finally ended. It was a major upset in every conceivable way.

A controversial late penalty, converted by ex-Chelsea striker Fabio Borini, saw Sunderland win 2–1 and sparked angry scenes in front of the Chelsea bench. Mourinho's assistant Rui Faria had to be restrained by his manager and goalkeeping coach Christophe Lollichon as he tried to confront referee Mike Dean over the disputed penalty. The same Dean who had earlier denied Chelsea two spot-kicks. Faria was sent to the stands and Stamford Bridge was sent into despair.

Mourinho sarcastically congratulated the referee after the game, saying, 'Mike Dean's performance was unbelievable and when referees have unbelievable performances it's fair to congratulate them.' He also took a swipe at Mike Riley, the man in charge of all match officials, adding, 'And congratulations also to Mike Riley, the referees' boss. What they are doing through the whole season is fantastic, especially in the last couple of months, and in teams involved in the title race. Absolutely fantastic. I also congratulate Mr Riley.'

Those mocking congratulations quickly led to an FA charge of improper conduct, with the game's governing body alleging that Mourinho's comments 'call into question the integrity of the referee and/or the integrity of Mr Mike Riley, General Manager of the Professional Game Match Officials Limited, and/or the comments bring the game into disrepute.' The FA also charged Faria with two counts of misconduct while Chelsea midfielder Ramires was also in the dock. He was charged with violent conduct after TV footage highlighted a clash with Sunderland's Sebastian Larsson in an incident that went unnoticed by referee Dean.

Severe ramifications, then, for Mourinho and his team on and off the field in the wake of that shock defeat by Sunderland. In terms of the league, it meant that Chelsea were now two points behind Liverpool with just three games left and their rivals had a crucial game in hand. Meanwhile, Manchester City were lurking only four points behind but with two games in hand on the Blues. Being champions again was suddenly looking a forlorn hope.

However, there was no time for prolonged recriminations, reproach or self-pity. Chelsea had to pick themselves up and go again. For while the league may have looked lost, the Champions League crown was still up for grabs. A successful campaign in the group stages had been followed with wins over Galatasaray in the first knockout round and then Paris St Germain (thanks to an away goal) in the quarter-finals. That all meant that Chelsea were to face Atlético Madrid in the semi-finals just three days after this damaging Sunderland defeat.

31

STUMBLING AT THE FINAL HURDLE

The tie with Atlético had been controversial from the moment the draw was made on Friday 11 April. The issue was that Chelsea had loaned goalkeeper Thibaut Courtois to the Spanish side and clearly did not expect him to play in such an important match against his parent club. It was revealed the Blues had even inserted a clause into the loan agreement to protect themselves against such a situation. It meant that Atlético would have to pay a fee of around £4.5 million if they wished to field Courtois in the two-legged semi-final.

It looked to have worked when the Spaniards complained they could not afford to play him because of the fee involved. However, immediately after the draw had paired the two teams together, UEFA intervened and insisted that the twenty-one-year-old Belgian must be allowed to take part. A strongly worded statement read:

The integrity of sporting competition is a fundamental principle for UEFA. Both the Champions League and the disciplinary regulations contain clear provisions which strictly forbid any club to exert, or attempt to exert, any influence whatsoever over the players that another club may (or may not) field in a match. It follows that any provision in a private contract between clubs which might function in such a way as to influence who a club fields in a match is null, void and unenforceable so far as UEFA is concerned. Furthermore, any attempt to enforce such a provision would be a clear violation of both the Champions League and the disciplinary regulations and would therefore be sanctioned accordingly.

I got straight in touch with José and asked him for his response to the draw and to whether Courtois should play. It was just before midday and his first reaction was calm and muted. He replied, 'Atlético is a very strong team,' and regarding Courtois there was a simple, 'UEFA wants him to play.'

It wasn't the only setback that he and his Blues had suffered as they closed in on European glory. On the day before the Champions League draw, Mourinho had been fined £8,000 by the FA after his sending off towards the end of the defeat at Aston Villa. Chelsea had also been thwarted in their efforts to move their upcoming Premier League match at high-flying Liverpool, which was a potential title decider. The Kop clash was scheduled as the big television game on the Sunday afternoon, right between the Atlético games. Chelsea had appealed to both the league and the Merseysiders to move the game to the Friday evening or the Saturday to give them extra time to prepare for the all-important second leg. Their appeals fell on deaf ears in London and Liverpool.

That whole frustrating scenario of recent events must have impacted on Mourinho as he cogitated on it all throughout that day, for José's humour had darkened considerably by the evening; since our first exchange at lunchtime he had gone from frustrated to furious, and was spoiling for a fight. With UEFA, with the FA, with the Premier League and with Liverpool. He raged, 'Courtois to play is a joke but the biggest joke is [we] play Liverpool on the Sunday. It is a disgrace that we play Sunday when next game we play the second leg. The game of the season we play for Chelsea and also for England. It is a disgrace. They hide behind walls and f**k us. Who are they? Do they have a name and a face? It is amazing.'

Then he turned on his old enemies, the FA, and their latest punishment: 'I don't accept the decision. I don't pay. I fight the decision and I kill the guys there. They want to f**k me and they do. Old guys, don't have a clue about football. I told them there that they are a disgrace.' I talked him out of going 'public' with those exact sentiments, but he did agree to me reporting the story of his unhappiness with the FA and using his rant as the basis of a quote from a Chelsea source. At the end of the chat he seemed placated, and his final words were, 'Let's see if we get a miracle!'

As José suspected, no one budged and nothing changed, so Chelsea just had to get on with it. They also had to ignore the fact that there was precious little time to recover, regroup and refocus after the Sunderland defeat. The challenge now was to go to Spain just three days later and get a result – and they did.

A tense, goalless draw at the Vicente Calderon stadium was a welcome result and there was now renewed optimism that a third final in seven years was a real prospect. The downsides were injuries to goalkeeper Petr Cech and skipper John Terry. There were also bookings for Frank Lampard and John Obi Mikel, which meant they would miss the second leg at Stamford Bridge.

First, though, there was the challenge of that trip to Anfield to face the league leaders. It was another huge game. Liverpool looked destined finally to end their twenty-four-year title drought after a thrilling run of nine successive wins had put them five points clear of the chasing Chelsea.

Sure enough, it turned into an eventful trip. Mourinho had threatened to undermine the big clash by announcing he was considering putting out a weakened side on Merseyside to keep his top stars fresh for the return with Atlético. It was partly his idea of revenge on the Premier League over their refusal to move the match, but also a bit of plain common sense. The chances of making the final were better than the chances of winning the league. Mourinho mused about it all publicly, saying, 'Me? I would play the players that are not going to play next Wednesday [against Atlético Madrid], but I can't decide by myself. I'm just the manager. I have to listen to the club.' He then explained his reasoning: 'When the Premier League decide to put that Liverpool game on Sunday, when Liverpool refuse to play on a Saturday, if the club [Chelsea] wants to go with everything in the direction of the Champions League I am ready for that. We represent English football and we are the only English team that is in European competition. Spain has four and gave them all the conditions to try to have success. We have a big match on Wednesday that can give Chelsea another Champions League final; we ask, ask and asked again to play on the Saturday. I know what I would do, but I'm not the club. I have to speak with the club.'

The mind games had started and José secretly used me to keep them going with the Liverpool game imminent. On the Saturday afternoon he contacted me with some inside information for me to write an article for the next day's newspaper: a story for match day.

It was a really funny episode. Mourinho was acting like a spy on his own team and sending me back messages to reveal his team's secrets. First he informed me that he was sick and might not make the match: 'JM ill. Arrived at hotel Formby Hall at 5 p.m. and went direct to room. Looks like he is ill and didn't travel with team.' Then he revealed: 'Team arrived one hour late and David [Luiz], Ramires, Terry, Hazard, Eto'o were not seen. Schwarzer, Cahill, Azpilicueta, Torres were there also with some kids from U21s, someone was saying they were [Andreas]

Cristensen and [John] Swift.' Of course I wrote the story and it appeared the following morning, the day of the game.

As suggested, Mourinho fielded a depleted team. There was no Cech, no Terry, no Hazard, no Luiz, no Eto'o and no Ramires. What's more, Willian, Gary Cahill and Fernando Torres were named in reserve on the bench, clearly in the hope they could rest up before the return with Atlético. The biggest news was that young, rookie defender Tomas Kalas was playing at centre half with the unenviable task of dealing with Liverpool's prolific striker Luis Suárez. Finally young prospects Nathan Aké and Lewis Baker were named among the substitutes.

Chelsea won 2–0. They were the first team to triumph at Anfield in the league that year. First of all an horrendous slip from Liverpool captain Steven Gerrard on the stroke of half-time allowed Demba Ba to romp through to put Chelsea in front. Then in time added on at the end of the match the Londoners counter-attacked ruthlessly to make it 2–0. Willian broke from deep and released substitute Torres for a free run on goal. The ex-Kop star zeroed in on keeper Simon Mignolet before unselfishly slipping the ball back to Willian, who almost walked the ball into the empty net. It completed a Chelsea double over the Merseysiders. Far more importantly it was a grievous blow to their title hopes.

Mourinho loved it. As Willian's late goal nestled in the back of the Liverpool net, he marched down the touchline towards the Chelsea fans pumping his arms in the air, then patting his Chelsea badge and shouting.

Suddenly, there were only two points in it – maybe he could win the league again after all. Three games to go and it could still be a Champions League and Premier League double.

Except that three days later Atlético came to London and won 3–1 to send Mourinho and his men crashing back to earth again.

Chelsea took the lead after thirty-six minutes when Fernando Torres scored against his old club, the team he had supported since boyhood. The lead didn't last long, though, with Adrián López scrambling in an equalizer just before the interval. The match was decided on and around the hour. First Atlético Madrid goalkeeper Thibaut Courtois made an incredible save from John Terry, which was all the more unbelievable to Mourinho as Courtois was a Chelsea player. Just 180 seconds later a chap called Diego Costa put Atlético in complete control by converting a penalty, before Arda Turan added a third to seal an all-Madrid final in Lisbon. In doing so he denied Mourinho the chance to face his old club Real Madrid in a final staged in his home country.

Now it was the league or nothing, and four days after their Champions League exit a 0–0 draw at home to relegation-haunted Norwich meant it was nothing. André Schürrle hit a post, David Luiz hit the crossbar and Chelsea just couldn't score. Meanwhile Liverpool were tossing away a 3–0 lead at Crystal Palace as Tony Pulis continued his remarkable rescue act at Selhurst Park.

All of which allowed Manchester City to glide to the top at just the right time. City were duly crowned champions having spent just fifteen days at the top of the table all season. Chelsea had blown it and Mourinho knew it. He was determined it wouldn't happen again.

32
COSTA BRAVO

It was 11:13 on the morning after the night before when I first learned that Diego Costa had agreed to join Chelsea. It was 1 May 2014. The night before had seen the very same Diego Costa score at Stamford Bridge to help his current side Atlético Madrid knock out his future team Chelsea in the semi-finals of the Champions League. It was a bitter blow for the Blues and their boss, and this was José's way of trying to promote some positive news out of an extremely negative situation.

His early email began by addressing the negative: his ongoing disbelief that a Chelsea player, Thibaut Courtois, had played a key role in helping knock them out. Mourinho moaned, 'Chelsea goalkeeper make an impossible save from Terry header … [it should not be] possible in a top club!!!' Clearly he was still upset that the keeper's loan move to Atlético had somehow backfired on his side. Then came the big news: 'Diego Costa is a Chelsea player next season.' One short sentence to instantly transform the mood.

The deal was supposed to have stayed secret until after Costa had played in the Champions League final and Atlético's season was finally over but Mourinho couldn't wait. He wanted the news out early to lift the spirits after such an anticlimactic conclusion to Chelsea's campaign. I wasn't complaining and wrote a world-exclusive story headlined 'José Bags £32m Costa' to help Mourinho get his message of 'We're already looking to next season and we're going to be stronger, much stronger' out there.

Finally José's tortuous, year-long search for a top striker to lead the Londoners' attack was over. Radamel Falcao, Edinson Cavani, Robert Lewandowski, Wayne Rooney and Mario Mandžukić had all been targets too, but Costa was eventually the man who agreed to put pen to paper.

The capture of Costa and the return of Courtois convinced Mourinho he was now very close to creating a group that could go on and dominate English football for the next decade. It was the culmination of a year spent assessing the strengths and weaknesses of the squad he'd inherited and then ruthlessly pruning and improving it. The emphasis was on blending an exciting crop of youngsters with established, experienced stars, but above all on players who had the belief and bottle to fight for their place and then fight for trophies.

By the December of his first season José had formed a clear idea of which players had the drive, the desire and the determination to make the club contenders again. I recall how, when I congratulated him on a 3–1 home win over Southampton, his response took me completely by surprise. He was very candid. 'With this team it isn't easy. The best players are old and the young ones are Mickey Mouses.'

No wonder it was a decisive, if controversial, transfer window in January 2014. Chelsea's Player of the Year Juan Mata was sold to Manchester United for £37.1 million, Kevin De Bruyne left for Wolfsburg in an £18 million deal, while Florent Malouda went to Trabzonspor and Michael Essien joined AC Milan. In came Nemanja Matić from Benfica for £21 million, Mo Salah from Basel for £11 million and young French defender Kurt Zouma banked £12.5 million for St Étienne.

The sale of Mata to Chelsea's big rivals Manchester United was the most contentious deal but José just shrugged off the criticism. He told me, 'We are not old-fashioned. We sell to rivals if the money is top for us.' So it wasn't that he didn't rate Mata as a player; he did. It was that £37.1 million had just been too good an offer to turn down, especially when he had Willian, Hazard and Oscar who could play the same wide right or number 10 role as Mata.

As for De Bruyne, José was a fan of his talents if not his attitude and didn't want to sell; it was the young Belgian who demanded to get away. The twenty-two-year-old winger was unable to cope with his lack of game time even though it was his first season with the first team and with Mourinho. Chelsea reluctantly let him leave but insisted on a 'buy-back' clause in the deal with Wolfsburg, one Mourinho and Chelsea declined to activate when Manchester City moved in with a £55 million offer for the player just eighteen months later. Much has been made of De Bruyne's departure from Stamford Bridge since, but the fact is that the incoming Nemanja Matić made a far bigger and more immediate impact on Mourinho's new team, especially in the 2014–15 season.

Mourinho couldn't get everyone and everything he wanted in that January transfer window, but he was very encouraged. When we chatted in February, just after the window had closed, he felt that if he could add a top striker and left back in the summer then his Little Horse would be ready to gallop off to glory.

The striker was dominating his thoughts. 'We give up on Roo [Rooney] for sure. Falcao no chance. We will put our money on Diego [Costa], Cavani and Mandžukić. One will be ours for sure because we will go strong, strong.'

José then mapped out his ideal first team for the future. Petr Cech and Thibaut Courtois would battle it out for the number 1 shirt, then the line-up would be 'Ivanović, Cahill, Terry and a left back; Ramires and Matić; Willian, Oscar, Hazard and a top striker and we have a top team'. He wasn't finished. 'Plus Azpilicueta, Zouma, David [Luiz] and Cole; Mikel and Lampard;

Schürrle, van Ginkel and Salah; Torres and we will have also a very good squad! So now we put our money all in one striker!'

It was intriguing to see former 'untouchables' Lampard and Cole down as squad players, but no surprise to see the unpredictable Luiz in there with the disappointing new boys Schürrle and Salah. Azpilicueta was clearly viewed as an understudy for Ivanović at right back, not a long-term solution at left back. So who did he have in mind for that job? I asked about Luke Shaw of Southampton but he wasn't keen, replying, 'Luke too expensive for his quality. I think Manchester United.' He was going to keep on looking.

At the beginning of April 2014 Mourinho had completely run out of patience with all of his forwards, exasperated with their repeated poor performances in attack. He told me, 'I want Torres, Demba, Eto'o out for sure.' Yes, that's right, he wanted all three of his front men out of the door in the summer. By then he was closing in on Costa, but José was also keen to bring Lukaku back from Everton.

The Goodison club had already made overtures about buying the big Belgian, who would finish the 2013–14 season with 18 goals for the Merseysiders. Again Mourinho didn't want to sell. He wanted a clean sweep of his existing front line and for Lukaku to be back-up for Costa. Just for good measure he wanted ex-Chelsea hero Didier Drogba back to mentor the young Romelu to the top. It was all great in theory, but not everything went according to plan in the summer.

Chelsea's transfer dealing did kick off in spectacular style. Costa was already in the bag and then on 12 June came a huge surprise. The Blues announced the £30 million capture of Cesc Fàbregas from Barcelona. It was not a deal that Mourinho had originally planned, mainly because he didn't think it was remotely possible, but once the opportunity arose he seized the initiative. He personally went to meet the ex-Arsenal captain to persuade him to sign and the Spanish star readily agreed. It was a recruitment that added extra quality and experience to an already exciting Chelsea midfield and José was thrilled that he'd clinched another piece of the jigsaw: his long-awaited 'quarterback' playmaker.

The next day the Blues balanced the books by selling David Luiz to Paris St Germain for £40 million. It was another bumper payday for someone who was a squad player in the manager's eyes. What's more, the windfall would more than cover the cost of signing Fàbregas, with cash left over to help fund what Mourinho believed would be the final piece of the jigsaw: a left back.

There were lots of rumours about who that would be but I didn't find out for sure until Wednesday 9 July. I was in Brazil at the 2014 World Cup finals, at that point at the Arena de Sao Paolo for the semi-final meeting between Holland and Argentina. My email pinged and there was a message from Mourinho. It simply said: 'Filipe Luís done.' Another gift of a back-page lead for me with the deal 'officially' confirmed a week later, and that should have been that.

Eto'o was out of contract, Ba had joined Besiktas in Turkey and Drogba was on his way back. Everything was falling into place. Well, everything but Torres. Mourinho, as we saw earlier, tried and tried to get him out but there were no takers. The days and weeks ticked by. Something had to give and just a week before the season there was a dramatic development.

Everton tabled a club record £28 million bid for Lukaku and that concentrated minds at the Bridge, but not for long. It was quickly concluded that this was another offer that was just too good to refuse. Like Manchester United's bid for Juan Mata six months earlier, it was huge money for a player who would not be an automatic first choice and so it became another pragmatic decision by the manager and the club's board of directors. If only they'd waited, though, for Torres did eventually move, going on loan to AC Milan at the end of August. Suddenly Chelsea only had two strikers, which had them scrambling to bring in Loïc Rémy from Queens Park Rangers as their third forward before the transfer window closed. In an ideal world José would have preferred Lukaku but he was still supremely confident that he now had a top team backed up by a top squad that could go on to truly compete for the top prizes.

33

FRANK'S A LOT!

Frank Lampard's defection to Manchester City in the summer of 2014 infuriated the hierarchy at Chelsea and left Mourinho desperately disappointed. The Blues boss was in favour of keeping the club's record goalscorer, even though he would be turning thirty-five on 20 June. To José, age has never been the determining factor in any decisions. It's about the number of top performances, not the number of big birthdays. Remember that at Inter he'd won Serie A and the Champions League with a bunch of thirty-somethings and a thirty-seven-year-old captain, and 'Lamps' still had two years on Javier Zanetti.

The stumbling block was that Chelsea had recently introduced a policy concerning players who were aged over thirty. They'd decided that once they'd passed that magic number, all new contracts would then be for one year only. Now, in many ways, that's an eminently sensible idea aimed at protecting the club from entering into a new long-term deal with someone whose best days may well be behind them and who could quickly become surplus to requirements. The difficulty then is offloading an ageing player whose form has gone and is sitting on the bench or, worse, sitting up in the stands, but still pocketing a very handsome salary. Those sidelined former stars don't want to give up their big pay packets and other interested clubs don't want to match them. So the misfits either demand a big pay-off to leave or stay put and carry on banking their bumper pay cheques.

The problem at Stamford Bridge was that Chelsea tended also to reduce the terms for these one-year contracts dramatically, asking players, even living legends like Lampard, to take huge pay cuts into the bargain. Ultimately, that's why Lampard left in 2014. Chelsea offered him a poor deal; Manchester City offered him a very good one.

In terms of cash in the bank it was a no-brainer, but in terms of Lampard's legacy at Chelsea it was a different story. That could be jeopardized by jumping ship to a Premier League rival, especially as Lampard had always portrayed himself as a 'true blue' who loved the club and its supporters. So which was more important?

It was a dilemma Lampard had wrestled with for some time. The free-scoring midfield star had threatened to leave the previous year, or more accurately his long-time agent Steve Kutner had stated he'd be leaving in the summer of 2013, miffed that Chelsea were playing hardball over the future of one of their greatest-ever players. Lampard's magnificent five-year contract was about to run out and negotiations for a new deal had all but collapsed. It was not signing a one-year deal that was the problem; the focus for discussion was on wages and Frank's future role at the club. Sensibly, on that occasion, Chelsea and Lampard had pulled back from the brink of an exit to thrash out a compromise deal and Lampard bit the bullet to sign on again.

The difference in 2013 was that the circumstances had been strongly in his favour back then as the England midfielder had enjoyed another landmark season with the Blues. He'd captained Chelsea to glory in the 2–1 victory over Benfica in the Europa League final; he'd become the club's all-time top goalscorer with a brace at Aston Villa, taking him beyond Bobby Tambling's long-standing record of 202 strikes for the Stamford Bridge side; and he'd finished the season as the club's top scorer in the Premier League with 15 goals and 17 in total. He'd done all that while playing for an interim manager, Rafa Benítez, who barely spoke to him and didn't always play him, which made his achievements all the more impressive.

The departure of the reviled Benítez and the return of the regaled Mourinho, with whom Frank had won two titles, two Carling Cups, the FA Cup and the Charity Shield, was also key in helping prevent a premature departure. Not that José was guaranteeing anything. The returning manager was quick to make it plain that his 'untouchables' from his first spell at the club, the likes of Lampard, John Terry, Petr Cech and Ashley Cole, were no longer a protected species.

The truth was that Mourinho had concerns about the number of games he'd be able to squeeze out of his older heads. It wasn't a question of ability – they were still arguably the best players in the squad – it was more a question of durability: how many times he could go to the well with them. Mourinho told me at the time, 'He [Lampard] is now thirty-five and he can't play sixty matches like he did before, but the quality of the player is exactly the same. We just have to be clever with him but, for me, performance is all about how good you are, not about your birth certificate.' The same went for JT, Cole and, to a lesser extent, goalkeeper Cech. José's bottom line, though, was that he desperately wanted to keep his old guard together because of their experience, loyalty and leadership qualities.

Unfortunately the following season, the 2013–14 campaign, did not match Lampard's usual high standards. He started 20 of 38 Premier League games, scoring just six goals and managed only eight in all competitions. He was more involved in the Champions League, though, with Mourinho clearly managing his man and his fitness as the Blues progressed all the way to the semi-finals. Lampard's European know-how was exploited in matches that tended to be far more tactical and technical and far less frenetic and lung-busting than the Premier League. It was a different Lampard in a different role, who was still good, but a long way short of his brilliant best. Everyone knew it: him, the club and the fans. So the pressure was really on as fresh negotiations began about another one-year deal.

Mourinho still wanted him to stay for the very same reasons as before but now he certainly saw Lampard as a squad player rather than a key first-teamer. José wanted to give the exciting, emerging talents of young midfielders Eden Hazard and Oscar more scope to grow, develop and flourish. For them to do that, Lampard would have to take more and more of a back seat. Nevertheless, the manager was still shocked when he learned just how much of a pay cut Lampard was being asked to take if he wanted to remain at the club. This time it looked like Lampard would be leaving for sure. After all, his record and reputation meant there would be no shortage of interested clubs keen to take him, regardless of his age. There were reports of lucrative deals awaiting him in Turkey and China, but especially from Major League Soccer in America, with LA Galaxy and New York City said to be in the frame.

On 23 May 2014, to no one's real surprise, Lampard was included on a list of players Chelsea would be releasing that summer. The caveat was that the club said there would still be talks about a new deal with Lampard, with the player himself insisting he would listen to Chelsea's offer before considering a move away. However, in the world of top-flight football such uncertainty inevitably invites speculation and the rumours of an imminent departure hit fever pitch towards the end of the month.

I was at Wembley Stadium on 31 May to cover a world-title boxing bout: the rematch between Carl Froch and George Groves for the World Super-Middleweight crown. I bumped into a top contact there who knew Lampard and his agent

Kutner and had been told that it was definitely all over for Frank at Chelsea and he was off to New York City. As a Chelsea fan and as a Lampard fan I hoped it wasn't true, but this was a guy who was definitely 'in the know'.

I immediately got in touch with José, asking him if it was right. His response all but confirmed that, yes, this was the end. 'Don't know but I believe it can be true. Chelsea pay him very short, so he looks for more. Maybe yes [he will leave the club] but I don't know.' It didn't sound good and sure enough, on 2 June, Lampard announced he would be leaving the club. Then on 24 July there was a fanfare announcement that he had signed for New York City.

Or had he? Just a few days later, suspicions surfaced about the whole deal when Manchester City, whose Qatari owners had created the New York City Football Club, declared Lampard would be playing for them at the start of the new season 'on loan' from NYC until January. It wasn't just me who smelled a rat: the announcement sparked plenty of debate and discussion in the media and especially on social media. The suspicion was that this had been the plan all along.

So imagine the reaction when in December it emerged that Lampard was to now spend the whole season in Manchester rather than go to New York to play in the MLS. Suddenly there were accusations of deceit and double-dealing over the whole transfer. Sure enough, on 8 January the Premier League confirmed that Lampard was registered solely as a player for Manchester City. Their statement read: 'Frank Lampard is registered with Manchester City FC until the end of the 2014–15 season. The Premier League has sought and received assurances from Manchester City that there is no agreement in place between the club or City Football Group with New York City FC relating to the player.' Lampard had never signed for NYC at all, but had apparently simply agreed a non-binding commitment that he would do so. It was a shabby, shameful affair that sullied Lampard in the eyes of many Chelsea fans and especially the hierarchy at the club.

Chelsea's director Michael Emenalo was certainly quick to email his thoughts on the Premier League's revelations to Stamford Bridge chairman Bruce Buck, director Marina Granovskaia and manager Mourinho. Emenalo wrote sarcastically, 'Interesting take from a family member of ours, and a staunch Chelsea fan, of course! I think City just screwed up admitting Lamps was signed to a deal thru 12/31 – that would violate rule T.11, no? The way they should have done it I think, if they didn't initially want a contract thru June 30, is to do monthly contracts under T.11.2 and just keep extending it every month thru 12/31. As I read the statute I think that would have worked. I want points docked!!' No points were docked. In fact, there was no punishment at all for slippery City.

There was a 'punishment' for Lampard after the 'deal' with NYC was revealed. When he returned to Stamford Bridge for the first time in the light blue of Man City in January 2015, the club where he'd spent thirteen years ignored the occasion. Previously they'd made on-the-pitch presentations to returning stars like Didier Drogba and Michael Ballack. Later they'd do the same for ex-boss Claudio Ranieri, but a man who contributed far more to the club than Ballack, Ranieri and even Drogba was totally overlooked. The fans didn't ignore him. Some welcomed him 'home' with banners like 'Lampard is a legend' and 'Frank Lampard forever in our hearts. Thank you for everything.' Others were clearly incensed by his actions, with one irate supporter brandishing a placard that read: 'Lampard you are not a legend anymore. You are a traitor to Chelsea FC and Chelsea fans.'

That sort of response was a far cry from the ovation Chelsea supporters had given Lampard in his first match against his old club when the Londoners had played out a 1–1 draw at City's ground the previous September. Lampard had come on as a substitute and even scored City's equalizer, which meant title-chasing Chelsea dropped two precious points, but 'Super Frank' was still given a hero's salute from his former fans. That was before the full story of his controversial switch to City had emerged and there are now some Chelsea folk who will never forgive him. At least they had the last laugh: Chelsea won the Premier League that season so Lampard missed out on a fourth winners' medal by quitting the club where he made his name.

34
FOOD FOR THOUGHT

Lampard jetted off with England to the World Cup in Brazil that summer. The great and the good of football, and quite a few of the evil and corrupt in the game, were also attending the greatest show on earth. Not José. He was heading to Africa to tackle the greatest scandal: 842 million starving people around the planet. The Chelsea boss was swapping the touchline for the front line in the fight to eradicate hunger around the globe.

It was 29 May 2014 and Mourinho was appearing at an afternoon press conference in central London to announce he had agreed to become an ambassador for the United Nations' World Food Programme. It was a cause close to his heart, particularly the aim of tackling the shocking and shameful fact that there are 66 million primary-school-aged children going hungry around the world, 23 million of them in Africa alone.

José was determined to do his bit and today was his big unveiling, but the sports desk didn't know anything about it until the last minute. This wasn't a sports story – it was a news event focusing on a global crisis – but we still should have been covering it. My attitude was: wherever José goes, we go. Best of all: wherever José goes, I go! So I hurriedly contacted the organizers to make sure my name was belatedly added to the press list for the event.

Everything was fine on arrival at the very impressive Prince Philip House on Carlton Terrace in swanky SW1. There was even time for a drink and some bits to eat before Mourinho emerged for his 3 p.m. conference. Sure enough there were a few other football hacks there asking the odd sporty question but the room was mainly full of news reporters following the news line. José was excellent and gave them some good answers but I was looking for something a bit more personal, a bit more specific, and so held back in the hope that I could see him one-on-one afterwards. Except the organizers weren't having any of it. They told me all requests for one-on-one interviews should have been made well before the event, and all the slots had gone so there was no way I would be able to see José. I tried to appeal to their better judgement: as well as being a pal of José's, I was from the nation's biggest-selling newspaper and could take their message to a huge audience; I was sure he'd agree to see me if only they'd ask him. No, no, no, came the replies.

Undeterred, I kept my eyes peeled and when the selected journalists with one-on-ones moved to a private interview room at the rear of the building I quickly tagged along. The WFP press officer was on me like a rash when she spotted me heading down the corridor. She gave me a real dressing down, told me I was not going in, that I was not welcome any longer and asked me to leave. I politely explained I was going nowhere and then ignored her and the various colleagues she'd sent for as reinforcements. Instead, I stood loitering in the corridor quietly and unobtrusively, but making it clear I was staying put until José emerged, at which point I would try my luck with the man himself. There was great huffing and puffing from the organizers, great consternation at my obstinate approach, and a Mexican stand-off developed with them standing between me and the door to the interview room just in case I was suddenly going to make a mad rush for it.

I must have been there for at least a couple of hours while Mourinho did his separate interviews with the selected television, radio and print journalists as planned. Finally he emerged flanked by more of the WFP team and his representative Luis Correia. He quickly spotted me and stopped for a swift 'hello', which gave me the chance to ask him for a couple of minutes so I could do my own article on his new project. He was absolutely fine with this, which surprised and placated the organizers in equal measure.

We talked on the hoof as he walked out front to his Aston Martin and then carried on the conversation in the car park for ten minutes or so. He was superb. It was clear that this was not a publicity stunt simply aimed at using his worldwide popularity to highlight a cause. This was something he was extremely serious about and committed to, and he pledged he would be heading to Africa that summer to get involved personally.

Mourinho was scandalized by the situation, confessing he simply couldn't grasp the huge scale of the problem or clear his head of some of the shocking images he had been shown in preparation for his upcoming task. He explained, 'Hunger is a terrible global problem and, when you become involved in something like this, you see some shocking images. I have some pictures in my head from award-winning photographers who have gone into these situations and taken unbelievable pictures of the hunger there, and even if you want to be the rock man, you just can't be the rock man, because you just collapse.'

Mourinho also addressed the stark contrast between his life of fame and fortune and the children's life of famine and misfortune. He admitted: 'I never had problems as a child; we were very far from hunger. Thank God I never had these problems but my area, the area where I was born, is not a rich area. Many years ago I was a teacher there with kids, not starving kids, but kids from difficult environments. So I know a little bit. My wife Matilde never had these problems but she was born in Africa so she also knows, and my kids, as you can imagine, are very far from these problems too, but we don't let them ignore them. We don't let them grow up not knowing about these problems. We develop in our kids a feeling of what we have and what others don't have because in our world it is so easy to forget there is another world. It's very, very important to me to make sure people don't forget this other world. A lot of times we see things on TV and it impacts not just on me but on my wife and my kids. We explain to them where we can help and the need for charity. We already do things privately with our own funds. Last Christmas my wife and kids went to Portugal and on Christmas Eve they went out with a big van distributing food wherever it was needed, but joining with the World Food Programme takes this all to another dimension.'

Now this was the sort of personal insight, the sort of raw emotion I had been after and it was all the more powerful because it was obviously genuine and sincere. He complained, 'There's 842 million people in the world with hunger. That's amazing. The numbers are shocking but the fact that the WFP is feeding eighty to ninety million of the most vulnerable is absolutely incredible. They have planes in the air, ships in the sea, trucks on the road and volunteers in place all over the world. It's absolutely amazing. I will be so proud to be one of them.'

He couldn't wait to get out in the field the following month, pleading with the WFP not to spare him and his emotions on the trip and demanding to go to where he could witness and highlight the children's plight the most. He added, 'I have been to Africa before. I went with Michael Essien once to Ghana. I also went to Senegal with Didier Drogba but it is a different scenario. You meet people, you smile, you raise awareness, you give out some Chelsea shirts to the kids. This time I go on my own with a different mission. This time I don't want to go to an easy place. I'm going where the real problems are, I'm going to see the real kids that are dying of hunger and they are going to receive from me and the other volunteers the food to try and keep them alive.'

It was touching and heartfelt stuff, and I told him so as I turned off my tape recorder and slipped it back into my pocket. As I thanked him he pulled me to one side and whispered, 'Ashley Cole has played his last game for Chelsea.' I gasped: 'Really? Where's he going?' José shook his head and added, 'I don't know, but he's leaving for sure.'

The next day I wrote the big back-page exclusive under the headline 'Cole Off', and the England and Chelsea defender confirmed my scoop on his Twitter account that very morning.

That was pretty cool, but I was far prouder of the two-page article that appeared on Sunday 8 June: my interview with José about the world's starving which we ran to coincide with him actually flying out on his trip to try to help the children of Africa on a quest he called the 'toughest challenge of my life'. Yes, while the Côte D'Ivoire [Ivory Coast] football team was preparing for its World Cup opener against Japan in Recife, Mourinho flew out to the nation's capital Yamoussoukro to begin his UN crusade.

35

CRIMINAL DAMAGE

Few people outside of Burnley and Brighton would have known the name of Ashley Barnes before 3 p.m. on Saturday 21 February 2015. By 5 p.m. the whole country knew it. Suddenly the small-club midfielder was big-time news all over the football world. His despicable, over-the-top, studs-up lunge into the shin of Chelsea's Nemanja Matić shocked a global audience. The failure of match referee Martin Atkinson to dispense any punishment at all to the hatchet man only added to the viewing public's disbelief, especially as the ref red-carded Matić for retaliation: a shove that pushed Barnes to the ground. However, it was the subsequent fury of José Mourinho that helped ensure his name would be remembered, even shamed, for long after the match itself had been forgotten.

The Premier League leaders Chelsea were winning 1–0 at Stamford Bridge when Barnes committed his X-rated tackle after sixty-nine minutes. They should have been home and hosed by then but for some other controversial decisions that didn't go their way. It was the referee's fourth non-decision that caused the biggest uproar, with Barnes escaping any sanction while the man he'd scythed down was sent off.

The resulting dismissal of Matić changed the match. The ten men couldn't hold out against the lowly strugglers from Lancashire and conceded a late equalizer and dropped two precious points in the title race. Mourinho had already suggested a 'campaign' was being waged against his side after a match at Southampton had also sparked controversy over refereeing before Christmas. He'd been fined £25,000 by the Football Association. However, he was so incensed by Barnes' and Atkinson's behaviour that he risked further punishment by embarking on a prolonged protest aimed at highlighting the mistakes of the day and claiming it all as further evidence that his side was being unfairly treated.

Mourinho's own campaign started straight after the game. At first he appeared reticent to comment too much, saying, 'I can't go through the incidents. I am punished when I refer to these situations and I don't want to be punished. I prefer just to say this game had four crucial moments: minute thirty, minute thirty-three, minute forty-three, minute sixty-nine. This is the story of that game. I cannot comment because it is difficult for me not to say the truth.'

Inevitably José couldn't leave it at that. He argued Barnes should have seen red for his first-half challenge on Ivanović. 'Normally the player, if I can call him a player, who was involved in minute thirty, should be in the shower. What happened to Matić was in minute sixty-nine. There wouldn't have been a minute sixty-nine if the person in charge had dealt with minute thirty properly.' And after seeing Chelsea's lead at the top cut to five points, he reckoned if the perceived campaign against his club continued it could cost his club the title. He warned: 'If you tell me the story that started a couple of months ago finished today and now we have twelve matches to play with an advantage of five points, I tell you we are champions, but I don't know if the story ends here or if you have more waiting for us.'

Mourinho's cryptic comments about the match, the Barnes incident and the referee's performance were all headline news that Saturday night and in the Sunday newspapers the next day. Yet the Chelsea manager was still not satisfied. He took the unprecedented step of contacting Sky Sports and asking to appear on their *Goals on Sunday* programme that day to give an even more detailed reaction. This time he pulled few punches. He was unequivocal in his view on the Barnes tackle, describing it as a 'criminal', career-threatening challenge. He said, 'This can be the end of a career. Matić is a very lucky guy. This is an end-of-career [tackle]. I cannot find the words to describe what that player did.'

He expressed empathy with Matić, though, explaining, 'I can clearly understand football is about emotions and sometimes you lose the emotions. Clearly Matić had a reason to lose his emotions. What could be the consequence of Matić's push? For the other player, nothing. One second later, he stands and goes. The consequence for Matić could [have been] end of career.'

The Blues boss was adamant that Barnes deserved to suffer some retrospective punishment, just as his striker Diego Costa had earlier in the season. The Spain international was banned for three matches after an independent disciplinary panel judged he'd stamped on Liverpool midfielder Emre Can during the Capital One Cup semi-final at Stamford Bridge in January. 'If you call Diego Costa's actions against Liverpool a crime, the minimum you have to say is this is a criminal tackle. You say Diego [commits a] crime because of a situation [in which] he put his boot on a hand. When Diego Costa had three matches banned, tell me how many this player [Barnes] deserves? I ask if Matić is going to get a three-match ban, if Diego got three matches, how many matches this player gets? I'm asking you. I'm asking the people at home.'

The people at home – that was exactly the point. Mourinho was going all out to build up a reaction from the media and the public against Barnes, but more importantly in support of his view that Chelsea were always being harshly treated. He was making as big a stir as possible, not just because he felt aggrieved again but in a bid to ramp up the pressure on referees, officials and even the FA to make sure it wouldn't happen again.

Naturally I offered to give him another opportunity to state his case the following day. First I gave him a heads-up I'd received from the FA that Barnes was unlikely to be punished, but that they wouldn't be charging José over his after-match comments or his *Goals on Sunday* appearance. Then I asked if he was 'happy' he'd got his message across on TV. He replied, 'Happy, yes. People know now what is happening.'

However he was far from happy about Barnes getting off scot-free. He vowed, 'If he is not punished, I will be, because I will kill them and the delegate's report I will bring also.' He was referring to the report the Premier League's match delegate gives on the referee's performance after every game, and that immediately gave me an idea. The match delegate at Stamford Bridge for the Burnley game had been a guy called Steve Greaves and I told José that it would be great to get a copy of Steve Greaves' report. The next thing I knew, the report had landed in my inbox. It certainly made very interesting reading and a great piece for the paper. For, unbelievably, Greaves backed up the ropey ref on every single incident, saying he'd called it all exactly right. That point of view flew in the face of all considered football opinion and made the whole farcical situation even worse. Our back-page story was headlined 'Reffin' Joke', which just about said it all. Inside we dedicated two pages to the story too, under the headline 'Is it any wonder José feels picked on?' We included Greaves' comments on the four key incidents direct from his report to his boss John Morton.

For minute thirty, Barnes' foul on Ivanović, he wrote: 'For me, NOT kmi (key match incident) – but I would appreciate your take on this … Barnes jump challenge with Ivanović.'

For minute thirty-two he wrote: 'Potential penalty decision – handball against Kightly, not given. In my opinion a correct decision as ball was hit with pace from close range and didn't seem deliberate.'

For minute forty-three, the second Chelsea spot-kick claim, he wrote: 'Potential penalty decision – foul on Costa, not given. (Damned if he gives it, damned if he don't!) For me, both in real time and on dvd, my opinion is that Costa is looking to go down as soon as contact is made. However, Shackell does put his hands on him so appreciate your thoughts!! Also to note, ref can't actually see Shackell's hands on Costa.'

Finally, for minute sixty-nine he wrote: 'Challenge by Barnes on Matić, nothing given – for me correct. In super slow-mo it obviously looks awful, but in real time live and dvd Barnes catches him as follow through from the challenge. (Does Barnes mean harm? – only he knows.) Also looks worse because Matić has his foot planted ...' And on the sending off of Matić he wrote: 'Straight red – Matić retaliation, correct.'

Mourinho summed it all up in his own inimitable way. 'It's amazing. Everybody must love to play Chelsea these days. There're no penalties, no cards and no action. It must be a great feeling.' I included his quote in the article, but after discussing it with him beforehand, I attributed it to a 'club insider' to protect him from any possible FA sanctions. He had the Capital One Cup final at Wembley the following Saturday and didn't want to risk being banned from the dugout. Having Matić ruled out was a big enough blow.

Ironically it wasn't the end of the midfielder's woes, for although the six-foot-four midfielder missed the final through suspension he ended up getting injured at the game. He damaged an ankle on the lap of honour as Chelsea celebrated a comfortable 2–0 win over Tottenham.

36
HAZARD WARNING

With the Capital One Cup safely secured, Chelsea's thoroughbreds ran on to win the Premier League at a canter, setting a new record along the way. The Blues were so dominant from the start to the finish of the campaign that they topped the table for an astonishing 274 days.

Captain John Terry joyously lifted his fourth Premier League title, the thirty-four-year-old skipper having played every minute of the league campaign. That made Terry only the second outfield player to ever achieve that feat, the other being Gary Pallister in the 1992–93 season.

New striker Diego Costa justified his fee with 20 goals, 7 of them coming in his first four games. New midfielder Cesc Fàbregas vindicated his fee with 5 goals and an incredible 18 assists, 7 more than any other player in the league that season. Eden Hazard enjoyed his best season, playing in all 38 league games and scoring 14 goals and boasting 9 assists. The brilliant Belgian playmaker was subsequently voted Player of the Year by his fellow professionals and Footballer of the Year by the country's football writers. Mourinho was presented with the Manager of the Year award.

The team's stats were equally impressive. Chelsea were seond-highest goalscorers with 71 to their credit, they conceded the fewest goals (32), they kept the most clean sheets (17) and they celebrated winning the league with three games to spare. Mourinho's new-look Chelsea were universally acknowledged as by far the best team in the land. They'd done it all in style too, combining fine, free-flowing attacking with mean and resolute defending. They were the real deal, the complete package and no one in England had come close to matching them. It had been a wonderful campaign.

Mourinho's men had kicked off at newly promoted Burnley and overcame the shock of going a goal behind to eventually win 3–1. Costa opened his account with the equalizer but Chelsea's second goal was the pick of the bunch, an early glimpse of the attacking quality they possessed.

Hazard weaved his way forward towards the Burnley box before sweeping the ball wide to full back Branislav Ivanović on the right. He pulled the ball back to Fàbregas on the edge of the area and, with one touch, he delivered an inch-perfect, slide-rule pass to set up André Schürrle to score a superb team goal. Ivanović finished off the newcomers and Chelsea were up and running. Costa scored again in a 2–0 win over Leicester and hit two in the 6–3 triumph at Everton as the Londoners made it three wins in three. Not surprisingly he was voted August's Player on the Month. Costa celebrated with a hat-trick in a 4–2 win over Swansea to continue an awesome start for him and his new team.

But Chelsea's winning ways came to a halt against champions Manchester City, even though they had taken the lead late on. André Schürrle had opened the scoring for Chelsea in the seventy-first minute, providing the killer touch to a brilliant, sweeping move as the league leaders turned attack into defence.

However, all the focus would be on City's equalizer, not because it was an even better goal but because of who scored it. For Frank Lampard was the guilty man, Chelsea's record goalscorer coming off the bench to slide in and side-foot home against his old club in the eighty-fifth minute. He didn't celebrate; he actually looked very sheepish and embarrassed, but there was no escaping the fact that 'Super Frank' had just cost Mourinho two precious Premier League points.

Chelsea were soon back to winning ways, though, and a 2–0 win over Arsenal sent them five points clear. Arsenal old boy Cesc Fàbregas was the creator for Diego Costa to notch his ninth goal in seven games after an Eden Hazard penalty had given the home side the lead in a match best remembered for a touchline clash between managers Mourinho and Wenger.

Away from on-the-field dominance and touchline controversy, Mourinho had also been busy behind the scenes. Courtois, Azpilicueta and Oscar had signed new five-year contracts, with playmaker Hazard having agreed, but yet to sign, a £52 million deal that would also tie him to the club for five more years. The manager worked to secure the young talent around him and reward them for their integral roles in the team's impressive displays and results. It didn't prevent Chelsea from having a worrying wobble in December and January, though.

First, they finally tasted defeat when they went down 2–1 to Alan Pardew's Newcastle at St James's Park. Then a 1–1 draw at Southampton in the last match of the year proved too much for the Chelsea manager. Sadio Mané put Southampton in front after just seventeen minutes, remarkably the first league goal Chelsea had conceded in 299 minutes of play. Hazard equalized on the stroke of half-time with a fine goal set up by a thirteenth assist by Fàbregas and the Spanish midfielder was in the thick of the action again just after the break.

Fàbregas was threatening in the Southampton area when he was tripped by Saints' Matt Targett. It looked an obvious penalty but referee Anthony Taylor did not give it; instead he awarded Southampton a free kick and booked Fàbregas for diving. It was a hugely controversial decision that dominated the after-match analysis of the game, especially from Mourinho's point of view. He called the decision a 'scandal' and talked about a 'campaign' being waged against his team by TV pundits, football commentators and even managers of other teams, which put referees under immense pressure when they were officiating at Chelsea games. Mourinho said, 'There is a campaign against Chelsea. I don't know why there is this campaign and I do not care. There's a campaign, a clear campaign. People, pundits, commentators, coaches from other teams; they react with Chelsea the way they don't react with other teams. They put lots of pressure on the referee and the referee makes a mistake like this. We lose two points. The season started in exactly the same way against Burnley, a penalty and Burnley goalkeeper red card and they transformed it into a free kick against Chelsea and a yellow card for Diego Costa. Eighteen matches after and four to five months after, the same thing: a yellow card for Fàbregas that we can't rescind and a good opportunity for a goal with a penalty that was not given.'

Those words would land Mourinho in the dock with the FA but he didn't care. Highlighting his growing sense of injustice was worth more to him than the cost of any future FA fine. José knew those two dropped points could prove even more costly. He was correct. For, although Chelsea were three points clear at the turn of the year, it was all square by New Year's Day as the league leaders suffered an even more shocking setback. The Blues were hammered 5–3 at White Hart Lane and suddenly their flying start and dominant position were evaporating away. Now they were only above second-placed Manchester City on alphabetical order, with the two teams equal in every other way: points gained, goals scored and goal difference. All the hard work of the first half of the season had been undone. The fear now was that City were making another well-paced push for the top.

Mourinho saw the danger signs and so did his team. He

demanded a response and his team delivered. In fact they delivered in the style of champions, going sixteen league matches unbeaten. In the fifteenth match of that run they had the chance to make the title theirs. All they had to do was beat Crystal Palace at home. So when Hazard stepped up to take a forty-fifth-minute penalty, Stamford Bridge was ready to begin the celebrations. Only he missed, seeing his spot-kick pushed away by Palace keeper Julián Speroni. It was his first miss in ten penalty attempts and could have proved so costly. Except that the ball rebounded straight to him and he was able to nod it home to win the day and the league.

The final table would show Chelsea 8 points clear of City, 12 ahead of Arsenal and 17 clear of fourth-placed Manchester United.

The Stamford Bridge trophy cabinet now displayed the Premier League trophy alongside the Capital One Cup. Goals from John Terry and Diego Costa had settled the issue against Tottenham and emptied the Spurs end of Wembley well before the final whistle, to land Chelsea's first piece of silverware since José's return. The victors had beaten Bolton, Shrewsbury, Derby County and Liverpool on the way to the 1 March showpiece showdown and then gained revenge on their North London rivals for that 5–3 New Year's Day beating. A beating that everyone felt had been the turning point of the season and which served to galvanize and inspire Mourinho's team to respond in commanding fashion.

One league defeat in the final eighteen games of the season made them worthy champions, and that defeat came a week after they'd lifted the Premier League crown. So when Chelsea did a final lap of honour after a 3–1 win at home to Sunderland on Sunday 24 May, the overwhelming feeling was that this would be the team to beat next season and quite possibly for many seasons to come.

There had been only a few disappointments that season. One very big failure in particular was the humiliation in January of losing at home to lowly Bradford in the fourth round of the FA Cup. Chelsea had been 2–0 up against the League One outfit but then inexplicably crashed to a 4–2 defeat to a side forty-nine places below them in the league pyramid. The Blues also suffered a bitter blow in the Champions League, losing on away goals to Paris St Germain in the last sixteen.

This was another occasion when a Chelsea old boy helped do the damage, this time David Luiz coming up with an equalizer just as Chelsea looked to be going through thanks to a Gary Cahill goal. The £40 million Brazilian changed all of that with his leveller in the eighty-sixth minute to send the tie into extra time. Unlike Lampard in the match at Manchester City, Luiz celebrated and celebrated big-time. The in-form Hazard put Chelsea back in charge ten minutes later from the penalty spot, only to see Thiago Silva's superb header settle the issue six minutes from the end. It was all the more galling as the Blues had enjoyed an extra man for ninety minutes of the match after Zlatan Ibrahimović had been sent off on the half-hour.

It was a worryingly flat and lacklustre display by Chelsea but it was such an uncharacteristic performance that season that it was regarded in the same way as the defeats at Tottenham and in the Cup against Bradford: a blip and nothing more.

37
POT, KETTLE

There was a significant backlash against Chelsea after their Champions League exit to PSG. The flat, feeble performance was panned but it was the so-called 'pathetic' and 'disgraceful' 'gamesmanship' of the Blues' players that brought the real criticism. The focus of the furore centred on the thirty-first-minute dismissal of Zlatan Ibrahimović. A gang of angry Chelsea players had protested to Dutch referee Björn Kuipers immediately after the PSG striker's lunging tackle on Brazilian midfielder Oscar. TV replays showed Oscar played the ball forward just before the Swede flew in from the side to flatten him.

The Chelsea players' reaction to the tackle was blamed in the media for the dismissal, although the referee had the red card out within seconds of the challenge and the PSG players' angry protests to the referee after the sending off weren't much better. Indeed, the referee was manhandled and Thiago Motta booked for dissent.

After the match the red-carded Ibrahimović gave his thoughts on being sent off. 'I don't know if I have to get angry or start to laugh. For me when I saw the red card I was like, "The guy doesn't know what he's doing or maybe he sees something else." But that was not the worst thing. The worst was when I got the red card, all the Chelsea players came around. I felt there were eleven babies around me.'

TV commentators on the match also pointed the finger at Mourinho's men. Former Liverpool defender Jamie Carragher spoke out strongly: 'The reaction from the Chelsea players is disgraceful and it's sad. It's something that's coming into the game and it comes from José Mourinho's teams. They have this reaction; it's not a one-off. I always think with José Mourinho's teams, they will always be respected but they will never be loved because of situations like this. They take winning to a level that no other team or manager does. You see the reaction of some of the players and it has definitely played a part. The worst bit of dirty tricks was from Chelsea, surrounding the referee; the reaction was disgraceful. José Mourinho could end up being the most successful manager ever with the trophies he goes on to win in his career but I don't think him and his teams will ever be loved because of actions like that. Does Mourinho care? I don't think he probably cares. I think it's sad.'

Fellow pundit and ex-Liverpool midfielder and manager Graeme Souness added, 'It saddens me and makes me angry that gamesmanship is deciding these big games. It's not a sending off, it is Oscar's studs that are high. If that's what our game is coming to we need to sort it out and sort it out quickly. This PSG team is just full of technique, a really good footballing team, and they had to put up with stuff which I find really, really unappealing. The reaction of the Chelsea players to the challenge on Oscar epitomized what I'm saying. To a man they surrounded the referee, [Diego] Costa ran fifty yards to get involved. That is something we can do without, that is not the British way of doing things, it's creeping into our game, which is, I find, totally unacceptable. We saw a bit of that in the first half and thank goodness the PSG team stood up to that and they leave here with credit. They're a proper team. When I played, when we played, if you got a kick, injured, you didn't want to show the guy who did it to you that it hurt, you stay on your feet. Today it's the exact opposite and that's crept into our game. There have been wonderful South American and Latin players come to this country, but they bring with them that tactic. I've worked in Latin countries, I've played in one. It was completely foreign to me when I went there in the Eighties and witnessed it close up. They thought it was good play if you got someone else in trouble, someone booked.'

Radio summarizer and ex-Liverpool star Mark Lawrenson added, 'Chelsea's reaction as a team almost seemed choreographed. It was as if someone pushed a button and said, "Go and surround the referee." I think Diego Costa ran fifty yards – what's it got to do with him?' He also had a dig at Chelsea's Brazilian midfielder Oscar, suggesting he'd play-acted to exaggerate the challenge. He reckoned, 'Oscar should be up for an Oscar!'

Mourinho wasn't having any of that. He emailed me a series of photos, some going back years, of other top English teams surrounding referees in exactly the same way. One message was tagged: 'For those with short memories.' Another was short and to the point: 'Mister clean Carragher and mister Souness in Benfica.' Sure enough there were two photographs featuring Liverpool, one of them with a certain Mr Carragher and colleagues confronting a referee in identical fashion. There was also one of Mr Souness when he was manager of Benfica, with the combustible Scot being restrained by a linesman as he lunged at opposing players.

There were shots of Jaap Stam, Roy Keane, Ryan Giggs, Nicky Butt and David Beckham haranguing a ref; of Patrice Evra, Ashley Young, Darren Fletcher and Rio Ferdinand doing likewise; of Vincent Kompany, Joleon Lescott, Nigel de Jong, David Silva doing the same on two different occasions with Manchester City. The point was that it was not new and it had been in British football for years, with British folk in the thick of it.

Mourinho hit back verbally at his Friday press conference, too. He sniped, 'The world is a bit strange, maybe because of diets and maybe because of the quality of the products we are eating, I think memories are getting shorter because when Jamie Carragher and Graeme Souness speak about it, it is because they are having problems for sure. Jamie stopped playing a couple of years ago and in two years he has forgotten everything he did on the pitch. And Mr Souness also forgets, but he stopped playing quite a long time [ago]. He also forgets that a couple of years after he left Benfica, I coached Benfica so I know a lot about him, I know so much about him. But I've a certain kind of education not just in football but especially in life and I prefer to laugh and I prefer to say "envy is the biggest tribute that the shadows do to the man".

Mourinho then continued the envy theme as he addressed the situation of his team in the wake of their Champions League exit, effectively defying his critics by predicting that Chelsea would cap a 'brilliant season' by being crowned Premier League champions. He claimed every other team would swap places with the Londoners, who already had the Capital One Cup in the trophy cabinet and boasted a five-point lead at the top of the table with a game in hand.

José maintained, 'Our situation is good. It's better than anyone else's. Everybody would love to be in our position, eleven matches to play in only one competition. So what we can do now for ourselves and our club is win the Premier League and I really believe we are going to win. We started the season with the same points as [Manchester] City, we have five more than them now. We have nine more than Arsenal and the reality is we haven't lost a game since the Bradford game and we have lost only two matches in the league all season. While in the Champions League, maybe it's a unique case to be out without a single defeat. So I have an unshakeable belief in these players. Absolutely unshakeable. The people who were out of the Champions League last Wednesday are exactly the same people who have been top of the Premier League from day one. The same people who won the Capital One Cup. The same people who are going to win the Premier League. So I like my players and I trust my players. I support my players and I still have the same belief in these players. We win together and we lose together.'

Mourinho also promised there would be no knee-jerk reactions to the PSG upset. He continued, 'It's one thing to be disappointed, and try and find the reasons why we didn't succeed in this game. Another thing is to lose belief in the players, but no, these are the same players who have been top of the league since day one. Not since yesterday, or in August and then down and up again. Since day one! And zero defeats in the Champions League. Zero!'

Mourinho did reveal that he'd held a team meeting at the club's Cobham training ground on the day after the away goals exit to PSG. Lasting thirty-five minutes, it addressed the Champions League failure and focused on moving forward to finish the job of winning the Premier League. Mourinho was delighted with how it went, revealing, 'The players responded the way I expected: open communication, nobody afraid to speak, nobody shy. Not everybody spoke, but lots of good opinions, different opinions: one opinion from a goalkeeper, another from a striker. Their opinions were based on what they felt on the pitch and were different from person to person. People on the bench also had a different vision watching from the outside. Then I closed with the players the chapter on the Champions League. When you are out, you are out, so we also spoke in that moment about our future, which is to try and win the Premier League and, if we do that, a season with a Premier League and a Capital One Cup is a brilliant season. A brilliant season. So this is what we want to do and I think our situation is good.'

José was right. They did exactly what he predicted and completed a league and cup double.

38
INSULTING BEHAVIOUR

With a roll of honour that guarantees Mourinho special status in football, you'd assume he wouldn't care about something as insignificant as the Manager of the Month award. That assumption would underestimate Mourinho and what makes him tick.

José wants to be acknowledged as the best at any and every opportunity. Now, no doubt his detractors will say that's typical of him because he craves recognition to feed his arrogance and vanity. José would simply argue he's seeking the due rewards to reflect his excellence. Which is why, in December 2014, José was convinced there must be a deliberate campaign against him in England over the Manager of the Month award. The two times European champion, the only man to win league titles in Portugal, England, Italy and Spain, the only man to win the treble in the history of Italian football, the coach boasting seventeen major trophies in the first fourteen years of his career, had the hump because he'd missed out again as Manager of the Month. So much so that this time he decided to react.

José got in touch and asked, 'Do me a favour, try to [find out] who decides that shit Manager of the Month. I don't care [about] that shit but till the end of November I was, from day one to the last day, top of [the] league and zero defeats. [But] I didn't win [the award] in August, September, October or November!!! The last one was [Alan] Pardew – [he] lost in November against West Ham and I won all, including Liverpool away and drew at Sunderland. This isn't normal!!! I need to know who are the people? Four years in Premier League, two titles, two seconds and I won Manager of the Month twice eh eh eh?' It was actually three times – the same as David O'Leary and Alan Curbishley.

I made some quick enquiries and was surprised to find out that the names of the people on the Manager of the Month panel were a closely guarded secret. When I did eventually find out some of the names, there were many journalists among them. Their collective 'wisdom' was perfectly illustrated towards the end of a title-winning season when they once again ignored Mourinho for the award. This time the man himself was in a rage, and he had a point. Chelsea were about to be crowned Premier League champions, incredibly a third success for José in five full seasons with the Blues. His Stamford Bridge side had dominated the campaign, leading the way virtually from day one. They were imperious and Mourinho was the mastermind. Yet he'd not won a single Manager of the Month award since his return to Chelsea and when he heard on 8 May that he'd been overlooked again, this time for the final award of the season, it was all too much.

He got in touch and fumed: 'Manager of the Month Nigel Pearson!!!!!!!!! A month where Leicester lost to Chelsea and Chelsea won four and draw at Arsenal. I was laughing all season but this one is the ice on the cake. What is going on??? Zero manager of the month when I am top of the league from day one, many months without defeat. Now I win against Leicester and Pearson win. Amazing!'

I told him it was 'a disgrace and an insult' and said if he subsequently went on to be named Manager of the Year he should refuse it. He replied, 'I don't win for sure,' adding, 'It's an insult, yes, I feel that way but everything has its limit and they should be ashamed of what they are doing.' Then he lightened up a touch and joked, 'My staff wants to buy me an award and give it to me.'

Picking up on this I dug out my own little award, a mini-footballer on a stand which I'd won as a player, and I took it along to his press conference the next day to have a bit of a joke about it all. When I showed it to him, he collapsed laughing and later, as I left the pressroom, I caught sight of him through the window upstairs in his office, dancing around his room and holding an imaginary trophy above his head in mock celebration. We both cracked up this time.

Later that month, Mourinho was announced as Manager of the Year despite having never won the monthly award. It was the third time he'd received the honour, each time after a victorious league title with the Blues. He had topped the table for a record 274 days: that's some feat and yet another first for the Special One, which even the Manager of the Month lot couldn't ignore.

José wisely didn't listen to my advice to turn down the award. Not surprising, I suppose, after all his complaints and anger about being overlooked during the season. At least he'd got the big one in the end, but he was hardly gushing in his reaction to the trophy.

José said pointedly, 'I was never Manager of the Month, so I wasn't waiting for this but obviously I'm happy with it. This is, as you like to say in England, the icing on the cake.' Then, in another put-down, he added, 'The cake is more important than the icing. The cake is the Premier League, the cake is the objective of the manager, of the technical staff, of the squad, of the club and of millions of supporters. And I work for the cake, I don't work for this ... But to be the Manager of the Season is nice for me and my people. I think it's a club trophy, not an individual trophy. It's me, my assistants, my players, everybody who works with me. It's not something you get on your own.'

True to his word, Mourinho was quick to share the award

with the rest of his coaching staff, posing for an official photograph alongside the rest of his team – assistant coaches Silvino Louro, Rui Faria and Steve Holland, goalkeeping coach Christophe Lollichon, and fitness coaches Carlos Lalin and Chris Jones – his face masking the anger he felt over all the insults along the way.

39
MEDALS, MEMENTOS AND MEMORIES

It's the winning, not the trophies; the memories, not the medals; and Mourinho even claims the lust for glory is sated within five minutes of being achieved. José argues the only medal he will truly care about is the last one he wins before he finishes his career.

It's not that José doesn't cherish his many achievements; he certainly does and can talk you through them. He'll remind you of them and how special his record is even when compared with the best of the best. It's just that he's not quite so sure about the whereabouts of all the baubles that have come along with his titles and trophies. He's even chucked some of them away over the years, choosing to throw medals into the crowd rather than keep them.

Like in April 2006 after Chelsea beat Manchester United 3–0 at Stamford Bridge. They were handed the Premier League trophy and winners' medals afterwards and José threw his into the Matthew Harding stand. He said at the time, 'The medal was for everybody but the person who caught it is lucky.' Mourinho promptly collected a second medal and hurled that into the crowd as well, and he joked, 'Whoever caught them has a great souvenir. Unless they put it on eBay and make a fortune.' One of the lucky recipients did just that in November 2008, by selling the medal at auction for £21,600. José did keep his 2015 Premier League winners medal, handing it to his daughter

Matilde for safekeeping after the presentation, but he was up to his old tricks again at the start of the next season.

After the traditional curtain-raiser to a new season, the Community Shield showpiece match at Wembley, he again threw his medal into the crowd. The difference was that this was a losers' medal and that's of even less value to a serial winner like José. It did make a young Arsenal fan from Coventry very happy, though.

It was on tour in the USA in 2013 that he explained to me why the medals and mementos don't mean that much to him: 'The memories and feelings you keep for ever. But life must be: you win, you keep the memories, you keep the medal or not ... but you keep going, you go for the next one. And I think the trophy I'm going to enjoy the most is the last one I win, that's the one I'm really going to enjoy. Like Sir Alex [Ferguson] in his last season.'

For him, the be all and end all is to be victorious. It's not the taking part; it's the taking charge. Mourinho even argues that it is a perfectly normal, natural instinct rather than a fault or a character flaw. He says everyone who takes up sport, at whatever level, has the same will to win and drive to succeed.

'When you are a kid you play in the street with your neighbours, three against three, four against four. You want to win. It's the basic thing about football, the most pure feeling: you go there, you want to win. It doesn't depend on the level you are. To be champions in the Premier League is not a different feeling to winning the Championship, League One, League Two or the Conference. It's about the happiness and also the frustrations. Everyone has his level, but in terms of human feelings, they're exactly the same.'

So, in Mourinho's mind, it is a feeling of euphoria and accomplishment rather than anything tangible like a gold medal or piece of silverware. He claimed, 'I don't care if we get the trophy, really. The meaning is the important thing. The feeling, the emotion is what stays forever. I have replicas of every cup I won but I don't care about the replicas or the medals. I have them, they're in my houses. I have some in Portugal, some here, some in my son's room but I really don't care. What stays forever is the feeling, the emotion, the memory of the moment and I have that clear in my head for every one of these moments I lived. Normally it's like a flash, the moment, the final or the game that gives you the league finishes. You have a flash of the people you love most, people who are with you, a little bit of the most important moments that lead to that trophy. It's like a quick flash and then, with me, five minutes later it's "move on".

Mourinho's drive to succeed gives him an edge, a focus and an intensity few in the game can match. His critics argue it is this single-minded, all-consuming approach that can 'burn out' players who can't cope with the constant demands and pressure that go with his rigorous style of management. They also argue it's why he has never managed to stay much more than three years at any club.

José would disagree with that, of course. He can't understand someone who is satisfied to win once without the hunger to go on and win again and again. It's the essence of his sporting existence and is why he is so ultra-competitive. He admits that if there is no contest he has no interest. 'Yes, I like the perspective of real competition. We don't go to a game of football not to compete, not to try to win. I would never go to football or any other sport for an exhibition match when it is not a competitive game. Even if you bring me the two best tennis players in the world – the number one and the number two – I would not go; it has to be competitive.'

There has to be something at stake for Mourinho to become engaged in the project and excited at the challenge. When he is, he wants to finish first. To him, second is nowhere. It's all about winning and being the best. That's the abiding memory, the long and lingering satisfaction of it all. The medals are mere trinkets.

40
GAME TIME

Mourinho's remarkable run of success means he is continually being asked to reveal the secret of his success. The answer is very simple. In fact, it's just one word. Winning. His raison d'être is to win games and his modus operandi to achieve that is to take one game at a time. It may be a football cliché, but it works. Match day for José is the 'be all and end all' of his football life. All his work is focused on delivering that one thing. All his energy is channelled into delivering that one thing. All his hopes and ambitions depend on delivering that one thing.

So no surprise then that it produces a combustible mixture of emotions, excitement and adrenalin when match day arrives. It's the ultimate challenge, Mourinho enjoying the chance to outwit and overcome his opponent, but not necessarily the spectacle of the game. This is business, not pleasure; work, not fun.

Mourinho sums it up this way: 'People used to say "let's go and enjoy the game", and yes that's true, but at the same time I go to the game and say, "Let's go and do our job!"' That's his focus first and foremost. Everything else is secondary. This is about putting into practice everything he's worked on in training, in his team meetings and in his team talk at the hotel before his team leave for the game – yes, he does his final team talk at the team hotel, not in the dressing room just before the game. In fact he does several team talks in the build-up to a match.

Mourinho explains, 'I start the team talk days before, when

I start preparing the team. Analysing our opponents, analysing ourselves and training in relation to that analysis. Normally the players feel the team before the team talk because of the way we work. Normally they feel the team that's going to play. Then that last team talk is usually in the hotel before we go to the stadium. When we arrive in the stadium there's a couple of individual words depending on something new, the line-up of the opponents; John is not playing, Tom is playing in his position. Attention to this, attention to that, but in terms of the team talk, that is before we travel to the stadium.'

Team talk done, there is then the lull before the storm after his team arrive at the ground. First there's the long, laborious build-up to the match and the boredom of nothing much to do until just before kick-off. The players get changed, go through their preparations and then go out for their warm-up with the coaching staff. Mourinho hates it.

'The period I call the empty part is the part I don't like. The players are preparing for the match and I'm waiting. That's an empty period but then, just before the game, is a spicy period and when you go to the tunnel and go to the pitch, everything is over. I'm never nervous but I can't control the moment, the urge to go out and play the match. When it goes to the countdown, I like the feeling that we have to force it, that we can't wait for it. The motivation is always the same. It doesn't change. We want to win every match. Okay, we know we can't do that but our approach doesn't change.'

It doesn't matter if the match is home or away, if the fans are with him or against him. Once the match commences Mourinho becomes engrossed in the game. Not the action necessarily, more the line-ups, the tactics, the individual duels and, most importantly, is his plan working? He says, 'I go to the touchline or sometimes I sit in the dugout and I am eating the game, I'm playing my game, not with the ball at my feet but I'm analysing, I'm trying to give feedback, I'm trying to support my players. I'm trying to read the game perfectly so I can have an intervention at half-time that can help the team play better in the second half than in the first. In that perspective I enjoy it, yes. I cannot live in a happy way without those ninety minutes but I go with the perspective that I'm going to do my job. So it doesn't matter if the stadium is supporting you because you are at home or if the stadium is against you because you are playing in the house of a football enemy. I'm going there to do my job and, to be fair, I enjoy both ways.'

What he can't abide is to see his plans go to pieces because his players have failed to implement them properly. His preparation is legendary. It is thorough, detailed and demanding. It focuses on the strengths and weaknesses of opponents with a thorough plan for his team to cope with those strengths and to exploit the weaknesses. Which is why the man is always convinced that if all goes to plan his team will succeed. The only way he can fail is if there's a freak occurrence or one of his players deviates from the script. He can accept the first of those options, but he just can't stomach the second.

'Because of the preparation I always feel confident but there is something I really hate: if you do mistakes with things that you were prepared for. I hate it! If you get mistakes because of the unpredictability of the game, okay that's the game. That's why football is the game it is and everybody in the world knows something about football, it's because of its unpredictability. So that's part of the game and I understand but when you know the opponent does this, this is their mechanic, this is the way they play, this is the way they create and you are going to make a mistake on something which you have worked on; yes, you feel powerless and I'm not happy. I feel betrayed because of the work you did [in training] but you could not express that on the pitch.'

Mourinho might accept 'unpredictability' is part of the game and will never be eradicated, but he works hard to try to keep it to an absolute minimum. In training he frequently works with ten men against eleven in case someone is sent off. He also plays eleven against ten to work on exploiting the scenario if the opposition has a player dismissed. He tries to factor in every conceivable scenario in a bid to ensure his team is as prepared as possible for any eventuality. 'What I do in a football match is try to reduce unpredictability. A game is an open space, where anything can happen. I can find myself with numerical superiority or inferiority, I can be winning 1–0 or losing 1–0, I can be playing well or badly.

'I try to study the possibilities to the maximum before a game, prepare myself and try to reduce the unforeseeable. A lot of times you don't succeed, and during the game we have to adapt to the situation and change the path we've set out. In a season I try to do the same thing. From the first day, in England, in Italy and Spain, I've tried to reduce unpredictability and get to know reality as much as possible.'

The reality is that there will be defeats, there will be setbacks, and Mourinho has a long-standing reputation as a bad loser. It's manifested itself in words and actions on numerous occasions throughout his career, especially when he feels his side has been cheated or if his players have let him down. He reacts, he complains, he accuses, he challenges. It's often sparked controversy, it's sometimes brought fines and touchline, even stadia, bans. It's an understatement to say he has a long list of 'previous'.

There have also been times when he's accepted crushing defeats and major setbacks with good grace and dignity. For instance, when Sporting Gijon won at the Bernabéu on 2 April 2011, it brought to an end Mourinho's remarkable record of remaining unbeaten at home in league games. It had lasted for

150 matches and stretched back more than nine years, from his time at Porto, throughout his first spell at Chelsea, on to Inter Milan and finally through to Real Madrid. And he went to the Sporting dressing room after the game to congratulate their players.

I remember witnessing another such episode when League One Bradford City humiliated Premier League Chelsea at Stamford Bridge in the FA Cup in January 2015. After the match he harangued his players for tossing away a two-goal lead and spoke of his own embarrassment. Then he went into the Bradford dressing room to shake hands and congratulate every one of their players.

Later that season José did a similar thing when Chelsea were knocked out of the Champions League at Stamford Bridge by Paris St Germain. Mourinho revealed, 'The game finished, I was in the tunnel and one by one I shook their hands and I told them "You deserved it" and "Good luck for the future."' When Chelsea lost to arch-rivals Arsenal at Wembley in the Community Shield at the start of the 2015–16 season it was more of the same. After the game Mourinho waited for the victors to descend the Wembley steps with their trophy and then shook hands with all of the Gunners' players.

It's something he learned from Sir Alex Ferguson, who behaved impeccably after Mourinho's Porto had put the Reds out in the Champions League at Old Trafford in 2004. José admits such a magnanimous approach doesn't always come easily to him but says the experience left its mark. 'That [match] was when I felt the two faces of such a big man. The first face was the competitor, the man that tried everything to win, and after that I found the man with principles, with the respect for the opponent, with the fair play. I found these two faces in that period, and that was very important for me. In my culture, the Portuguese and the Latin culture, we don't have that culture of the second face; we are in football to win and when we don't there is not a second face most of the time but when we beat United in the Champions League I got that beautiful face of a manager which I try to have myself. I try.'

The repetition of the word 'try' is deliberate, it is honest, it is hopeful but it is not a solemn pledge. Mourinho is just too volatile for that and he knows it. Even now, in his fifties, he'd admit that 'knowing' doesn't always equate to 'doing'. He tries, but even he doesn't always succeed.

41
BEATING WENGER

When you publicly denounce someone as a 'specialist in failure' and 'a voyeur', it's abundantly clear you don't like them much. What must José Mourinho's views on Arsène Wenger be like away from the cameras and microphones?

Unsurprisingly, they're even more damning. Put simply, on such occasions the gloves have been well and truly off whenever the matter of Monsieur Wenger has been raised. A couple of times José even talked about wanting to physically fight the Frenchman. That's how bitter and basic their rivalry has become over the years. It's a deep dislike that has festered into one of the longest-running feuds in football, with the pair clashing ever since Mourinho first arrived in England in 2004. Relations have deteriorated steadily since then and now both men find it impossible to hide their scorn.

To say it's all down to a clash of personalities and football philosophies is too simplistic. It is a good starting point, though.

In 1996 Wenger arrived in England very much an unknown quantity, dubbed 'Arsène Who?' by the English press, with even some of Arsenal's players admitting they didn't know who he was. By 2004, though, Wenger was a well-established and respected manager with a glowing reputation for championing beautiful football and winning top trophies – at the time he had claimed three Premier League titles, three FA Cups and three Community Shields. His nickname was 'the professor' because of his scholarly ways, and he was reigning supreme at one of England's most traditional and historic clubs.

Contrast that with Mourinho, who was thirteen years Wenger's junior for a start. A cocky young newcomer with big ambitions, a big ego and a big mouth. The man who, on first arrival, had dubbed himself a 'special one' after winning the Champions League, the UEFA Cup and back-to-back league titles with unfancied Porto in his native Portugal. The new, swaggering upstart of a boss at the helm of a brash new Chelsea Football Club being bankrolled by a Russian oligarch outsider.

Trouble erupted almost as soon as Mourinho and his team started to live up to all the hype. Chelsea and Mourinho quickly toppled Arsenal and Wenger, with the Blues sweeping to successive Premier League titles in 2005 and 2006, the Gunners and all other rivals simply being blown away. Wenger felt that the millions of Abramovich had distorted the transfer market and the league, and in the summer of 2005 he also sniffed at Mourinho and Chelsea's style, saying, 'I know we live in a world where we have only winners and losers, but once a sport encourages teams who refuse to take the initiative, the sport is in danger.' When Wenger again criticized Chelsea's transfer policy the following season, it was time for Mourinho to hit back in typically controversial and colourful fashion.

Mourinho famously said, 'I think he is one of these people who is a voyeur. He likes to watch other people. There are some guys who, when they are at home, have a big telescope to see what happens in other families. He speaks, speaks, speaks about Chelsea.'

Wenger retaliated, responding, 'He's out of order, disconnected with reality and disrespectful. When you give success to stupid people, it makes them more stupid sometimes.' And so it all started.

When I visited Mourinho in Madrid in early January 2013, he couldn't resist a dig at Wenger, even though he was now managing in a different country and was no longer a direct rival. José, who'd won Spain's La Liga in fine style the previous season, noted Arsenal's French boss had failed to win a trophy since 2005. Mourinho confessed he was envious of the Frenchman's longevity and job security but he added he could never stomach so long without silverware. 'Yes I would love to have that stability at a club but at the same time I think for my mentality I also need the pressure to succeed and if no one imposes that pressure on me then I would impose that pressure on myself. The pressure to win things. Yes it's possible to be one or two seasons building for the future and not being at the level to win things, but no longer, because my mentality is I always need the pressure of winning things. Maybe it could happen soon for Arsenal. They play good football and produce good players, and they're always buying players in every transfer window so surely sooner or later they should do something, should win something.'

In the summer of 2013 Mourinho returned to the Premier League and to Chelsea, determined to restore the Blues as the dominant force in English football, and it wasn't long before hostilities were renewed.

In January 2014 Wenger had spoken out about Chelsea's plans to sell star midfielder Juan Mata to Manchester United for £37.1 million. Asked if he was surprised at the move, Wenger replied, 'Yes I am because Juan Mata is a great player and they sell a great player to a direct opponent.' He then made the point that Chelsea had already played United twice that season so Mata could not hurt them but his quality could hurt teams like Arsenal who had only played United once. 'They could have sold him last week [Chelsea's second game with United] but it opens up again questions about the dates of this transfer window. Some teams have already played twice against one opponent and some others not. I think if you want to respect the fairness for everybody exactly the same, that should not happen.' Mourinho saw this as yet more evidence of Wenger's obsession with all things Chelsea but for once he bit his tongue.

That all changed when José delivered his 'specialist in failure' speech the following month. Wenger had made a thinly disguised dig about Mourinho deliberately playing down Chelsea's chances of being crowned champions because of a 'fear to fail'. It was too much for the ultra-competitive Mourinho to resist, especially with the jibe coming from a man without a trophy for eight years. So when he was asked about Wenger's comments, Mourinho let fly. 'You know, he is a specialist in failure. I'm not. I'm not. So if you suppose he is right, I'm afraid to fail, it is because I don't fail many times. Maybe he is right, maybe I'm not used to failure, but the reality is he is a specialist because eight years without a piece of silverware, that's failure. If I do that at Chelsea, eight years, I leave London and I don't come back.'

It was a Valentine's Day massacre. Mourinho had carried out a cold-blooded assassination of his enemy in broad daylight. Inevitably it was too gory for some, who believed José's brutal honesty was too vicious and vindictive. Not to him it wasn't.

A few days later he was still pumped up about it all, telling me, 'When Mr Wenger criticizes CFC and Man United over the deal with Mata ... I will find him one day outside a football pitch and I [will] break his face.' Sure enough, a few weeks later José did give Wenger a beating. It was 22 March 2014, the day of the Frenchman's thousandth game as a manager, and it just happened to be an away match at Chelsea. It was as painful an experience as you can imagine for the Arsenal manager. Final score: Chelsea 6 Arsenal 0. Wenger was utterly humiliated, so much so that he ducked out of the usual after-match press conference at Stamford Bridge. His excuse was that the Arsenal team coach was about to leave so he had to dash off.

José was quick to mock Wenger for that, joking with me afterwards, 'Next time I lose a game I don't go to the press conference because the team bus is waiting for me.' No sympathy, no remorse, no regrets. Wenger had become the man Mourinho just loved to hate.

The following week I had an exclusive interview with Mourinho ahead of Chelsea's trip to Crystal Palace. José tipped me off he was flying to Basel in Switzerland for a promotion with classy watchmakers Hublot, who were making Mourinho and Chelsea watches. He invited me to meet him there. I didn't need a second invitation. It turned out to be a far-reaching interview, which discussed the title race, the struggles of David Moyes at Manchester United, whether United had tried to get José to Old Trafford, the progress of his friend Brendan Rodgers at Liverpool, his thoughts on Manchester City and his view on the evolution of his Chelsea side.

I said to him, 'Chelsea are top of the table and in the last eight of the Champions League but you could still end up without a trophy for the second year running. That doesn't happen to Mourinho, does it?' He replied, 'I think I win anyway because this is a special season for me and my Chelsea, even if we don't win anything. If we don't win and don't see any evolution, yes, okay, then that's bad, but I see evolution in the players, in the team, in the mentality, in the approach. To push to win the Premier League and to go from the Europa League to the last eight in the Champions League is an important step. It's a new feeling for a lot of the players and let's see what happens next but obviously there can only be one champion in each competition.'

That sounded to me like Mourinho was giving himself some wriggle room just in case he came up empty-handed again, so I tweaked his tail with a Wenger quote. The Arsenal manager had previously commented that finishing in the top four of the

Premier League was akin to winning a trophy so I teased José with it by saying: 'Yes, because isn't finishing in the top four like winning a trophy?'

Mourinho bit. He snapped: 'No, we don't want a trophy for finishing second, third or fourth like some other guys want. We don't want that! I want my team to feel that there is only one champion and, if you finish second, you are not a champion!'

Gotcha. The headline for the two-page spread I wrote was: We don't want a trophy for 2nd, 3rd or 4th ... unlike others', and everyone knew exactly who he meant by 'others'.

The war of words between the pair actually became physical on Arsenal's next visit to the Bridge, 5 October 2014. Chelsea won 2–0 but the game is best remembered for an angry shoving match between Wenger and Mourinho on the touchline.

The next day I asked José what had happened and he revealed, 'He was asking for a red card and pressing the ref in my technical area. I told him to go back to his area. He pushed me. I told him, "Here you do that, you know I can't react, but I will meet you one day in the street." Now I don't think José was ever serious about having fisticuffs with the Frenchman, he was just huffing and puffing and letting off steam. I gave him the benefit of the doubt on this occasion, even though an article for me with José saying 'Let's sort this out in the street, Arsène' would have been huge. Forget the back page, this was front-page news all around the world. There are times, though, when you have to be a friend first and a reporter second. This was one of those occasions. So I told José, '"Push me again and I'll see you in the street" could be a good story to show you took no nonsense from him but I think it's best to leave it. All the focus is on him and how he lost it and how stupid he looked and I think that's perfect. We got the three points. Happy days. Well done.'

José took it on board, replying: 'Yeah, yeah, he is in a bad situation for his clean image but if I do what he did I would be dead by the media and the FA.' He was probably right.

Later in the 2014–15 season there was more astonishing stuff from José. Chelsea won 5–0 after a superb performance at Swansea to make a real statement of intent. I was at the game and the Blues were looking every inch potential champions. When I congratulated Mourinho on the thumping victory he was already looking forward to the next day's clash between Manchester City and Arsenal. He declared, 'Yes was good, now let's see shit Arsenal.'

We were both convinced City would win, and win easily, but we were both wrong. Arsenal won 2–0 with a very uncharacteristic performance. I told José they'd actually done a 'Chelsea' and copied his game plan from a year ago, which had been regarded by many as a masterclass in how to win at City. I joked, 'I'm sure I have seen that "Arsenal" game plan somewhere before! Ha. Imitation is the sincerest form of flattery so Arsène loves you really!'

His emailed response left me gobsmacked. First he joked, 'Mr Wenger new 5 years contract', but then he claimed, '[One of the players] sent me an SMS to say players did themselves, organized themselves during the week. Wenger did nothing.' When I expressed my amazement he replied that his information was: '100 per cent.'

It may well have been, but that was another story that didn't get published, not because I didn't believe José or because I thought the story was ill-advised. I only had one source for the story and couldn't find a second person to confirm it so there was no way the lawyers would allow it to be printed. What was undeniable was the depth of Mourinho's dislike for Wenger. That could certainly be proven beyond all reasonable doubt.

José boiled over again when Arsenal were trying to sign Chelsea's long-serving goalkeeper Petr Cech for £10 million in the summer of 2015. Mourinho wasn't interested in the money; he wanted to keep the Czech international stopper but was overruled by owner Roman Abramovich. He took his frustration out on Wenger, who he blamed for unsettling Cech and causing this unwelcome problem.

He immediately hatched a plan to try to turn a straightforward cash sale into a swap deal in a bid to prise away, or at the very least unsettle, a couple of young Arsenal stars in retaliation. He told me in an email, 'Mister Wenger wants Cech and he thinks about money ... he is wrong!!! What I want is to f**k him ... want Cech? Okay, I want Walcott or Oxlade-Chamberlain!!! Want a top [goalkeeper] ... okay ... I want a young player, shit with you but I can make him top.' The inference was clear. He could make Oxlade-Chamberlain and Walcott top, top stars and succeed where Wenger had failed. I didn't use Mourinho's actual rant in my article but I did write the story of a possible swap deal for Cech, and inevitably it made yet more headlines and was further evidence of the ongoing feud between two of English football's top managers. On this occasion the Frenchman had the last laugh for once, landing Cech without sacrificing any of his players and then seeing Mourinho sacked by Christmas 2015 after just two and a half seasons back at the Bridge. Wenger ended that season a runner-up in the Premier League, albeit ten points behind champions Leicester City, and celebrated nineteen years at the helm at Arsenal in the process.

Almost two decades at one club is an incredible achievement, something Mourinho craves but can never seem to achieve. For all his stability and security, Wenger has never matched José's array of successes – yet in the final analysis, Mourinho puts silverware first and security second.

42
YOU'RE NOT WANTED HERE

It's easier to explain Mourinho's bitter dislike for Rafa Benítez. That was born out of a bitter rivalry and bitter disappointments. While Mourinho was king of English football during his first spell at Chelsea, boasting two league titles and a runners-up spot in his three seasons at the helm, it was Benítez who proved his nemesis in Europe and in one-off matches. Two Champions League semi-final exits to Rafa's reds from Liverpool really hurt and there was also an FA Cup semi-final defeat and a Community Shield failure.

It was baffling, as Chelsea had always proved far superior to the Kop club over the course of a season and undoubtedly had a far better team capable of sustaining a serious challenge on all fronts. Yet it was Benítez who delivered the most painful hammer blows to Mourinho between 2004 and 2007. Mourinho didn't like it.

The two men arrived in English football within days of each other in the summer of 2004. Mourinho was a European champion and had won the league with Porto two years in a row. Benítez came from Spanish club Valencia where he'd won La Liga twice in three seasons and had just lifted the UEFA Cup. These were two quality additions to the top flight of English football and both went on to make their mark.

It was Mourinho who set the pace and the standard. In that first season he raced to three wins in a row against his new rival, completing the league double over the Merseysiders and mas-terminding a 3–2 Millennium Stadium triumph in the Carling Cup final in Cardiff. Their fourth meeting that term came on 27 April at Stamford Bridge in the first leg of a Champions League semi-final. It ended goalless. A fourth successive failure for Rafa in trying to overcome the Blues boss.

It was a different and controversial story in the second leg, Benítez and Liverpool finally coming out on top thanks to the now infamous 'ghost goal' by Luis García. What was worse was that Benítez went on to win the Champions League that season, and in stunning fashion, recovering from 3–0 down against AC Milan to level at 3–3 and finally succeeding on penalties.

That incredible night in Istanbul earned the Spaniard the UEFA Manager of the Year award for the second season running. Mourinho had lost one game in five against him, had won the Premier League and set all sorts of new records, had lifted the Carling Cup and had finished an astonishing 37 points ahead of the Kop boss, but was still deemed second best. Now that was never going to be acceptable to Mourinho.

The 2005–06 season saw the sides meet twice at Anfield in five days. First there was a goalless draw in the group stages of the Champions League, then Chelsea returned to Merseyside at the weekend to thrash Liverpool 4–1 in the league. In December the two sides had both already qualified for the knockout stages of the Champions League when they played out another goalless draw in the return group match at the Bridge. The result meant that the European champions topped the group, with the English champions in second place. That would cost Chelsea dear. They were matched with Barcelona for the knockout stages, losing 2–1 at home followed by a 1–1 draw at the Camp Nou. Liverpool's defence of the trophy also came to an early conclusion, beaten home and away by Benfica.

Both clubs had more joy in the FA Cup, reaching the final

four where they were once again pitched together, just one step away from a major final. The semi-final was staged at Old Trafford in front of a capacity 64,575 crowd. Chelsea were on course for a second successive league and cup double but once more struggled to find their true form against the Anfield side on a day when it truly mattered.

The Blues were a goal down after just twenty-one minutes when John Arne Riise drilled home a trademark free kick. Luis García made it 2–0 with a brilliant half-volley in the fifty-third minute, making sure there could be no doubts this time about the legitimacy of the goal. Didier Drogba scored with twenty minutes left and finally the Londoners came to life, but Liverpool defended defiantly to book their place in the final at the Millenium Stadium on 13 May.

Benítez again finished the season with a trophy, and once more it was in the most dramatic fashion. Liverpool finally overcame West Ham on penalties after coming from 2–0 behind to scramble a 3–3 draw. Mourinho trumped that, though, by clinching back-to-back Premier League titles, finishing nine points ahead of third-placed Liverpool.

Benítez came out on top again in the Community Shield clash in Cardiff in the kick-off to the 2006–07 campaign, wining 2–1. Riise scored again and Peter Crouch got an eightieth-minute winner after Andriy Shevchenko had crowned his debut with a goal just before half-time. That was just the opener for another season of epic conflict and confrontation.

Chelsea won 1–0 in the league at Stamford Bridge in September but in the New Year lost 2–0 at Anfield, a disap-pointing reverse as they went in search of a third successive title. Worse was to come as the season entered its climax. The Champions League pitched the two rivals together in the semi-finals for a second time in three years, with Mourinho handed the chance to avenge the controversial outcome of 2005.

A 1–0 home win gave them the upper hand thanks to Joe Cole's goal, but Liverpool had the advantage of staging the decisive second leg at Anfield. Defender Daniel Agger put the home side in front after twenty-two minutes to leave the tie wide open, but neither side could conjure up a winner in ninety minutes or extra time so it was down to penalties, Liverpool's speciality. Sure enough they won the shoot-out 4–1 with goalkeeper Pepe Reina the hero after saving from Arjen Robben and Geremi.

It was Chelsea's third semi-final in four years and they were still waiting for a first final. In contrast Liverpool were through to a second final in three years and for the seventh time in their history. They didn't add to their five European crowns, though, this time losing 2–1 to AC Milan.

Chelsea enjoyed some consolation by reaching the final of the FA Cup, where they faced Manchester United in the first final staged at the new Wembley, in the last game of the season. Didier Drogba scored to settle it and ensure more silverware for Mourinho, completing his full set of domestic trophies. The quest for a third title ended in failure, though. Chelsea finished six points adrift of Sir Alex Ferguson's Manchester United in second place, and 15 points ahead of third-placed Liverpool.

The final meeting between Benítez of Liverpool and Mourinho of Chelsea came in August 2007 at Anfield. New boy Fernando Torres scored for the home side but a Frank Lampard penalty ensured a share of the points, the spot-kick sparking more controversy with Liverpool contesting referee Rob Styles' decision.

Remarkably, Mourinho was gone from Chelsea a month later, however. Not that his dramatic departure stopped the rivalry. That remained as keen as ever because the careers of both men became strangely interlinked. Benítez left Liverpool by mutual consent in 2010 after winning three trophies in six years. The

Spaniard subsequently followed in Mourinho's footsteps to take charge at Inter Milan, Chelsea and Real Madrid, although only in Italy did the Spaniard become manager immediately after José had gone. That's something Benítez should have told his wife, for she really got Mourinho's back up by suggesting otherwise.

In a newspaper interview in Spain, shortly after Benítez had become the boss at the Bernabéu in 2015, Mrs Benítez said, 'Real Madrid are the third of José's old teams Rafa has coached. We tidy up his messes!'

Mourinho promptly put her right and in the process put his old rival down. 'The lady is a bit confused. Her husband went to Chelsea to replace Roberto Di Matteo and he went to Real Madrid and replaced Carlo Ancelotti. The only club where her husband replaced me was at Inter Milan, where in six months he destroyed the best team in Europe at the time. And for her also to think about me and to speak about me, I think the lady needs to occupy her time, and if she takes care of her husband's diet she will have less time to speak about me.' That was a dig at Rafa's increasingly rotund appearance, which had earned him the derogatory nickname 'the fat Spanish waiter'. José never called him that, but he was aware of the unfortunate nickname and so couldn't resist the jibe.

It wasn't the first time Mourinho had insulted Benítez or that Rafa had targeted José. Neither made any secret of their contempt for each other. As with Arsène Wenger, Mourinho had made his views very clear and very public. The pair had numerous spats over the years and increasingly chipped away at each other as the antagonism between them and their teams intensified.

It didn't really become a topic for discussion between us until the Spaniard became interim manager of Chelsea in November 2012. When the news broke we were both stunned.

José's message was on the money: 'fatb rafa in cfc'. It's fair to say he was not impressed.

A lot of Chelsea fans took umbrage too. As soon as he was appointed there was resistance, hostility and protest. Benítez was booed and subjected to abusive chants at his very first game, a goalless draw with Manchester City at Stamford Bridge. Afterwards, he said, 'I can understand the rivalry in the past [between Chelsea and Liverpool] but I am sure the majority of fans will understand I am a professional and I just want to do my job.' He vowed to win over the fans by 'working hard, doing my best and winning games', but the supporters were having none of it. Their fury at his appointment wouldn't be a one-off protest; it became a prolonged campaign.

Banners and placards were a popular choice of protest, featuring messages such as 'We don't want Rafa to be our Gafa', 'Worst Manager since Mr A [Abramovich] took over. FACT', 'No one ordered a fat Spanish waiter, Roman', 'Di Matteo Chelsea legend. Rafa Chelsea reject. FACT'. But the most frequent was simply 'Rafa Out'.

If Benítez and Abramovich thought the protests would die away with time they were both sadly mistaken. They got worse and more vociferous as we entered 2013. Ironically, Mourinho was experiencing something similar at Real Madrid that January and messaged me: 'Chelsea fans love Benítez more than RM fans love me.'

By the end of the month I sent him a video to prove he was wrong. The footage was taken at half-time of Chelsea's FA Cup tie at Brentford on Sunday 27 January. The Blues had been knocked out of the Capital One Cup at Swansea a few days before and were now trailing 1–0 to a team from the third tier of English football. The travelling fans bellowed their anger, singing, 'You're not wanted here, you're not wanted here.' They didn't sing it once; they sang it repeatedly to ram home their feelings. There was also booing, jeering and other insults hurled in his direction. Chelsea scraped a 2–2 draw in the end, twice coming back from the brink, but it was a miserable day for all Chelsea followers, who wondered why Benítez was ever given the job.

By February 2013 I knew José was leaving Real that summer and was keen on a return to Stamford Bridge. In the meantime Chelsea fans had to suffer. That month Chelsea scraped through against Sparta Prague in the Europa League, Eden Hazard scoring two minutes into stoppage time after a night of impotency and profligacy in front of goal, particularly by the £50 million Fernando Torres. The next day Mourinho emailed his opinion that 'Rafa was lucky last night'. He also looked ahead to the Blues' upcoming match with Manchester City, adding, 'let's see our cfc against city'. He didn't sound confident and he was right. Chelsea lost 2–0.

Benítez was increasingly between a rock and a hard place, and on the evening of Wednesday 27 February it all came to a head. Oddly it was a 2–0 FA Cup win at Middlesbrough that proved to be the final straw. After the match a clearly exasperated Benítez announced he'd had enough of it all. 'If they continue singing and preparing banners and wasting time I think it will be a problem. If they want to achieve the Champions League this year, if they want to be behind the team in the Champions League next year, they have to support the team. I have a contract to the end of the season. I will finish. I will leave so they don't have to be worried about me. I will leave at the end of the season.'

It worked. The mood changed. At the next game, a 1–0 home win over West Bromwich Albion, Chelsea fans were now singing Mourinho's name and waving banners and placards urging him to return. He was delighted when I told him. He said every time he heard the fans singing his name it made him more determined to go back to Stamford Bridge.

Replacing Benítez and trying to clear up his mess had become his priority. He said as much later in 2013 when he finally made his long-awaited return to Stamford Bridge. José announced, 'I want Chelsea to be the Chelsea of everyone. I want them [the fans] to be with us in good matches, bad matches, cold weather, sunny weather, home, away, win or lose; be with us as a Blue family, which at certain moments it looked like the family was broken, and I want to try to bring the family back together.'

The Spaniard managed just six months at Inter after taking over from Mourinho. At Chelsea his brief 'interim' role only lasted from November 2012 until June 2013. And then Rafa got the Real Madrid job in 2015. It was another appointment that amazed Mourinho and me. I'd been given a strong tip it was in the offing and checked the info with José saying, 'Hearing rumours Rafa is in line for the Real Madrid job!!!' Within minutes José emailed back: 'No way.' He revealed he'd turned down an approach to go back saying, 'President loves me and wanted me to go and clean it, clean shit people pepe, casillas ramos marcelo. I told him too late, now I don't go. Presi thinks Zidane because of name and status but he did shit with B team and he is afraid of that risk. Klopp is only one he can bring ... rafa no wayyy.'

This time José was wrong. Just after midnight he got back to me to say, 'I was told Benítez RM!!!!!!! Can't believe but the source is good.' The source was very good. A month later, in June 2015, Benítez became the boss at the Bernabéu. Sadly for him it was another short stay. He was out by January 2016. The contrasting fortunes of Madrid and Benítez after that parting of the ways were stark. Zinedine Zidane took over and Madrid recovered their form and won the Champions League. Benítez became Newcastle United boss and was relegated to the Championship. But no matter the divisions in which José and Rafa find themselves, there will be no let-up in their rivalry.

43
POOR RELATIONS

Mourinho lost his job in December 2015. Winning the league and the Capital One Cup the previous season counted for nothing as Chelsea mounted the worst defence of the title in Premier League history. The Blues were abject. They'd gone from dominant to dominated in a matter of months. Their fall from grace was as difficult to fathom as Mourinho's impotence in finding a solution. It was a sudden, dramatic and totally unexpected decline but it wasn't as sudden or unexpected as it appeared.

The very first indications that there were problems for Mourinho during his second spell at the Bridge actually surfaced a year earlier, in the winter of 2014, the middle of a title-winning season. Chelsea were top of the Premier League and had been there almost from the start of the season. However, all of those end-of-season celebrations only served to mask a growing sense of frustration over player recruitment for Mourinho, which had returned and reignited midway through the campaign.

José has spoken several times over the years about his preference to try to use every transfer window to improve and fine-tune his squad. So in November 2014 I decided to try a pre-emptive strike to find out who he might be buying or selling in the upcoming January 2015 transfer window. Obviously I was looking for an early scoop. After all, the previous season Chelsea had brought in Nemanja Matić and Mo Salah during the January transfer window and Matić in particular had gone on to make a dramatic impact on the team and the campaign. So who had the Special One got in mind for this winter window?

There was a quick, one-liner reply: 'No money to spend in January.'

I was surprised. At this point of the season Chelsea's eventual title success was still a long way off and by no means guaranteed. An astute signing or two at the midway point could have made all the difference, but no cash was being made available. I tried to clarify the scenario, asking, 'So if you want to deal, you need to sell?' Quick as a flash he came back: 'Yes but I don't want to sell the good ones.'

Now we were getting somewhere, so I thought I'd tempt fate with a couple of suggestions as to which players he might consider offloading to generate funds. I told him, 'There's a couple I can think of you might want to upgrade! On current form Salah and Schürrle.' His quick reply said it all, 'Of course.'

Great, I'd got my scoop and duly wrote that Schürrle and Salah were fighting for their Chelsea futures and could be heading out of the club in January. Sure enough, two months later they were both gone.

The other nagging worry at the turn of the year was veteran goalkeeper Petr Cech. He had eighteen months left on his contract but was unhappy about having lost his number-one spot to Thibaut Courtois, the young Belgian international keeper. Courtois had returned the previous summer from a loan spell in Spain with Atlético Madrid, had signed a new long-term contract and had now been made first choice by Mourinho. It was a tough call, especially as Cech was arguably still the better man, but José was looking to the future so went with the younger guy. He had done the same when he first came to Chelsea in the summer of 2004, axing first-team regular Carlo Cudicini and giving youngster Petr Cech his chance.

Now it was Cech's turn to have to play second fiddle. Not that José wanted him to leave – he was delighted to have two top-class keepers at the club and said as much, boasting Chelsea had two of the best three goalkeepers in the world. The problem was that it wasn't all down to Mourinho. Cech had initially agreed to stay and fight for a place but as the season progressed he became more and more disillusioned at being stuck on the bench. He was also being courted by other clubs who thought they might be able to prise him away, either in that January transfer window or at the end of the season. The general consensus was that Chelsea would sell while they could, probably at the end of the campaign, rather than risk him going for free at the end of his contract.

José frequently refuted that point of view, saying he was prepared to keep him for another year, until the end of the 2015–16 season when Cech's contract finally ran out. Well, that was his public position anyway, and that's what he wanted, but he admitted to me he had no clue what would actually happen. After being ignored over Lampard just six months earlier, he now feared he'd be overruled on another big decision about another key figure on the playing staff. He was right, but it didn't happen in January. Cech was staying, at least for the time being.

All in all it turned out to be a pretty mundane January transfer window for the Blues. Just a bit of late wheeling and dealing: striker André Schürrle and defender Ryan Bertrand sold for £22 million and £10 million respectively, Juan Cuadrado bought for £26 million and Mo Salah loaned to his former club Fiorentina as part of the deal. So José lost three players to gain one.

He could stomach that in January, but he was stunned when he was told he needed to sell again before he could buy new recruits in the summer. It was a baffling decision to have to accept, especially hot on the heels of having achieved a league

Homecoming: José achieves his heart's desire in a move back to
Chelsea in 2013.

(**Above**) José shows his passion for the club as he begins his second spell as Chelsea manager.

(**Below**) Mourinho celebrates in unusual fashion after winning his first trophy since returning to Stamford Bridge.

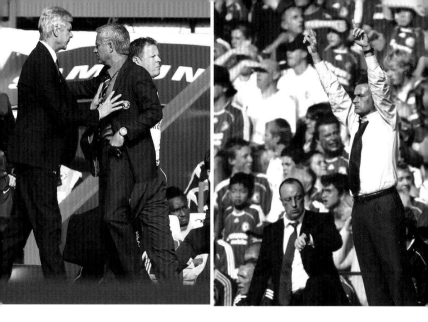

Mourinho has cultivated some of the most notorious rivalries in Premier League history – his spats with Arsène Wenger and Rafa Benítez often threatening to turn physical.

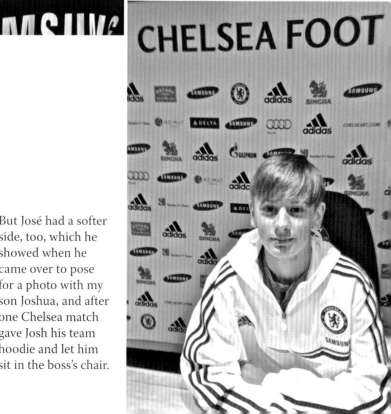

But José had a softer side, too, which he showed when he came over to pose for a photo with my son Joshua, and after one Chelsea match gave Josh his team hoodie and let him sit in the boss's chair.

(**Above**) José shows off his picture with Al Pacino to me, proving even the most famous can still get star-struck.

(**Below**) Thanks for the memories: Mourinho no longer throws his medals into the crowd, instead saving them for his son, José Jr.

(**Left**) José celebrates winning his third Premier League title with Chelsea.

(**Below**) But a lot can change in a few short months in football . . .

TAKE THAT MANCHESTER
JOSE'S
"BACK FOR GOOD"

(Right) Mourinho stuns the football world by signing for Manchester United in May 2016.

(Left) Part of the family: José shakes United legend Sir Bobby Charlton's hand before the 2016 Community Shield, with new signing Zlatan Ibrahimović, pictured behind, reuniting with his old Inter manager.

Start as you mean to go on: Mourinho sends out a powerful statement of intent by winning a trophy in his first official game as United manager, beating league champions Leicester 2–1 to win the Community Shield.

and cup double. Mourinho had wanted at least a couple of marquee signings to make a statement of intent that he and Chelsea were in unrelenting mood, that they weren't going to rest on their laurels and bask in the glory of a fine season. With rivals Manchester City and Manchester United both preparing to spend big that summer to try to bridge the gap, it did seem an essential requirement. Certainly the media thought so, linking Chelsea to huge deals for the likes of Paul Pogba, Antoine Griezmann, Douglas Costa, Isco and Mario Götze.

None of them happened, which was no surprise to José or me. His card had already been marked by an increasingly frugal Chelsea board when he first discussed new signings for the 2015–16 season. I caught up with the situation at the start of July, two months after Chelsea won the league, when he'd just returned to work after his holidays. I emailed him to ask if there was anything imminent regarding incoming transfers and José's reply was caustic and sarcastic. There was 'no news' of any deals because the 'club think I make miracles and don't need players ah ah ah'.

So José moaned and he moaned and he asked for more and I tried to help by writing about it all in the newspaper. He was desperate to deal, especially to buy a centre half to complement and compete with ageing skipper John Terry, England defender Gary Cahill and the emerging Kurt Zouma. He could see Chelsea's defence was an area that needed urgent attention and he still hankered after Real Madrid's Raphaël Varane, but after trying to sign him in the spring of 2015 he confided that he had 'no chance' of sealing a deal.

By the summer he had turned his attention to Everton's John Stones. So began a saga that would dominate the summer months. Ultimately, and infuriatingly for Mourinho, it became a carbon copy of the failed pursuit of Wayne Rooney in 2013. Mourinho did all the talking, saying how much he liked the player, admired his qualities, but the club again tried to be clever and play a cagey game of poker with Everton.

At first they didn't make a bid, they just let the Merseysiders fret and sweat a while. Then they came in with a low, opening offer of £20 million to test the water and to sound out Everton's resolve. Everton said 'No'. Chelsea then upped the stakes to £26 million. Everton still said 'No'. There was a pause before a £30 million bid was tabled and this is where Stones did what Rooney never did: he handed in a transfer request to try to force the deal through.

It didn't work. Everton stood strong, refused to sell and even some last huff and puff from the Londoners could not make them change their minds. Chelsea had yet again failed to deliver one of Mourinho's top targets.

Chelsea's other transfer activity that summer, apart from the pursuit of Stones, was pretty unremarkable. Abramovich overruled Mourinho and allowed Cech to join Arsenal for £10 million. That went down well: a hard-nosed football decision ignored in favour of a benevolent, sentimental one. The Blues then spent £8 million of the Czech's cheque on Asmir Begović from Stoke City. One in, one out. They brought in Monaco striker Radamel Falcao on loan to replace the departed Didier Drogba, even though Falcao had been a miserable failure at Manchester United the season before. One in, one out. They sold Oriol Romeu to Southampton for £5 million and brought in Brazilian prospect Kenedy from Fluminense in Italy for £6.3 million. One in, one out.

The rest was small change. Two young centre halves were signed for their potential: Michael Hector from Reading for £4 million and Papy Djilobodji from Nantes for £2.7 million, with both immediately farmed out on loan along with £1.25 million signing Danilo Pantić, who'd just joined from Partizan. Ones for the future, perhaps.

Then finally, towards the end of July and into mid-August, it started to hot up. Unsettled left back Filipe Luís returned to Atlético Madrid after just a year away, bringing in £16 million. That helped fund the £21.7 million needed to buy his replacement, Baba Rahman, from Augsburg in Germany. Again it was one in, one out, with little money actually spent. That is until the Blues suddenly paid £21 million to Barcelona to capture Spain's international winger Pedro. It was still one in, one out, though, as he was coming in to replace flop Juan Cuadrado. The trouble was that no one wanted to buy Cuadrado, at least not at the money Chelsea were asking anyway, so he'd gone back to Italy on loan to Juventus after just a few miserable months in London. And that was it. Stones stayed put, Chelsea missed out and José had to go again with pretty much the same squad as he finished with in May 2015.

All Chelsea's rivals had strengthened significantly. The Londoners' total spending that summer was £65 million, with £31.75 million recouped in sales, meaning Chelsea had invested £33.25 million. Liverpool paid there or thereabouts for Christian Benteke alone. Manchester United actually spent more than that on one player, handing Monaco £36 million for Anthony Martial, not to mention the £25 million to Southampton for Morgan Schneiderlin. United's neighbours Manchester City easily topped that by recruiting Kevin De Bruyne from Wolfsburg for £55 million to put their £44 million purchase of England winger Raheem Sterling in the shade. In all, moneybags City spent £137.5 million and recouped just £22 million. They'd made a £115 million investment to try to recapture the Premier League crown and finally, perhaps, make a dent in the Champions League, a competition in which they had an abysmal record. In comparison, Chelsea were very much the poor relations and José knew he'd got his work cut out on and off the pitch.

44

FAME AND FORTUNE

When you are as big a star and celebrity as José Mourinho, life off the pitch can be just as testing and problematic as life on it. Have you ever imagined what it would be like to be someone like him? The fame, fortune, football and following. A global superstar with all the trappings such worldwide adulation and status brings: beautiful homes, supercars, expensive watches and jewellery, the smartest designer clothes, spectacular holidays. A fantastic, fantasy life.

But in reality it's not a life without its share of problems. A virtually 24/7 existence in the public eye, a constant pressure to succeed, an incredible, sometimes intrusive scrutiny of your work and your personal life – a relentless existence where every time you step out of your front door you are being watched, photographed, followed and, yes, fêted too. 'Can I have an autograph?' 'Can I get a selfie?' Back-patting from your admirers but backbiting from the haters – on the street, at the supermarket, in the cinema, the restaurant and on the beach.

So what's it really like being José Mário dos Santos Mourinho Félix? It was a question I just had to ask the Special One.

It was back in August 2013 and we were sitting together in the Executive Lounge of the plush Mandarin Oriental Hotel on the bank of the Potomac River in Washington DC. Mourinho was the 'Happy One' after returning for a second spell as manager of Chelsea Football Club after five seasons away. Back in Chelsea blue, back at the club he loved and where he was loved. José was in the American capital because the Blues were on pre-season tour in the United States again, this time competing in the Guinness International Champions Cup alongside Real Madrid, Juventus, Inter Milan, AC Milan, Valencia, Everton and LA Galaxy. As the tour came towards its conclusion we spent an afternoon chatting and discussing all things Mourinho, including what it's like being him.

Mourinho attempted to sum it all up, saying, 'The good is much more than the bad. The bad is about moments. Any person that is public because of their job, there are things we lose, but that's a little bit of the price. The fame I don't enjoy, for sure. If I could spend some of my money to go outside shopping with my wife and family and nobody [would] disturb me, I would. If I could use some of my money to say "on this beach it is forbidden to take photographs" then I would pay for that, so that I'm on the beach just like every other person without every telephone taking pictures of me and my family. So to be famous, for sure, I don't enjoy. But I don't cry a lot because of what football took from me, because football also gave me a lot.'

A lot of money for starters, although Mourinho reckons he's not that fussed about the fortune bit, either. He continued, 'I'm a very normal person. I would say I would live almost the same way without the money I have ... As a family man, as a father, it is nice that you can support your kids, your family. That if they want to go to university in any corner of the world I can say, "Yes, let's go!" If they want to marry, if they want to buy a nice flat anywhere in the world to live with [their] husband or ... wife, I can support that. But only for that, because me and my wife are very normal people.

'We live basically the same way we did when we started together twenty-five years ago and we educate our kids to live the same way. I remember when we were married twenty-five years ago, looking and waiting for the day of the next salary.

Me and my wife, we have this amount, we are going to get the school salary on the twenty-fifth of the month and [it is] now the twenty-first so for those four days we have to control this and that. We speak a lot about that, explain it to the kids, how life is. I remember exactly how it is, although we didn't have [too many] problems, to be fair ... but we remember perfectly to have this balance, to think, to be organized and to take the money for the things we have to pay every month – the monthly expenses. I remember perfectly to save some to try and buy a new car, refurbish a room ... and this is the organization we had at the time.'

This sounds like the sensible and pragmatic Mourinho. But contrast that with his dark side. With the fame also comes the infamy, with seemingly more people against him than with him, no matter where he goes or which club he manages. In fact, the bigger the club, the bigger the animosity, as he found out at Real Madrid. And not even the man himself would dispute that he is a 'Marmite' character who people either love or hate.

Mourinho also accepts he has his faults; he knows he's made mistakes, he knows his intense attitude and drive to succeed alienate him from many, some of them his players. That sometimes he does go too far. Yet he says he will never change and in Washington he insisted he had no regrets over anything he has said and done. 'There's no conditions to regret – you can't go back and change things. For sure there would be some decisions, some behaviours, some things that, if you could [change them] you would, but I never spend one second thinking about it because there's no way to do it.'

He may not regret, but he does apologize when he is in the wrong, and he was never more wrong than in August 2011 when he attempted to gouge the eye of Barcelona's assistant manager Tito Vilanova in an unsavoury flare-up when he was manager at Real Madrid. That was one incident that will never be forgotten. He publicly apologized for it afterwards, saying on Fox Sports, 'I obviously should not have done what I did, obviously not. The person who messed up there was me. I failed and I am not looking for excuses. If I failed, I failed. The image will remain forever, the negative image is more important than any words. Between me and him there are no problems, we have greeted each other since, when we have met in games since then, and that's that. Story over and we will try to ensure nothing similar happens.'

As for being hated by so many, he understands it – to a degree. He told me, 'It depends on the reason why they hate me. If they hate me for the right reasons I respect that hate. If they hate based on lies and projects to make people hate, I feel it is not fair and I don't enjoy it so much. Football is what it is; [the feelings] are because of this game. I'm what I am because of this game so you have to live with it.'

And on the question of being perceived as arrogant, he would agree, to an extent. He once told the *Daily Mirror*, 'If people say I am an arrogant football manager, maybe they are not so wrong. These people don't know me personally – they are not my friends, they are not my family. But if some family or some friends say I am arrogant, then I am upset. Because I am not an arrogant friend, I'm not an arrogant family member. I am soft.'

When all's said and done, he is who he is and you either like it or loathe it. As he told the world when he was unveiled as the new boss of Real Madrid, 'I am José Mourinho and I don't change. I arrive with all my qualities and my defects.' Which of those he has more of will depend on whether you love him or hate him, but that's often the price of fame.

45
THE HOME FRONT

While in public Mourinho is the outspoken, charismatic superstar, at home it's a rather different story. Once he steps through the front door everything changes. Suddenly he's a mere mortal and José wouldn't have it any other way. He told me, '[At home] I'm treated like what I am: a husband, a father. I'm very normal. I do what I can do. I don't do things I'm a disgrace at doing. I can't cook, for example; I don't need to clean but I love to go to the supermarket to do the shopping or go with my kids to do things they like to do, to go to a movie and help with homework if it's something I can do. I love to be normal.'

The man makes no secret that the love of his life is his wife Matilde. He calls her 'Tami', but also affectionately describes her as the mother hen of the family. They met as teenagers and still behave like it at times. Like in 2013 when Tami had a tattoo and challenged her husband to do likewise. He did, having her nickname and those of his children inked on to his left wrist. It read 'Tami, Tita, Zuca'. Tita is his daughter Matilde, Zuca his son José, which clearly avoids any confusion at home!

But there's no confusion about the secret behind their long and loving relationship. In one interview Mourinho summed it up, saying, 'My wife trusts me, my wife knows me. She has been with me since I was seventeen and she was fifteen. Everything is so crystal clear for us. I have my professional work and I have my family life. I am not the kind of guy with a social life and I am so happy the way I am. The secret in everything is love. If you are successful in football, it is because you love football. If you are successful in any job, I believe it is because you are in love with that job and if you have a successful family it is because people are in love with each other. Love is the basic.'

The fact is that while football is José Mourinho's passion, it is his family that is his true love. Without football, he says, he would be miserable. Without his family, he would be finished. 'After my family it is football. Without family I would say there is no life. Without football for sure there is no happy life. So football is important for me and I felt that most, not when I'm working every day, [but] in that period when I left Chelsea at the end of September [2007] and I made a decision not to work until the end of the season. So between September and May I would say: October was enjoyable, November so-so but from December to May I was in trouble.' He coped, though, because, although he didn't have a job, he did have the love and support of his family.

José's certainly a doting dad. For instance, I remember him getting in touch in March 2014 asking me to highlight an exhibition of photographs by his daughter Matilde. It was a school project and they were being displayed at the IB Art & Film Show in London's Conway Street. He gave me the address and said, 'It's a photo show, my daughter made pictures of me. It's very funny!' José wanted the photos in the newspaper to highlight how well his girl was doing at school. However, he didn't want Matilde to know he was responsible for arranging the coverage. He added, 'She doesn't know I told you but anyone can go there and see the art show. My pics are very, very funny because [they] are about emotions: anger, happiness, disgust.' The other proviso was, 'I don't want people to know which school she is at.' That was no problem; I just wanted the pictures because I felt it would make a great piece.

It should have been easy. Turn up to the exhibition, takes

snaps of the photographs and stick them in the newspaper. It turned into a nightmare. Three times we went to the exhibition, three times we failed to even get inside. So I emailed the school saying I had heard of the exhibition and asking for their help in highlighting Matilde's work, but guaranteeing everyone's privacy. I did not mention that José was involved at all but just for good measure I kept him in the loop. He remained keen, explaining, 'My pics are very private and I only did it [for] her, so nice really.'

The school refused to cooperate, leaving me and José frustrated. He couldn't believe something that should have been so simple was now so complicated. He decided to intervene, telling me, 'I will try to make it happen and speak with a teacher there.'

After four days of trying I finally thought we'd cracked it. José emailed to say, 'My wife and daughter now give permission to school to let the *Sun* make it!! Only thing Matilde ask is that she ask u to write that her decision to do my pics was because her first show was on the Father's Day.' That was perfect. It actually gave the feature an extra edge: this was now a daughter's Father's Day treat for her dad, a brilliant photo exhibition of him at his best, at his happiest, at his worst and at his angriest. This was going to be a great piece, well worth the time and trouble.

Except that the very next day José emailed again with the worst of news. 'Finally this morning they decided in school to stop [the article] ... better for other students bla bla bla. Sorry for u and sorry also for myself.'

Like most dads, José is very proud of his children. He once sent me a photo of the two of them at a London film premiere posing on the red carpet with Hollywood actress Jennifer Lawrence. That was in November 2014. The message with it? 'Not a bad way to celebrate Liverpool.' Chelsea had just won 2–1 at Anfield and here he was revelling in the victory and in being able to treat his children to the extra-special experience of meeting a superstar.

More photographs of his children take pride of place in his office. On his desk at Real Madrid was the shot of a young goalkeeper diving full length to make a flying save. He was so proud that José Jr was trying to emulate his grandfather and make the grade as a goalie. Obviously José could help his lad a lot in that ambition, with his contacts and influence. In Madrid the young José played for local side Canillas and when his father returned to Chelsea in 2013 the teenager had successful trials at nearby Fulham and was signed up.

When he wasn't playing football, José Jr was a regular at Chelsea's home games at Stamford Bridge, sitting just a few rows back from the Blues' dugout and his dad. It wasn't always so. His season ticket seat used to be behind the away team's dugout, but that all changed after a dramatic last-minute win over Manchester City at Stamford Bridge in October 2013. Fernando Torres notched a ninetieth-minute winner to spark a controversial celebration by the Chelsea manager.

Mourinho jumped out of his dugout, ran in front of City boss Manuel Pellegrini and the City bench, to jump into the crowd behind them. It looked an outrageous act of provocation and disrespect, but the Blues boss insisted it was nothing of the sort: he was just trying to share the moment with his boy who was sitting in that area.

He explained, 'Chelsea is guilty because I want to buy a season ticket for my son and they give a season ticket for my son behind the opponents' dugout. Now they have to give my kid tickets behind my dugout. I promise that I went for him but this is the drama of the last minute. Last year I beat Man City in the last minute in Madrid, I slid on my knees, I destroyed my trousers. This is the emotion of the game. If they believe that my son is there, great. If they don't believe,

I apologize if they feel that I did something wrong.'

José Jr is also the reason Mourinho no longer throws his medals into the crowd. The youngster has started to keep mementos of his father's triumphs so all medals and awards are passed on to him. Even daughter Matilde has to give way to her younger brother on that front. Mourinho handed her his 2015 Premier League Winners' medal after a 1–0 home win over Crystal Palace secured him his eighth title in twelve years, but it was only because José Jr couldn't make the match and his sister was under strict instructions to pass it on when she got home. Mourinho, in his after-match press conference, said, 'My son wasn't here today. I gave the medal to my daughter, but she knows she has to give it to him.'

Mourinho's focus on family is so strong that he's sure his desperate need for football is all to do with his genetics and DNA. He believes being born into a footballing family has played a crucial role in him creating his own life and career in the sport.

His father, José Manuel Mourinho Félix, had a nineteen-year career as a top goalkeeper in Portugal, even winning one international cap. José's dad then went into a long career in management, stretching from 1971 to 1996, and so Mourinho says he's been living and breathing football from the very moment of his birth.

He recalled, 'I was born the son of a footballer; I grew up the son of a manager. In fact on the day I was born my father played a big match; he just came home to see me born. Afterwards he went to the stadium to play a big game so I was born into that environment. Of course I don't remember that big game against Sporting Lisbon.

'The match I remember well was my father's match against Ireland: Portugal against Ireland in Brazil [25 June 1972 in front of 13,000 fans in Recife]. I was a kid, I don't know – eight years old. I remember perfectly all the details and emotions of that and after that I remember so many things because my life was inside football. I started my own little career as a kid who wants to play football in every category. Then there was my formation as a coach and my youth experiences as a coach, then into professional football so my life was football and football.'

Mourinho tried hard but, ultimately, failed to emulate his dad to become a top player, although in 1981 Mourinho was on the books as a striker for his father's Rio Ave team, who were in the Portuguese top flight at the time. However, his career as a player never really ignited, although his desire for the game could not be extinguished. He turned to coaching instead, and the rest is history.

It was in his genes all along, something Mourinho is proud to point out. 'I think genetically you are what you are; what you have in your DNA means there's no way back. It doesn't matter how, but you are always going in that direction.' So maybe his son 'Zuca' can go on now and make it three generations of Mourinhos in the game. Now that would make dad and grandad proud.

46
CLOSE AND PERSONAL

Out of a close professional relationship came a close personal relationship. It simply evolved, and certainly wasn't something I deliberately or cynically tried to engineer. I can honestly say I never once tried to ingratiate myself with Mourinho; quite the opposite, in fact.

Yes, I complimented him; yes, I bigged him up at times; and, yes, I even pumped him up at times, especially after a setback. I'd remind him what he'd achieved and how special he was. There was a balance, though. I never gave him an easy ride. I always asked him tough questions and volunteered strong opinions on performances and players. My match reports were harsh and critical when necessary. I can't say for sure, but I think he respected that. I certainly respected him. But there was far more to the friendship than simply respect.

We'd always got on, possessed a similar sense of humour and outlook, were honest with each other and trusted each other. Neither of us took any crap, we both tell it as it is and we both wanted what was best for 'the Chels'. So there was a bond, one that meant that on many occasions we simply chatted about family and life in general, not football. We became close but I reckon Mourinho was a much better friend to me than I was to him. What could I do for someone like him, someone with his life and in his position? Yes, I could be a sounding board for ideas; yes, I could give him feedback; and yes, I could push his message out in the press, either on or off the record. I could give him inside information via my contacts at other clubs, at the FA, Premier League or in the football world. However, he gave me so much more, and not just me: he was also generous to my children, my family and my friends. Generous of time and generous of spirit.

Like when my mum and dad celebrated their sixtieth wedding anniversary. They got a card off the Queen and a card off the King of Stamford Bridge. Inside, José wrote, 'Happy 60th – Amazing!' My folks loved it, and so did the local paper, who did a big article about it.

When my boy Joshua turned thirteen, his birthday coincided with Chelsea's first home game of the title-winning 2014–15 season, a Premier League match against Leicester City. As a gift José gave us three tickets for the Directors' Box at Stamford Bridge, which came with full hospitality. A slap-up meal before kick-off; tea, coffee, cake and biscuits at half-time; and more food and drinks afterwards. That wasn't all, for José had also invited us to the Chelsea team hotel at Chelsea Harbour on the Friday afternoon before the game to hand over the tickets in person to Joshua. José and his assistant Rui Faria then spent an hour sitting with us talking football, talking Chelsea and talking family. It was a neat follow-on to the last home game of the previous season, a 0–0 draw with Norwich on Sunday 4 May.

José had again arranged special seats for Joshua and Saskia for that game, this time right behind the Chelsea dugout, just along from his own children José Jr and Matilde Jr. Josh and Sask were even allowed into the pressroom afterwards to see Mourinho's after-match press conference. Then, as he was leaving, José stopped to say a quick hello to the pair of them, before whipping off his white Chelsea training jacket and handing it over. We quickly got photos of them in the pressroom sitting in José's chair wearing José's top, and we emailed him copies the next day. Photographs which forever captured a magical moment for them both. He was pleased they were so chuffed. 'Hug – happy they enjoy', was his response.

It wasn't the first time they'd received a jersey from him either. When he was still boss at the Bernabéu, two Real Madrid tops arrived in the post at Christmas. On one he'd written 'For Saskia' and on the other 'For Joshua', followed by his signature. The kids were thrilled but never wear them because they're scared to wash them in case the writing fades or disappears.

When José came back for his second stint at Chelsea, both Joshua and Saskia visited the club's Cobham training ground to watch a Mourinho pre-match press conference and meet some of the players. To the children he really was the guy that keeps on giving.

There were plenty of 'wish you and yours good' and 'big hug' messages throughout the year and special greetings at Christmas and New Year. When he saw me appear on television he'd send a 'well done', 'top man' or 'hugs' message. If he thought I'd done a good article in the newspaper it was the same.

There was banter, too. When I informed him I'd had a knee operation and so wouldn't see him for six weeks or so he replied: 'F**k man, take care. You are getting old, don't do stupid things.' I wasn't having that, replying: 'Ha – me growing old??? I can remember a certain someone without the grey hair!!!'

When I missed one of his Friday press conferences because I was receiving a long-service award for working twenty years at News International, he quipped, 'F**k 20 years ... I hope they pay you a good salary', clearly hoping I was being well looked after for my loyalty. But then, when I told him my reward for twenty years' service was the grand total of £300, he added: 'F**k Murdoch.' He often made me laugh like that.

José is also incredibly selfless, which may surprise you. Nothing ever seemed too much trouble, even when I was asking for favours on behalf of family or friends. My cousin

Iain wanted a signed Chelsea shirt for one of his friends. Done. My niece Becky wanted a signed Chelsea shirt for her fiancé's aunty. Done. My close friend Philip Morrison wanted a signed Chelsea shirt to present to his wife Jane on their wedding day. Done, complete with the message 'You are the Special One!' My buddies Colin Lester and Grant Black wanted Chelsea tickets for a Champions League match away in Galatasaray. Done, and VIP tickets too!

Now that particular favour worked out especially well. Colin is manager of international pop star Craig David, while Grant is the record producer/songwriting son of legendary lyricist Don Black, an Oscar winner no less. Typically Colin was keen to show his gratitude and offered José and his family free tickets for Craig David's upcoming concert in London. And guess what? José's daughter Matilde is a big Craig David fan. It's wonderful when it all works out like that. A favour given, a favour returned. The problem with José is that he gives out so many favours it is nigh on impossible to repay them all.

47

THE SACK RACE

As José and I sipped Cristal champagne at Stamford Bridge on 24 May 2015, neither of us imagined for one moment that we'd both be out of work in a few months' time. He'd just won the Premier League and the Capital One Cup in fine style and been rewarded with a new four-year contract. I'd just enjoyed a string of big exclusive stories, including one that was nominated for Sports Story of the Year 2015: my scoop on Chelsea's signing of Diego Costa. Neither of us would see the end of the next season, though.

Like Mourinho with his transfer woes, my troubles started even before a ball had been kicked. New management at the newspaper didn't like my style and quickly made that clear. I was told that I was 'a dinosaur' living in the 1990s if I thought exclusive stories were the main focus of the newspaper nowadays. I was told that the *Sun*'s fantasy football game Dream Team, Sun Bingo and Sun Betting were the three most important things that would determine the future success of the publication. I was also told I needed to file more filler content to 'feed the beast' of the internet, even though hardly anyone was hitting on our website because we were behind a paywall. Finally, I was told that my relationship with Mourinho was 'exaggerated', that the Chelsea boss would talk to anyone on the paper, not just me, so I would no longer be covering Chelsea. It didn't need anyone else to tell me that I was on my way out. I gave José the heads-up and he was shocked, replying,

'I can't believe they f**k you!!' For my part, I couldn't believe what then happened to him.

It was the opening day of the Premier League season when José's problems began. It wasn't the result that was to blame – a 2–2 draw with Swansea at Stamford Bridge was an acceptable outcome, especially after the fifty-second-minute dismissal of goalkeeper Thibaut Courtois. No, it was a touchline bust-up with Chelsea doctor Eva Carneiro that would dominate the day's headlines and the sports pages for weeks to come.

The clash happened after Carneiro and physio Jon Fearn had run on to the pitch to treat a stricken Eden Hazard towards the end of the match. Mourinho was incensed as it meant his star player would now have to leave the pitch, reducing Chelsea to just nine men. He screamed at the medics and made his displeasure clear again in his after-match press conference, branding the pair of them as 'impulsive and naive'. He later removed them from their match-day positions on the bench.

The media frenzy surrounding those actions would not die down. Carneiro would not return to work and instead instructed lawyers to bring a case for constructive dismissal against the club and their manager. Mourinho would not back down, but what he did do was bunker down. What he also did was change his email address and that suddenly made life a lot trickier for me. Short of driving from Warwick to London and knocking on his front door, it had been my only way of communicating with him after being removed from the day-to-day coverage of Chelsea. Now that line of communication had disappeared too and it couldn't have been at a worse time.

José was also having the worst of times. On top of the Carneiro controversy came an even more alarming crisis – he was embarking on the worst run of results of his entire career as Chelsea scrambled just one win in the first six games of the season, which included a Community Shield defeat to Arsenal, a

3–0 thrashing at Manchester City, a 2–1 loss at home to Crystal Palace and a dismal 3–1 reverse at Everton. It was desperate stuff, especially watching on from the outside, not knowing what was happening on the inside.

I had repeatedly tried to contact Mourinho since the opening day of the season but each time the emails bounced back. Finally, on 27 August I sent a message instead to his trusted assistant Rui Faria to try to clarify some information I'd been given about what would happen if José did get the sack. I'd been told he would not get a bumper pay-off, as he had done first time around; the information this time was that Chelsea would simply carry on paying him until he got another job.

My plan worked. Within an hour José had responded personally. His opening line explained a lot: 'No emails … dangerous!!' I'd later learn his emails, past and present, were under scrutiny as part of the Carneiro case, which explained it all, including his change of email address. And he was right to be concerned, as at least one extract from José's email files was produced at Carneiro's subsequent case for unfair dismissal in June 2016.

The worry about his messages being examined and scrutinized by third parties didn't stop him from clearing up my query about his pay-off. José gave me chapter and verse on what would happen if he were dismissed. 'I have four-years contract. If Chelsea sack me they have to pay two years; when I have only two years contract they have to pay one year.' Then he concluded: 'But don't lose your time with something stupid.' Clearly he had no expectation that he'd be losing his job any time soon although those subsequent defeats to Crystal Palace and Everton didn't make it sound such a 'stupid' idea.

The 3–1 loss at Everton in September was a big blow, in particular for Mourinho and was also a key day for me. I wasn't at the game; my assignment that day had been to cover West

Bromwich Albion against Southampton. Nevertheless, as it was the lunchtime kick-off, I managed to watch the Chelsea game from the Albion pressroom.

It was not happy viewing and I started to realize the situation was now becoming serious. So I decided to stay put in the pressroom to await Mourinho's after-match press conference, rather than go to the press box for the kick-off of the West Brom game.

It was no dereliction of duty – quite the opposite. We had two reporters at the game: my colleague Graeme Bryce was writing the match report for the Sunday newspaper while it was my responsibility to file the report for Monday's paper. I told Graeme of my plans and he agreed it was sensible. We both felt that the mushrooming Chelsea crisis was a much bigger story than the Baggies against the Saints.

Mourinho's demeanour in the press conference was downcast; he was effectively throwing in the towel on the title after just five games. Yes, it was that dramatic.

In the circumstances I decided to risk the wrath of Mourinho by pinging him a quick email to try to find out more despite his 'no emails ... dangerous!' warning. I then made my way to the press box to watch the last hour or so of Albion and Southampton playing out a goalless draw, and waited in vain for a reply from the Under Pressure One.

I was on a day off on the Sunday but still got a message from the office asking me about the Chelsea story. It wasn't much of a message. No pleasantries or even a 'hello'. It bluntly said, 'This is where your relationship with him [Mourinho] needs to come to the surface. What do you know? What have you got? Is he expecting it to go tits up?'

It should have made me angry. It just made me smile. Remember, I'd been taken off the coverage of Chelsea and told my 'relationship' with Mourinho was exaggerated and he'd talk to anyone on the paper! But here they were asking me to bail them out even though I hadn't even been at the game. In fact, I hadn't covered a Chelsea match at all that season. I hadn't seen Mourinho since sharing a glass of bubbly with him the previous season. Yet now the same people who had exiled me from Chelsea wanted me to tell them exactly what was happening at the club and precisely what he was thinking. Priceless.

I said as much in my reply and for good measure added that José was no longer responding to my emails. How could I possibly help? I knew nothing, I had got nothing and I had no idea if Mourinho thought it was all going to go 'tits up'.

On the Monday I was informed by the Head of Content that he could 'only view ... [my] unwillingness to provide any help on Chelsea as requested as a failure to carry out a reasonable instruction of management. For this reason I believe your actions warrant formal investigation under the Company Disciplinary Policy.'

It simply backed up my suspicion that they wanted me out and, sure enough, the following month, I had to go through the mockery of a disciplinary hearing. I'd now ceased to care about the job and was strongly tempted to tell them exactly how I felt. Except I was a father with two children in school, I had a mortgage and bills to pay, and had responsibilities in relation to the future welfare and well-being of my family. And anyway, in my eyes it was such a pathetic and obviously trumped-up charge that I thought I'd fight it, if only to embarrass the lunatics who had taken over the asylum.

In contrast, three Chelsea wins in a row seemed to have stopped the rot and steadied the ship: a 4–0 beating of Maccabi Tel Aviv in the Champions League and a 4–1 win at Walsall in the Capital One Cup were sandwiched around a far more meaningful 2–0 victory over Arsenal at Stamford Bridge. I thought Chelsea's season had belatedly kicked into action. So did Mourinho. We were wrong. It was a false dawn, the slump became more prolonged and soon afterwards I was saying to him, 'I thought Arsenal was the turning point!!!' to which he replied, 'It was but then the FA f***ed Diego.'

So in José's eyes it was the win over Arsenal that actually served to derail Chelsea once again. What should have been a huge boost, after a Kurt Zouma header and a deflected Eden Hazard shot had seen off the Gunners, actually turned into another damaging setback and another negative scenario. Chelsea striker Costa was retrospectively charged with violent conduct by the FA after a clash with Arsenal defender Laurent Koscielny and was subsequently banned for three games. It seemed Mourinho and the club were staggering from calamity to calamity. There was just no escape from the rapidly increasing pressure of it all. But José still had time to try to help a friend in need despite being under immense pressure amid an ongoing crisis.

I devised a plan to save my neck. Who could be my first witness? José Mourinho, of course. These were extreme times so you have to take extreme measures. I again decided to try an email to José in the hope that he would respond, especially considering the circumstances. Hopefully he would confirm to the haters in the office that I had repeatedly tried to keep a dialogue going with him from afar but that he had not responded. Just for good measure I sent him copies of the various emails I'd received from work that had led to and included the disciplinary procedure. Pitiful stuff, and as I hoped, he saw it in the same way. Whether emails were dangerous or not, the manager of Chelsea was there for me. This time he did reply, and what a reply it was.

From: José Mourinho
Subject: Not fair!!
Date: 21 September 2015 12:24:11 BST
To: Rob Beasley

I dont think your situation is fair ... of course we are
friends and of course i want to help you but sometimes
there is no way, there are no storys ... our club is different
now and we are calm no wars no problems with owner
nothing ... so i couldnt give anything.

And because eva story our emails are under control i cant
change mails with you.

But when u keep [your] job we find a way to help u for
sure ... u are the only journalist in [England] i have some
contact and [your] paper shouldnt loose it.
Regards to [your] family
Jm

Soon afterwards Mourinho even spoke at one of his press
conferences about journalists losing their jobs when the subject
of his own future was being discussed. He said, 'What I'd like
to understand is why some people can be so excited and happy
with the perspective of somebody losing his job. If you tell me
your newspaper is going to sack 20 people, first of all I will be
worried for you, I promise you. And, secondly, I would be very
disappointed even if I don't know the other 20 guys who are
going to be sacked.' These were not empty words as his email
in support of me proves. Not that it changed the increasingly
inevitable outcome for either of us.

Chelsea's form did not improve just as my job prospects
did not improve. A 2–1 Champions League defeat in Porto was

swiftly followed by a 3–1 home defeat to Southampton at the start of October. West Ham inflicted more woe with a 2–1 win at Upton Park and on Halloween night there was the nightmare of another 3–1 home defeat, this time by Liverpool.

November was a better month for Chelsea: they lost at Stoke City but beat Norwich City and Maccabi Tel Aviv in Israel and held Tottenham to a goalless draw at White Hart Lane. It wasn't a better month for me: first there was my disciplinary and I decided not to use José's email to try to rescue my job. Maybe I should have done. Looking at it now, it is a powerful statement by him, clearly saying that we are friends and that he wanted to help. He also explained in it that because of the Eva Carneiro case his emails were under tight control, meaning he couldn't exchange any emails with me at all. It was also heartening to hear his confirmation that I was the only journalist in the country that he had some contact with, and that my newspaper shouldn't throw that away.

But something inside me told me not to produce it at the disciplinary. My attitude was that I had done everything right and nothing wrong. That this was a sham of a process, with a prejudged conclusion, and so I would maintain the higher ground and keep Mourinho and his email out of it. I had too much pride to stoop to their level and dignify their proceedings with something as important to me as my relationship with José.

Sure enough the disciplinary went against me. I was given a written warning and I knew there and then that there was no way back. Incredibly, though, I lasted longer than José. It wasn't until the beginning of March 2016 that I received a pay-off of just over two years' salary. I was 'lucky' in that I had a break from my ordeal, a long-overdue ankle operation that would keep me off work for three months, but although I was out of the firing line there was no respite for the Chelsea manager. On 5 December the reigning champions lost at home to Bournemouth. I was sitting with my son Joshua watching Wasps play Exeter Chiefs in a big rugby union clash when the result came through. I turned to him and said, 'That must be it now. José will be gone after this.' He nodded. Neither of us could see any escape now. Amazingly, though, he lingered a little longer.

There was still time for a 2–0 home win over Porto in the Champions League before he was sacked on 17 December, just seven months after being crowned a champion and Manager of the Year. A good source in Cobham rang to tell me that it was about to happen. Straightaway I tried to message José on his new email address. It bounced back immediately. His Chelsea email account was no longer in service and shortly afterwards it was announced he was no longer in a job.

His demise followed a 2–1 defeat to Leicester City, who surprisingly went on to be worthy champions that season. Unbelievably it was a ninth defeat in sixteen league games and the Blues were sixteenth in the table. It was a sad final chapter for the man who had brought unprecedented success and silverware to the club we both loved. Three league titles, three League Cups, three Champions League semi-finals, an FA Cup and a Community Shield. What a record and what a legacy.

48

FROM BLUE TO RED
2016

At 9.30 on the morning of Friday 27 May, 2016, an announce-ment was posted on the official Manchester United website, confirming what was by then football's worst-kept secret. Underneath a colour photograph of a smiling José Mourinho – aptly suited and booted and proudly holding a Manchester United shirt in front of him – came the news that the fifty-three-year-old Portuguese coach had agreed a deal with the Old Trafford club which could see him in charge at United until 2020.

United chief executive Ed Woodward declared, 'José is quite simply the best manager in the game today. He has won trophies and inspired players in countries across Europe, and, of course, he knows the Premier League very well, having won 3 titles here. His track record of success is ideal to take the club forward.'

Mourinho himself added, 'To become Manchester United's manager is a special honour in the game. It is a club known and admired throughout the world. There is a mystique and a romance about it which no other club can match. I have always felt an affinity with Old Trafford; it has hosted some important memories for me in my career and I have always enjoyed a rapport with the United fans. I'm looking forward to being their manager and enjoying their magnificent support in the coming years.'

Later that day the club's television channel MUTV aired the first interview with the new Old Trafford manager. It wasn't great. José was a little tongue-tied in his excitement as he stood under the TV lights in front of the Manchester United sponsors' board. Still, he managed to get his message over: he was coming to win matches, win trophies and couldn't wait to get started.

Mourinho clearly believed the timing was perfect – that his great experience was capable of matching United's high expectations. He said, 'I feel great. I think it comes in the right moment of my career. Man United is one of those clubs where you really need to be prepared for it because it is what I used to call a giant club and giant clubs must be for the best managers and I think I'm ready for it. So I could say I'm happy, I'm proud, I'm honoured, I'm everything, but the reality is that what I love is to work and I can't wait for the seventh of July to go on the pitch.' He then addressed the fall from grace of the Red Devils since the departure of his friend Sir Alex Ferguson in 2013. 'I think we can look at our club now in two perspectives: one perspective is the past three years and the other perspective is the club's history. I think I prefer to forget the past three years. I prefer to focus on the giant club I have in my hands now. I want to focus on the history of this giant club. I will give absolutely everything to try and go in the direction that we all want.'

Then José saluted the United fans, who he said had been fair with him over the years, despite his numerous triumphs at Old Trafford with former clubs Chelsea and Real Madrid. 'I think I know what they can give me. I think also they know what I can give them. Obviously the most important thing [is] the players and the relation the players establish with them [the fans], but it is very important and curious that I play so many games against Man United and at Old Trafford with other clubs and there was empathy, no problems, and in fact I was pushed by that feeling to say sometimes things that my club were not happy with. I remember, for example, when I won at Old Trafford with Real Madrid. I [said] that the "best team lost" and not many people were happy at Real Madrid.'

It wasn't until July 5 that Mourinho followed up the initial announcement of his appointment with his first face-to-face press conference with the media. And the first question was how he felt. His response was typically unconventional: 'It is difficult to find the right words to describe this club. I don't like the denomination that many people use like "dream job". It is not a dream job, it is reality. I am Man United manager but the reality is I think it is a job everyone wants and not many have a chance to have and I have it and I know obviously the responsibility, I know the expectation. At the same time I know the legacy, I know what is behind me, the history of this club, I know what the fans expect from me. This challenge doesn't make me nervous because my history in the last ten years or more was always to live with big clubs' expectations and I think it comes in the right moment of my career, I feel very prepared, very stable and with a great motivation. I can say I am where I want to be – in this club, in this country, in the Premier League and in the domestic cups, I feel a bit frustrated I am not playing Champions League. Obviously Manchester United is more important than myself and Man United is a Champions league club so we have to make sure in July 2017 that this club is where it has to be, which is obviously the Champions League.'

Typical Mourinho, he has never aimed low. The nature of the man is to always strive to be the best, or at least battling with the best, even if those lofty ambitions bring added pressure, extra scrutiny and the prospect of widespread criticism should he fail. He explained: 'I was always much more aggressive in my approach with the risks that can bring. It would be easy – and even honest and pragmatic – to focus on the last three years, on the fact that we don't qualify for Champions League and so on, and be quite pragmatic to say: "Let's work and try and be back to the Champions League, try and be back to the top four." I prefer to be more aggressive and say we want to win. What is playing well? It is scoring more goals than the opponents, conceding less, making your fans proud because you give everything and you win. It is everything at the same time. It is an aggressive approach by myself. I want everything. Of course we are not going to get everything but we want to.'

His ignominious exit at previous club Chelsea – where he was sacked just four months into the 2015/16 season – after a dismal run of 9 defeats in 16 league games – was a focus for journalists wondering if the Special One had suddenly lost his sparkle. Did he feel he now had something to prove after that abject failure?

José's response was typically blunt and uncompromising. He quickly compared himself to other top managers in the Premier League and although he didn't name names it was all pretty obvious, just think Arséne Wenger and Mauricio Pochettino. For Mourinho replied: 'There are some managers ... the last time they won a title was ten years ago. Some of them, the last time they won a title was never. The last time I won a title was one year ago [with Chelsea], not ten years ago or fifteen years ago, so if I have a lot to prove, imagine the others. But the reality is, that was never important for me. I play against myself. That is my feeling many times. I feel I have to prove not to the others but to myself. I would never be able to work without success. I have always many questions towards myself and the people working with me. That is my nature. I could approach this job in a defensive point of view by saying the last three years the best we did was fourth. I can't – it is not my nature. Manchester United – for many years success was just routine and in this moment the last three years are to forget. I want the players to forget. I don't want the players to think we have to do better and finish fourth. Finishing fourth is not the aim.'

That was the gauntlet thrown down to a United side that had badly under-performed for three seasons in a row. It was time to step up and deliver, to restore the Old Trafford club to its former glory. With that in mind Mourinho also splashed the cash to bring in £145m worth of new talent to strengthen the squad up front, in midfield and in defence. Paul Pogba was the biggest outlay with United spending £89m to bring their former player back from Juventus. Defender Eric Bailly, signed from Villarreal for £30m, Borussia Dortmund star Henrikh Mkhitaryan cost £26m and veteran striker Zlatan Ibrahimovic joined on a free from Paris Saint-Germain. Four big-name stars brought in to return United to the big time. Could they and Mourinho work their magic?

EPILOGUE: GLORY GLORY, MAN UNITED

It started well. A 2–1 Wembley win over Champions Leicester City in the Community Shield was the perfect curtain-raiser for Mourinho the Red. What's more it was new signing Zlatan Ibrahimovic who scored with a late header to clinch that first piece of silverware for the new Old Trafford boss – grabbing the headlines after Jamie Vardy had earlier wiped out Jesse Lingard's stunning opener for United. Cue celebrations all around. Yes, okay, the Community Shield's not much of a trophy in the great scheme of things, certainly not for a club as huge as Manchester United, but José will have quickly added it to his long list of Successes, and used it to try and instill a winning mentality into his new charges.

The winning start continued as the season kicked off in earnest,with three league victories in a row, setting up a mouth-watering home clash with neighbours and arch-rivals Manchester City, now managed by Mourinho's old adversary Pep Guardiola. It turned into a reality check for José, his team and their fans. City took United apart in the first half with ex-Chelsea star Kevin De Bruyne – whom Mourinho sold in 2014 – scoring after just fifteen minutes. Kelechi Iheanacho made it 2–0 after thirty-six minutes and City were good value for their lead. However, a howler of a mistake by City's debutant goalkeeper, Claudio Bravo, just before half-time gifted Ibrahimovic a goal to haul United back into the game. The Reds were far better after the break but couldn't overcome a resilient

City, who held out for the win and topped the table with 4 wins out of 4. It was a body blow for United and they wobbled.

Further defeats to Feyenord in the Europa League and at Watford in the Premier League showed there was plenty of work to be done to lift the club out of the doldrums of the last three years. A 6-match unbeaten run in all competitions, albeit with only 1 win and 2 draws in the Premier League, steadied the ship but United were sunk completely when Mourinho returned to face former club Chelsea at Stamford Bridge in the league on Sunday October 23.

It was a humiliation for the Special One who'd won 3 league titles and 7 trophies in all with the Blues. Incredibly Chelsea were ahead after just thirty seconds when Pedro Rodriguez pounced to stun the visitors, and Gary Cahill reinforced that early breakthrough with a twenty-first-minute strike from close range to put the Blues in full control. Their dominance saw Eden Hazard and N'Golo Kante complete the rout with goals in the sixty-second and seventieth minutes. Chelsea fans were delirious and some taunted their ex-boss by singing, 'You're not special any more!' – adding insult to his already injured pride.

The man himself was far from happy. Mourinho moaned afterwards, 'You come with a strategy, you cannot concede a goal in the way we did. We were coming to have an offensive approach. We wanted to create chances; we showed that after the 1–0. The second and the third were counter-attack goals. It is one of those days when you give the advantage to opponents by doing nothing. In terms of points, we got zero points, we lose 3 points. We are 6 points from the top, 3 from the top four. We need to win our matches now, which are not easy. We need to win to close that gap – after these last 3 matches, we made 2 out of 9. We now need points.'

Mourinho clearly knew even then that he could not afford any more slip-ups if a top four finish was to remain a realistic target – and here he was drilling home that message to his new players. It had the desired effect. United responded by setting a club record of 25 matches unbeaten in the Premier League, winning 13 and drawing 11. What's more they never conceded more than 1 goal in any of those 25 games. The problem was the number of draws, especially the 9 at home – many in matches that United would normally expect to win: Burnley, West Ham, Hull, Bournemouth, West Bromwich Albion, Everton and Swansea. Those draws would ultimately prove costly at the end of the season but at least the mark of Mourinho was beginning to appear, United were becoming devilishly difficult to beat, even if they were all too often squandering chances to make them serial winners in their manager's image.

In the midst of that long, unbeaten league run United returned to Wembley for an EFL Cup final showdown with Southampton. The incredible Ibrahimovic was the match winner again as United finally triumphed 3–2 in a dramatic and controversial game. Controversial because Southampton were the better side and should have taken a first-half lead when striker Manolo Gabbiadini scored a perfectly good goal, which was wrongly disallowed for offside. It was a huge let-off for United who took full advantage; Ibrahimovic and Jesse Lingard scoring to give United an undeserved 2–0 advantage. Gabbiadini would not be denied, though, and showed his class with goals either side of half-time to level an enthralling match that looked destined for extra time. That was until that man Zlatan grabbed a last-gasp winner three minutes from time to claim the trophy and spark another round of celebrations, not least for the manager. It was Mourinho's fourth League Cup crown in all, equalling the record of legends Sir Alex Ferguson and Brian Clough, despite José only having served six full seasons in English football. More surprising was the news that Mourinho had also become the first Manchester United manager to win a major trophy in his first season.

So this debut-season triumph meant a lot to the highly-decorated Portuguese boss. He confessed: 'Winning is always special. The day I don't get emotional when I win is the day I go home. So yes I'm a bit emotional. It's not easy to win titles so many times, it's not easy to cope with the pressure I put myself under all of my career.' But José showed that he was not dazzled by the trophy or the success, for he was also magnanimous in the victory, praising Southampton's performance and admitting they were unlucky. He added: 'It was a game I felt was difficult, so credit goes to Southampton. We have the cup in our hands but we should be playing extra time.' Mourinho then singled out Ibrahimovic for particular praise, adding, 'He won the game for us, he was outstanding in a match where our opponent was better than us for large periods of the game. They deserved to go to extra time, they didn't deserve to lose, but Zlatan made the difference and won us the cup.' The Swede's 25th and 26th goals of the season proved crucial and vindicated Mourinho's eagerness to bring the veteran frontman to England. Ibra's great ability, huge confidence and amazing aura making him the outstanding talisman for a pretty ordinary United side.

As a result of the big man's goals and performances, this underwhelming United team was right on track for a successful season. It was now the end of February, two thirds of the way into the season, and United still had their sights set on a top four finish, the FA Cup and the Europa League too. The campaign actually looked as if it could turn into a special one. A relentless, insatiable Mourinho tried to drive them on. He wanted his men to maintain their unbeaten league-run AND strive towards more glory in the Cups as the season entered a critical phase. Three games in one week would help determine the scale of those ambitions: a last-16 double header against Russia's FC Rostov sandwiched around a meaty clash with Chelsea back at The Bridge in the FA Cup. This would be a huge test of the team's hunger, desire and belief and José urged his team to deliver. Unfortunately United struggled to meet the challenge. They could only draw their first-leg Europa League tie on a disappointing night in Rostov but at least the result put them on the brink of a quarter finals spot with the deciding leg at United. Before that came a return to Stamford Bridge. And, not for the first time, it didn't go well there, either. Mourinho again suffered defeat on a ground where he had once been so imperious.

It was a tempestuous affair. United were without star man Ibrahimovic, who was suspended, and matters worsened when they saw Ander Herrera sent off ten minutes before the break for a second foul in quick succession on a lively and dangerous Eden Hazard. The rash challenge brought the feisty midfielder a second yellow card followed by the inevitable red. Mourinho and Chelsea manager Antonio Conté clashed on the touchline shortly afterwards and again in the second half.

It was similarly spiteful on the pitch, with United's Marcos Rojo appearing to stamp on Hazard but escaping punishment at the time and – more surprisingly – retrospectively too. United were charged by the FA after the game, though, for failing to control their players in the aftermath of the Herrera dismissal, when the Spaniard refused to leave the field while a crowd of red shirts surrounded referee Oliver to protest the decision. Chelsea's N'Golo Kanté settled a stormy quarter final with a superb twenty-five yard drive into the bottom corner with fifty-one minutes gone.

To make matters worse for Mourinho, a section of the home fans taunted him with cries of 'Judas' – even though it was the SW6 club that had jettisoned José, not the other way around. Mourinho was understandably unimpressed. He'd won 3 league titles, 3 League Cups and the FA Cup during his two spells at the club, between 2004–07 and 2013–15. He made the point during the game by holding up three fingers to the hecklers, one for each title he'd given them, and he went further afterwards, snapping: 'Until they have a manager who has won 4 titles, for them I am the number one. Judas is number one.'

What those few, fickle Chelsea fans didn't know was that Mourinho was still in touch with a lot of his old friends at the Bridge and relations were pretty warm and friendly. For instance, just a month earlier, in mid-February, when the London club's long-serving press and accreditation officer Thresa Conneely celebrated forty years working at Chelsea, Mourinho filmed a special video message to send to her to mark the occasion. In it he said: 'Hi Thresa. Many congratulations for your forty years. Here from Manchester, I just want you to know that I will never forget your support. In the good moments you were there, in the bad moments you were there. You were a real friend and the great thing is that every Chelsea manager can say and feel exactly the same. So big kiss and all the best to you.'

And then on that fateful and hurtful Monday night in March, even despite the FA Cup defeat, the Herrera red card and the abuse he'd been subjected to by a certain section of the fans, a caring José still found his friend Thresa after the game to give her a hug, pose for a photograph and say his 'thank you' in person. That's some Judas hey?

There was little time to dwell on this FA Cup setback. Three days later it was Thursday night Europa League football, with the quarter finals beckoning. It was another nervous, frustrating night for an uncertain and insecure United. Juan Mata finally settled the issue with a seventieth minute goal but the home team had goalkeeper Sergio Romero to thank for two late saves, which kept United in front and on course for more silverware.

United's advance meant that by April the matches were coming thick and fast; 9 games in that month alone. Impressively the unbeaten league run was still going and in mid-April Mourinho's side enjoyed a memorable week. In the middle of a 3–2 aggregate win over Anderlecht in the Europa League they comfortably beat league-leaders Chelsea 2–0 at the Theatre of Dreams.

Suddenly United fans really dared to dream of a big finish on both fronts. It didn't last long. Once again the draws did for them. Stalemates at Manchester City and at home to Swansea saw the league push becalmed again, as Mourinho moaned about the stress, strain and hardship of playing every three or four days.

As May began, Mourinho decided enough was enough, and that his men were so jaded by their relentless programme of games that he had no choice but to decide between the two competitions. He needed to make either the Premier League or the Europa League the priority. Both offered the prospect of Champions League football, but going for both could destroy the prospect of a return to rub shoulder's with Europe's elite.

First game up that month saw United away to Celta Vigo and Mourinho made his decisive move. He announced: 'In relation to the Premier League, I think it's too late because in the past month of April we played 9 matches, 7 of them in the Premier and we had too many problems, too many players absent. So in this moment the perspective is different because the Europa League becomes even more important for us. Of course, it depends on the result and the way we analyse the situation on Friday after the match, but if we have to rest players next weekend we are going to do that.'

United dominated in Spain and won 1–0, but left frustrated because the scoreline did not accurately reflect their superiority. Nevertheless the considered view was that they effectively had one foot in the final, with a home leg still to follow and that was enough for José. His mind was made up and unapologetically he made the Europa League his top target. The immediate consequence was a reshuffled side losing 2–0 at Arsenal in the league to bring about the end of a long, unbeaten run that stretched all the way back to the 4–0 drubbing at Chelsea on October 23. The flip was that just four days later United duly claimed their place in the Europa League final. It was another nervy, unconvincing display in which they struggled to draw 1–1 and squeezed through thanks only to that narrow away win in Spain. So what? They'd done it and were just one match away from another trophy and a much-needed return to the glamour and riches of the Champions League.

Inevitably the Premier League campaign duly fizzled out. A 2–1 defeat at Tottenham, a goalless draw at Southampton and a 2–0 win at Crystal Palace completed United's league campaign and confirmed them in sixth place in the final table. They'd won 18 games, drawn 15 and lost only 5 – the same as Chelsea – to amass 69 points. That was a hefty 7 points shy of Liverpool, with the Merseysiders celebrating claiming fourth place and the final Champions League place. Even more damning was that United had finished an astonishing 24 points behind Champions Chelsea. The Premier League table certainly made sober viewing and no one knew that better than Mourinho. It was not good enough, nowhere near the exacting standards he demands and expects. The only redeeming fact was that a win against Dutch giants Ajax in Stockholm, on the night of Wednesday May 24, would turn their topsy turvy season into a resounding success. Tragically there was a late, devastating twist to the scenario that focused eyes even more fervently on that final.

At 10.30pm on Monday May 22 a suicide bomber blew himself up at an Ariana Grande concert at Manchester Arena. Twenty-two people died and more than fifty were injured. The horrific event left a nation in shock, especially Mancunians. The following day, in the aftermath, Mourinho and his Manchester

United side flew to Sweden for their cup final. The mood was sad and sombre. United scrapped the usual pre-match press conference that evening and although the players visited the match venue, the Friends Arena in Stockholm, they did not train there to prepare themselves for the following night. They announced they would be wearing black armbands for the match, in mourning for the dead, and that there would be a minute's silence before kick-off in memory of the victims. All this with the team facing their biggest match of the season – actually United's biggest match in four seasons! But footballing fortunes suddenly seemed insignificant and inappropriate in such appalling circumstances.

Mourinho and his men had to fight to separate themselves from the high emotion of the moment. They had to be professional and to focus on their job and the final. That was difficult. There was already plenty of 'football' pressure with the match dubbed 'the game that will define United's season'. It would also determine their standing next season too – in or out of the Champions League. This pressure was heightened further by repeated calls from back home that United should 'Win it for Manchester' at a time when the city was hurting so badly.

United rose to the occasion. Mourinho's tactics were immaculate and his players implemented them to perfection, so the result was never in question. United comfortably won 2–0 thanks to goals from Mourinho signings Paul Pogba and Henrik Mkhitaryan. And yes, despite everything, they celebrated their football triumph, celebrated wildly in fact. The relief was almost tangible in players and manager. After a long, hard, fluctuating and frustrating season they had done it. United were back in the Champions League and back in the Winners' Enclosure with three trophies to show for their efforts. In the process the club had captured the one major prize to have eluded them during their long and proud, trophy-laden history – the Europa League.

It was a magical moment for Mourinho the manager. A moment of elation, occasion and vindication. This trophy was a hugely important one for him, even among all the Champions League and League titles he has won in England, Spain, Italy and Portugal. It was a powerful statement, not only about him and his unique ability to plunder silverware here, but also about his new club, Manchester United, who had rediscovered their winning habit and were back where they belonged, among the world's biggest clubs. He summed it up saying: 'It is the end of a very difficult season but I think a very, very good season. And we prefer this way [to qualify for Champions League] than to finish fourth, than finish third, than finish second. We made the objective of going back into the Champions League by winning a title and an important title – a title that gives the club the lot. The club is now a club that has won every title in world football and we are very happy because we fought hard for this from the beginning. We always thought that we could win the Europa League and now we have won three trophies in the season and made the Champions League. I'm really happy with my players in probably my most difficult season as a manager. Now I'm on holidays!'

There was also Mourinho the Man out there that night. Mourinho the father. Mourinho the human being. He joyously hugged, jumped and rolled on the pitch with his son José Jr as the celebrations began. A precious family moment being shared at a showpiece event and occasion. He explained how difficult it had been to concentrate on winning the Cup at such a sad time:

'We just came here to do our job. We came without the happiness we should bring with us, because when you come for these big matches you go happy, you go proud. We didn't. We just came to do our job.'

José also pledged: 'If we could, we would change obviously

the people's lives for this Cup. Immediately. We would not think twice.' And I believe he meant every word too. My experience is that he's a man, husband, father, friend first – a football manager second – and he's a 'special one' at all.

Acknowledgements

To José Mourinho. He's the Special One for sure, as a manager and a man. Thanks for everything, boss!

Special thanks to my sister, Dr Joanne Opie, and my big buddy, Philip Morrison, for their proofreading skills and unstinting support for this book.

Thanks, too, to my mum and dad, whose love has never wavered, even during those times when I tested it to the limit.

Big hugs for my sister Alison, my nephews and nieces Helen, Tom, Samuel and Becky.

And enduring gratitude to the late, great Roger Jeffery, editor of the *Nuneaton Evening Tribune*, who gave me my first chance in journalism in the summer of 1977.

Finally to my hometown Nuneaton, the place and the people that shaped me into the man I am today and which will always be home.

Picture Credits

Page 1: Andy Hooper / Daily Mail / REX / Shutterstock (top); © Bret Thompsett /Alpha (bottom).

Page 2: Christopher Lee / Getty Images (top left); Adrian Dennis / AFP / Getty Images (top right); Darren Walsh / Chelsea via Getty Images (bottom).

Page 3: Paul Ellis / AFP / Getty Images (top); © Alpha (bottom).

Page 4: Darren Walsh / Chelsea via Getty Images (top); Phil Cole / Getty Images (bottom).

Page 5: Giuseppe Cacace / AFP / Getty Images (top); Pedro Armestre / AFP / Getty Images (bottom).

Page 6: Giuseppe Cacace / AFP / Getty Images (top); Jasper Juinen / Getty Images (bottom).

Page 7: Ander Gillenea / AFP / Getty Images (top); Cesar Monso / AFP / Getty Images (bottom).

Page 8: Alex Cid-Fuentes / ALFAQUI / The Sun (top); Glyn Kirk / AFP / Getty Images (bottom).

Page 9: Richard Heathcote / Getty Images.

Page 10: Clive Mason / Getty Images (top); Glyn Kirk / AFP / Getty Images (bottom).

Page 11: AMA / Corbis via Getty Images (top left); Shaun Botterill / Getty Images (top right); Adrian Dennis / AFP / Getty Images (bottom).

Page 12: From the author

Page 13: Jamie McPhilimey / The Sun Online (top); Michael Reagan / Getty Images (bottom).

Page 14: Mike Hewitt / Getty Images (top); AMA / Corbis via Getty Images (bottom).

Pages 15 & 16: John Peters / Man Utd via Getty Images (all)